$ 45.00

THE ARCHITECTURE OF COLLAPSE

The Clarendon Lectures in Management Studies are jointly organized by Oxford University Press and the Saïd Business School. Every year a leading international academic is invited to give a series of lectures on a topic related to management education and research, broadly defined. The lectures form the basis of a book subsequently published by Oxford University Press.

Clarendon Lectures in Management Studies:

The Modern Firm
Organizational Design for Performance and Growth
John Roberts

Managing Intellectual Capital
Organizational, Strategic, and Policy Dimensions
David Teece

The Political Determinants of Corporate Governance
Political Context, Corporate Impact
Mark Roe

The Internet Galaxy
Reflections on the Internet, Business, and Society
Manuel Castells

Brokerage And Closure
An Introduction to Social Capital
Ron Burt

Reassembling the Social
An Introduction to Actor-Network-Theory
Bruno Latour

Gatekeepers
The Role of the Professions in Corporate Governance
John C. Coffee

Science, Innovation, and Economic Growth
Walter W. Powell

The Logic of Position, The Measure of Leadership
Position and Information in the Market
Joel Podolny

Global Companies in the 20th Century
Leslie Hannah

Material Markets
How Economic Agents are Constructed
Donald MacKenzie

Corporations in Evolving Diversity
Cognition, Governance, and Institutions
Masahiko Aoki

Staying Power
Six Enduring Principles for Managing Strategy and Innovation in an Uncertain World
Michael A. Cusumano

The Architecture of Collapse
The Global System in the 21st Century
Mauro F. Guillén

THE ARCHITECTURE OF COLLAPSE
The Global System in the 21st Century

MAURO F. GUILLÉN

OXFORD
UNIVERSITY PRESS

OXFORD
UNIVERSITY PRESS

Great Clarendon Street, Oxford, OX2 6DP,
United Kingdom

Oxford University Press is a department of the University of Oxford.
It furthers the University's objective of excellence in research, scholarship,
and education by publishing worldwide. Oxford is a registered trade mark of
Oxford University Press in the UK and in certain other countries

First Edition published in 2015

Impression: 1

Published in the United States of America by Oxford University Press
198 Madison Avenue, New York, NY 10016, United States of America

British Library Cataloguing in Publication Data

Data available

Library of Congress Control Number: 2015936868

ISBN 978-0-19-968360-4

Printed and bound by
CPI Group (UK) Ltd, Croydon, CR0 4YY

For Andrea Isabel Guillén

PREFACE

The global system evolves incrementally and, at times, in markedly punctuated ways. This book focuses on the last few decades, arguing that the global system has become more fragile, afflicted by disruption, and prone to breakdown. I advance a novel argument about the interplay between complexity and coupling at the node and network levels that creates "an architecture of collapse," a situation in which deviations or shocks spread quickly throughout the system, wreaking havoc around the world. I use the global financial crisis that started in 2008, the dyadic relationship between the U.S. and China, and the complex and tightly coupled subsystem known as the Euro Zone as case studies to illustrate how well the theory applies at different levels of analysis, from the organization to the industry, and from the dyadic relationship between pairs of countries to the global system.

Although I did not anticipate the final form of my argument when I started writing this book, I was relieved to conclude that there are ways to defuse the dangers of complexity and tight coupling in the global system. I initially thought that, at the global level or within subcomponents of the global system, complexity might be shock-absorbing as opposed to shock-diffusing. I was wrong. The case studies in the book indicate that complexity can be as conducive to the spread of disruptions and crises as tight coupling normally is. The difference lies in that complexity at the level of the network diffuses shocks while certain types of complexity at the level of the node absorb them. In particular, my argument contributes to the growing awareness that we need strong state apparatuses in the nodes of the global system in order to address the mounting problems generated by the architecture of collapse.

The idea for this book belongs jointly to my wife Sandra Suárez and I. We started to work together on the global financial crisis and the

Great Recession shortly after the meltdown of 2008. As a result of that collaboration, we published an article analyzing the causes of the crisis from a combined organizational and political perspective. I thank her for letting me update and expand that article, which appears in this book as chapter 4, and more importantly for allowing me to pursue the argument at the level of the global system and subcomponents within it. My foremost gratitude goes, as usual, to Chick Perrow, who initially criticized us heavily for allegedly misusing his theory of normal accidents in the context of the implosion of the financial system, thus helping us refine the analysis. I hope that the distinction between node and network complexity and coupling, absent from the original version of the argument, and the renewed emphasis on human agency and on ideologies, will persuade him that certain elements of his theory can be fruitfully applied in this context.

This book would not have come to light without the invitation extended by Oxford University Press and the Saïd Business School to deliver the 2014 Clarendon Lectures in Management Studies. I am especially indebted to David Musson and Dean Peter Tufano for their guidance, and to Chris McKenna for hosting me at Brasenose College and introducing me to a sampler of time-honored Oxford traditions. A few days at Oxford are a treat for any scholar, especially one interested in port wine, architecture, and design. Several colleagues provided me with access to data, comments, and suggestions, including Heather Berry, Miguel Centeno, Randy Collins, Paul DiMaggio, Martine Haas, Ann Harrison, Arun Hendi, Witold Henisz, Zeke Hernandez, Victoria Johnson, Donald Lessard, Daniel Levinthal, Emilio Ontiveros, Lori Rosenkopf, Nancy Rothbard, Adrian Tschoegl, Peter Tufano, and Mark Ventresca. I have also benefited from conversations with Tony Davis and Barbara Thomas. I thank Woody Powell for sharing his advice as to how to approach the series of lectures. Gerald Parloiu, an undergraduate student at Penn, provided able and timely research assistance.

I am indebted to Wharton Dean Thomas Robertson and Deputy Dean Michael Gibbons for offering me the chance of organizing and leading a pro-seminar on the global financial crisis during the spring and fall terms of 2009. This experience enabled me to learn from my Wharton colleagues and from the more than 300 students who took the class, thus sharpening my understanding of how crises develop and unfold. I also benefited from the process of preparing, videotaping, and delivering my massive open online course on Analyzing Global Trends for Business and Society, which invited me to think through some of the arguments contained in this book, especially those related to the ways in which isomorphic forces fuel complexity and coupling. Finally, I must thank Teresa Sanjurjo, Director of the Princess of Asturias Foundation, for inviting me to serve on the social sciences award committee, and later to join its Board of Trustees. I cannot possibly enumerate the myriad conversations I had with my fellow jurors and trustees, and with some of the awardees, regarding the arguments contained in this book.

I would like to dedicate this book to my younger daughter Andrea. She is superb at keeping me in line when I make arguments that do not hold up to scrutiny, and that discipline has helped me improve this book.

New York City,
February 2015

CONTENTS

LIST OF FIGURES

ABBREVIATIONS

BRICS	Brazil, Russia, India, China, and South Africa
CDO	collateralized debt obligation
CDS	credit default swap
ECB	European Central Bank
EEC	European Economic Community
EMU	Economic and Monetary Union
EU	European Union
EZ	Euro Zone
FDI	foreign direct investment
FDIC	Federal Deposit Insurance Corporation
GATT	General Agreement on Tariffs and Trade
GDP	Gross Domestic Product
IMF	International Monetary Fund
OECD	Organization for Economic Cooperation and Development
OTS	Office of Thrift Supervision
PIIGS	Portugal, Ireland, Italy, Greece, and Spain
R&D	Research and Development
SEC	Securities and Exchange Commission
TARP	Troubled Assets Relief Program
UN	United Nations
WTO	World Trade Organization

1

The Global System

The global economy has the capacity to "work as a unit in real or chosen time on a planetary scale."

> —Manuel Castells, "Toward a Sociology of the Network Society"
> (2000: 694)

The conventional wisdom suggests that the global system has become intricate, interconnected, unwieldy, and unpredictable. Frictions, conflicts or crises proliferate and become the subject of daily media coverage. But is it really true that the global system has become riskier and more likely to experience instability, disruption, and crisis? Are we going through a period of systemic vulnerability and danger that is unprecedented in recent history? Do we have any tools at our disposal to bring these problems under control, to reduce the global system's proneness to instability? Can the global system and its various sub-components survive as presently structured?

These are the tantalizing questions addressed in this book. I will use perspectives and theories borrowed from the fields of sociology and organizational theory to answer them in a hopefully persuasive way. The overarching argument is fairly simple: The global system has become more unstable due to the way in which it is structured. Most demographic, economic, financial, political, social, and cultural indicators suggest that the evolution of the global system towards instability is here to stay. I refer to this current structure of the global system as the *architecture of collapse* because of its intrinsic propensity to instability, disruption, and crisis.

Let me illustrate the problem with data about economic and financial crises. It is very clear that the frequency of currency, inflation, stock market, domestic debt, external debt, and banking crises has increased markedly in recent times. The top panel of Figure 1.1 shows the evidence for 70 countries between the years 1800 and 2010. The number of crises and the number of countries affected has been much larger since the mid-1980s than during any other period. It is sobering to observe that during the two decades between the early 1990s and the late 2000s, more than 50 of the 70 countries included in the chart were affected by at least one type of crisis. Most importantly, the average number of crises experienced by countries in a given year has also risen to an all-time high (see the bottom panel of Figure 1.1). Thus, the conventional wisdom that the global system has become more prone to these types of crisis is entirely accurate.

The Global System as an Idea

The notion that we live in an interconnected world is at the core of several influential schools of thought in the social sciences. Prominent among them is world-system analysis, pioneered by sociologist Immanuel Wallerstein beginning with the first volume of *The Modern World-System* (1974). This book advanced a structural view of the global system as a hierarchical one in which "core" industrialized countries play a qualitatively different role than the countries located in the "periphery," which provide cheap labor and raw materials (Smith and White 1992; Van Rossem 1996). The developing and industrializing "semi-periphery" lies somewhere in between, although the hierarchical structure is still preserved as the industrialized core has moved into higher-value activities associated with manufacturing design, capital goods, and services (Gereffi and Sturgeon 2005). The intense relationships between the core and the periphery serve to cement the global system, solidifying the differences between them.

The idea of a global system is also central to the world-society approach in sociology, which adopts the nation-state as the locus of institution-building and therefore as the fundamental node in the system (Meyer et al. 1997; Beckfield 2010). The distinctive aspect of this theory is to emphasize the process of expansion and diffusion of rationalized activities, which acquired a momentum of their own during the twentieth century, fueled by the "exigencies of global social

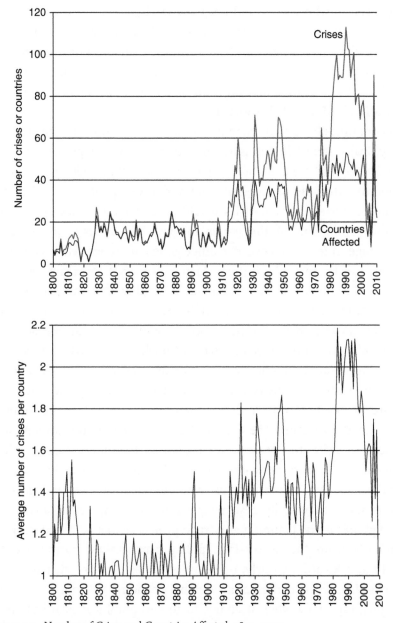

Figure 1.1. Number of Crises and Countries Affected, 1800–2010

Note: Based on 70 countries.

Source of the data: Reinhardt and Rogoff (2009), and subsequent updates.

organization whose logic and purposes are built into almost all states" (Meyer et al. 1997:152). Conformity with global norms is driven by the world-culture of rationalized modernity, which promotes the formal acceptance of "matters such as citizen and human rights, the natural world and its scientific investigation, socioeconomic development, and education" (Meyer et al. 1997:148).

Economists have also made important contributions to the study of the global system. No discussion of the contemporary global economy can ignore the concept of comparative advantage, which underlies economic analyses of foreign trade and investment. In 1776 Adam Smith proposed that countries would be better off if they specialized in the production of the goods for which they have the greatest advantage in terms of cost. For other goods, he suggested engaging in trade in order to procure them. Half a century later, David Ricardo modified Smith's original argument by adding that the principle of comparative advantage held even if the country did not enjoy the absolute lowest cost. In other words, countries should specialize in the production of the goods for which they have the most comparative advantage relative to other countries or the least relative disadvantage.

Economists spent the next century and a half refining and extending Ricardo's insights until Paul Krugman (1979, 1980) laid the foundations for the so-called "new trade theory," which assumes increasing returns to scale, the presence of monopolistic competition, product differentiation, and network effects. The main implication of this approach is that industries cluster in certain locations, and governments may successfully reshape patterns of comparative advantage through industrial planning and trade protection, a result that deviates markedly from the laissez-faire policy prescriptions formulated by Smith and Ricardo. Clearly, one cannot understand the structure and functioning of the contemporary global economy without Krugman's insights, especially when it comes to the geographical distribution of production.

For their part, political scientists have approached the study of the global system from the point of view of the decisions that governments make as to how their country relates to the rest of the world, and to what extent the domestic economy is open to international flows of capital, labor, goods, and services. The field of international political economy seeks to elucidate why, when, and how states decide to join the global economy, noting that full integration or openness is historically rare and politically problematic (Gilpin 1987). Research in this area has established that, in spite of globalization, governments retain a considerable degree of autonomy when it comes to formulating and implementing policy (Boix 1998; Garrett 1998).

Culture, Social Organization, and the Global System

The global system, however, is not only shaped by factor endowments, economies of scale, network effects, and domestic politics. The theory of "societal comparative advantage" sees the social organization unique to a country, not as an obstacle to economic action but as a resource for action (Biggart and Orrù 1997; Biggart and Guillén 1999; Portes 1997; Stinchcombe 1983). Preexisting institutional arrangements are the path-dependent context of action, which guides and enables socially-embedded action (Douglas 1986; Geertz 1973:220; Granovetter 1985; Swidler 1986). Following a comparative institutional perspective, Biggart and Guillén (1999:725) have argued that organizing logics vary substantially across different social contexts. For example, in some settings it is entirely normal and legitimate to raise business capital through family ties; in others, this is an "inappropriate" imposition and fostering ties to banks or to foreign investors might be a more successful fund-raising strategy. Logics are the result of historical development, are deeply rooted in collective understandings and cultural practices, and relatively resilient in the face of changing circumstances. Thus, culture and social organization provide not only ideas and values, but also strategies of action.

If local patterns of social organization are resources for action, then countries may play different roles in the global system and succeed to different degrees depending on the match between logics of social organization at the country level and the opportunities offered by the global economy. A comparative institutional approach warns that it is futile to attempt to identify the best practice or model in the abstract (Guillén 2001; Lazonick and O'Sullivan 1996; Whitley 1992). Rather, countries and their firms are socially and institutionally equipped to do different things in the global economy.

For instance, German, French, Japanese, and American firms are justly famous for their competitive edge, albeit in different industries and market segments. Germany's educational and industrial institutions—dual apprenticeship system, management–union cooperation, and tradition of "hands-on" engineering or *Technik*—enable companies to excel at high-quality, engineering-intensive industries such as advanced machine tools, luxury automobiles, and specialty chemicals (Hollingsworth et al. 1991; Murmann 1998; Soskice 1999; Streeck 1991, 1995). The French model of elite engineering education has enabled firms to excel at large-scale technical undertakings such as high-speed trains, satellite-launching rockets or nuclear power (Storper and Salais 1997:131–48; Ziegler 1995, 1997). The Japanese institutional ability to borrow, improve, and integrate ideas and technologies from various sources allowed its companies to master most categories of assembled goods, namely, household appliances, consumer electronics, and automobiles (Cusumano 1985; Dore 1973; Gerlach 1992; Westney 1987). And the American cultural emphasis on individualism, entrepreneurship, and customer satisfaction enables its firms to become world-class competitors, producing goods or services that are intensive in people skills, knowledge, or venture capital, such as software, financial services, or biotechnology (Porter 1990; Storper and Salais 1997:174–88). Trade economists have demonstrated that countries' exports differ in the degrees of product variety and quality depending on their social-organizational features (Feenstra, Yang, and Hamilton 1999). Thus, the global system is highly structured and differentiated as a result of a complex set of economic, technological, sociological, political, and cultural factors, with national economies playing a variety of roles.

Nodes, Network, and System

Before formulating the argument about the architecture of collapse that characterizes the contemporary global system, it is necessary to discuss its various components. At the lowest level of analysis, we find nodes. States constitute the basic nodes of the global system. They are sovereign entities associated with a territory and a population, and they undertake all sorts of activities internally and in relation to other states (Meyer et al. 1997).

The network is the next level, and it is made of dyadic relationships between pairs of nodes. It comprises different kinds of relationships, including exchanges of goods, services, capital, people, information, and so on. At the highest level of analysis, the global system includes both the nodes and the network of relationships among them. Thus, this book differs from much contemporary network analysis in that dynamics both internal to the nodes and external to them are taken into consideration.

The nodes, the network ties, and the global system have become so much more interesting to study because of recent trends and events. Consider the example of the economy. The global economy nowadays is very different from the world economy that emerged in the sixteenth century or the trade-and-investment-driven economy of the late nineteenth and early twentieth centuries. It is an economy in which information plays a crucial role. Thus, the global economy of the twenty-first century has the capacity to "work as a unit in real or chosen time on a planetary scale." (Castells 2000:694). It is certainly one in which national economies become more interdependent in terms of trade, finance, and macroeconomic policy (Gilpin 1987:389). What is perhaps most distinctive about the global system today is that there is a new level of intensity regarding our consciousness of the world as a whole and of each of its constituent parts (Robertson 1992:8; Albrow 1997:88; Waters 1995:63). We have become keenly aware of the fact that many aspects of our daily experience are dependent on what happens in other parts of the world, and we make decisions and act accordingly.

Diversity and Isomorphism in the Global System

One key characteristic of the contemporary global system is that practices, crises and other events spread from one country to another. These processes of diffusion have been conceptualized from a neo-institutional perspective by examining the impact of normative, coercive, and mimetic forces tending towards "isomorphism," i.e. similar forms, structures, and practices (DiMaggio and Powell 1983). At the cross-national level, world-society theorists argue that these forces operate under the umbrella of overarching narratives and rationalized normative orders spanning the globe (Meyer et al. 1997). Various sociologists and organizational scholars have studied the global spread

7

of economic practices and policymaking institutions from the dual perspective of world-level rationalization and isomorphic pressures (Dobbin et al. 2007; Kogut and Macpherson 2008; Polillo and Guillén 2005; Henisz et al. 2005; Weber et al. 2009), finding robust effects of a normative, coercive, and mimetic kind.

Crises and other forms of systemic breakdown spread from one country to another following a number of mechanisms, including cohesion, structural equivalence, and role equivalence (Guler et al. 2002). Cohesion means that two closely interrelated countries are likely to experience the same events or to adopt the same practices. Structural equivalence, by contrast, implies that a pair of countries relating to the same set of third countries is more likely to experience the same events or to adopt the same practices (Burt 1987). Role equivalence means that countries playing the same role in the global network, regardless of whether they relate to the same set of third countries or not, are more likely to experience the same events or adopt the same practices (Mizruchi 1993; Guler et al. 2002). We will examine in this book if any of these network-based isomorphic effects are at play in the global economy.

Tendencies towards isomorphism create situations in which all actors are exposed in the same way to similar events, disruptions, and shocks, thus potentially contributing to systemic failure. Institutional diversity, by contrast, prevents such occurrences. Isomorphism operates through the three traditional mechanisms of normative, coercive, and mimetic convergence (DiMaggio and Powell 1983), and also through trait-based emulation of the leader in the field, i.e. the country or countries perceived as being the most effective or successful (Westney 1987). As I will argue in the concluding chapter, institutional diversity creates buffers, degrees of freedom, and other devices that prevent disturbances from diffusing system-wide. This idea is a central piece of the analysis in this book.

Complexity, Coupling, and "Normal Accidents"

In his landmark book, *Normal Accidents* (1984), sociologist Charles Perrow proposed that when systems are simultaneously complex and tightly coupled they become prone to instability and failure. He defined interactive complexity as the extent to which a system has many moving parts in intricate arrangement, interacting with one another in non-linear ways. Coupling is the extent to which the constituent parts of a system are tightly related to one another, thus reducing the buffers and/or limiting the degrees of freedom, the tolerance, or the margin for error. When a system is tightly coupled, it cannot easily accommodate deviations from the normal state of affairs. Any such departure has the potential for disrupting the overall system as the disturbance spreads from one tightly-coupled component to another. When the system is also complex, the non-linear interactions of tightly-coupled components make it very hard to return the system to equilibrium when there is a disturbance.

Perrow illustrated his theory with a variety of examples drawn from the worlds of nuclear power stations, shipping, defense systems, and biotechnology. While there are several key differences between the concept of the normal accident and the argument in this book concerning the architecture of collapse in the contemporary global system, the fundamental theoretical premise is that systems can indeed become too difficult, or even impossible, to manage, with consequences that may be catastrophic in nature (Palmer and Maher 2010; Schneiberg and Bartley 2010; Harford 2011).

It is important to note that systems are oftentimes designed to be tightly coupled or to approximate tight coupling in order to increase efficiency or profitability. This is especially true of financial markets, where investment banks leverage themselves by borrowing money so as to preserve capital and increase their profitability (Guillén and Suárez 2010). In his prescient analysis of the financial sector in the United States, Richard Bookstaber (2007), a former trader and chief risk officer at Solomon Brothers, identified complexity and coupling as contributing to higher systemic risk. It is also the case that manufacturing systems and supply chains often become more tightly coupled in order to reduce costs or optimize delivery times (Goldin and Mariathasan 2014). Thus, high degrees of coupling create a situation in which the system cannot easily return to equilibrium if something throws it off balance. Eliminating buffers, cushions or circuit breakers contributes to efficiency, but facilitates the diffusion of disruptions from one component to another, eventually reaching the entire system.

Complexity:	Coupling:	
	Loose	Tight
High	**Complex interactions with built-in buffers** There is room to adapt in response to deviations and mishaps, even if systemic	**Complex interactions without buffers** Potential for systemic crises
Low	**Linear interactions with built-in buffers** Very easy to manage	**Linear interactions without buffers** Deviations and mishaps not of systemic nature

Figure 1.2. Four System Configurations in terms of Complexity and Coupling
Source: Adapted from Perrow (1984).

Perrow argued that "normal accidents" are inevitable — they are accidents waiting to happen — and become especially likely when both interactive complexity and coupling are high. As reflected in Figure 1.2, systemic disasters tend to occur when there are complex interactions among system components without buffers. When interactive complexity is low, i.e. interactions among system components are linear, tight coupling may produce mishaps, but rarely of a systemic nature. An even less dangerous situation obtains when complexity is high but coupling is loose, meaning that there are built-in buffers in the system creating room to adapt in response to deviations, even if potentially systemic. Lastly, when both complexity and coupling are low, it is easy to manage disruptions to the system.

One should not equate the concept of tight coupling to that of dependence or interdependence. Two nodes or parts of the global system may be interdependent but not necessarily tightly coupled. For instance, Wallerstein's (1974) core and periphery are interdependent in the sense that one cannot exist without the other. However, there are considerable degrees of freedom built into the world-system as long as there are multiple core and multiple peripheral countries. Let us illustrate this situation with a specific example. The bargaining power between a buyer and a supplier of a natural resource, or between a foreign investor and a local government, depends on how many alternative sources of supply exist and how mobile the investment is. If there are several sources of supply for a given mineral and the investments to extract it can be easily moved from one location to another, then the system is not tightly coupled (Haggard 1990).

It is also fundamental to realize that complexity and coupling can be defined and measured at the levels of the node and of the network as well as at the level of the overall system. In fact, node complexity and network complexity both contribute to system complexity. Similarly, node coupling and network coupling contribute to system coupling. In Perrow's (1984) classic analysis, the potentially catastrophic effects of tight coupling get multiplied in the presence of high interactive complexity because non-linear systems are less predictable and harder to return to equilibrium than linear systems. Thus, Perrow's theory of normal accidents is fundamentally about complexity and coupling at the level of the network of parts and units, i.e. the system or the subsystem. His theory does not apply within nodes, i.e. the parts or units: "An *accident* is a failure in a subsystem, or the system as a whole, that damages more than one unit and in doing so disrupts the ongoing or future output of the system. By contrast, an *incident* involves damage that is limited to parts or a unit, whether the failure disrupts the system or not" (Perrow 1984:66).

In this book, I examine the effects of complexity and coupling within nodes as well as at the level of the system or subsystem. Within nodes I examine banks and other organizations in the financial industry to show how complexity and coupling at that level can generate instability and crisis at the higher level of the economy. Like Perrow, I also focus on dyadic relationships between nodes, subsystems of nodes (e.g. trade blocs), and the entire system.

In his own account of the financial crisis, Perrow (2010:309) emphasized human agency as well as political and regulatory factors, relegating structural variables to the background. "Financial elites, to serve personal ends, crafted the ideologies and changed institutions, fully aware that this could harm their firms, clients, and the public," he argued. I agree that greed and deception played key roles in the crisis (see chapter 4). However, it is important to highlight that the meltdown could only bring about the kind of systemic repercussions on a global scale that it provoked in the presence of unusually high levels of complexity and coupling at the levels of the node and the network, as

Perrow (2010:309) himself recognizes: "Complexity and coupling only made deception easier and the consequences more extensive." In other words, greed and deception would have had purely local implications as opposed to global ones in the absence of complexity and coupling.

In the chapters that follow I adopt a theoretical perspective aligned with the proposal by Anthony Giddens to avoid the extremes of pure agency-based and pure structural explanations: "The notions of action and structure *presuppose one another*; but that recognition of this dependence, which is a dialectical relation, necessitates a reworking of both a series of concepts linked to each of these terms, and of the terms themselves" (1979:53). Action or agency, in his view, "does not refer to a series of discrete acts combined together, but to a continuous flow of conduct" (1979:55), while "structure" involves the "rules and resources, organized as properties of social systems" (1979:66). The concept that brings all of these elements together is that of "structuration," or "the *duality of structure*, which relates to the *fundamentally recursive character of social life, and expresses the mutual dependence of structure and agency*" (1979:69).

In a previous analysis of the financial crisis, Sandra Suárez and I borrowed selected aspects from the theory of normal accidents so as to be attentive to both agency and structure, invoking cultural, political, and structural factors at the levels of the organization, the financial sector, and the global system (Guillén and Suárez 2010; see also: Bookstaber 2007; Harford 2011). In this book I generalize this argument, noting the shock-diffusing and shock-absorbing characteristics of complexity and coupling at the level of the node and at the level of the network, which includes the dyad, the subsystem, and the system. While the case studies analyzed in subsequent chapters do not represent instances of pure normal accidents, the concepts of complexity and coupling are still useful to understand the causes and the widespread consequences of systemic disruptions, shocks, and crises.

Nodes, Networks, and Crises in the Global System
Complexity and coupling dynamics may have different effects on subsystems and entire systems (see Figure 1.3). I argue that a country (node) that has a complex economy and society is in principle more likely to sustain shocks coming from the rest of the global economy, as

	Complexity	Coupling
Definition:	An entity is complex when it has many moving parts in intricate arrangement, interacting with one another in non-linear ways.	An entity is coupled to the extent that its constituent parts are tightly related to one another, thus reducing the buffers and/or degrees of freedom, the tolerance, or the margin for error.
Levels of Analysis:	System > Network > Dyad > Node	System > Network > Dyad > Node
Main Advantage:	Redundancy	Efficiency

Figure 1.3. Basic Characteristics of the Global System: Complexity and Coupling

political scientists and political economists have argued (Katzenstein 1985; Rodrik 1998). However, following Perrow's theory, I submit that a node that is not only internally complex, but also tightly coupled, is more prone to instability and crisis. I will demonstrate this effect in chapter 4 with the chain of events that started in the United States in 2007, and led to the Great Recession. Further, if a highly complex and tightly-coupled node is also tightly coupled with other nodes in the global system, the probability of the shock diffusing to those other nodes is much higher. I will examine this dynamic in chapter 4 when examining the spread of the U.S. crisis to Europe, and in chapter 5 when analyzing the dyadic relationship between China and the United States.

The impact of network complexity, however, requires further analysis. In principle, a complex network can be both shock-absorbing and shock-diffusing. A network structure is shock-absorbing when the pattern and structure of relationships among the different nodes makes it hard for a disturbance to spread and become systemic. There are several features that can make a network shock-absorbing. The first is when not all nodes are connected to one another, i.e. the network has firewalls or circuit breakers built into it in the sense that there are several clusters of nodes that are internally very cohesive but do not relate to other clusters. A second shock-absorbing situation refers to the presence of nodes in the network that are both impervious to global pressure and occupy a strategic position in the network because they are the only nodes linking different clusters, as in Burt's (1987) structural-hole theory.

A high density and redundancy of diverse ties between nodes may make it possible for the network to respond to shocks by reconfiguring itself in real time. Most importantly, the complexity of relationships makes it possible for the nodes to find alternative ways to relate to one another in the wake of a widespread disturbance or failure. For example, researchers in the field of ecology and ecosystems have argued that the "redundancy of components and pathways, in which one can substitute for another, is also a key element in the robustness of complex systems" (May et al. 2008). From this point of view, complex systems are those in which no particular node and no particular part of the network is indispensable. In linear or sequential systems with low complexity, the absence of one part splits the system into two disconnected subsystems.

The design for the ARPANET, the precursor of the global Internet, is a good illustration of why complex, redundant networks are shock-absorbing. The key idea has to do with the distinction between circuit switching and packet switching. In traditional telephone communications, for instance, voice travels back and forth between two people over a dedicated line or circuit. Packet switching allows for a sharing of the link and for communication with multiple destinations simultaneously. While there is no evidence that the initial design was meant to survive a nuclear attack, "the later work on Internetting did emphasize robustness and survivability, including the capability to withstand losses of large portions of the underlying networks" (Leiner et al. n.d.).

By contrast, a network can become shock-diffusing when it has the opposite characteristics; namely, there are few firewalls and redundant ties between nodes, ties are of a homogenous type as opposed to diverse, and the opportunities for finding alternative arrangements are diminished. Tightly-coupled networks, those in which relationships between nodes are operating at the efficient frontier with little margin for error, are especially shock-diffusing. When a disturbance occurs in some part of the network, tight coupling makes it hard for the nodes to adapt and to find alternative arrangements because the degrees of freedom are small or nonexistent.

Central to the argument that complexity is shock-absorbing is the idea that complexity in systems plays two different roles. As a recent IMF study put it (Minoiu and Reyes 2010:4, 6),

> higher interconnectedness [i.e. complexity] in the financial system is
> believed to improve risk sharing and reduce the risk of contagion
> (through better ability to absorb shocks) but to also increase it

(through a wider outreach or reverberations). Financial systems have been shown to display *robust-yet-fragile* tendencies (Gai and Kapadia 2010) and to react differently to shocks depending on the pattern of interconnectedness (Allen and Gale 2000). [...] The trade-off between shock absorption and shock diffusion in financial networks is a recurring theme in the economics literature, with complex network structures being seen as both better able to diversify away idiosyncratic risk and more capable of propagating financial distress.

A variation on this argument is to make a distinction between the diffusion of losses and the actual bankruptcy of one node in the network:

> In a highly connected [i.e. complex] system, the counterparty losses of a failing institution can be more widely dispersed to, and absorbed by, other entities. So, increased connectivity and risk sharing may lower the probability of contagious default. But, *conditional* on the failure of one institution triggering contagious defaults, a high number of financial linkages also increases the potential for contagion to spread more widely. In particular, high connectivity increases the chances that institutions that survive the effects of the initial default will be exposed to more than one defaulting counterparty after the first round of contagion, thus making them vulnerable to a second-round default. The effects of any crises that do occur can, therefore, be extremely widespread. (Gai and Kapadia 2010:2403)

Therefore, three points need to be highlighted. First, certain patterns of complexity in interconnectivity may increase the rate at which a shock diffuses throughout a network and how far it diffuses (Rogers 2003; Burt 2005; McKinsey Global Institute 2014). Second, certain patterns of complexity can make shocks diffuse less quickly and to fewer and less far-flung nodes (for a review of the evidence, see: Minoiu and Reyes 2010; Gai and Kapadia 2010). In particular, saturated, i.e. very complex, networks are shock-absorbing because they make it possible for the interconnected nodes to absorb losses or other problems (Allen and Gale 2000; Gai and Kapadia 2010). Most importantly, network complexity means multiple pathways, and such redundancy allows for the network to reconfigure itself in response to disturbances, even if they diffuse quickly and throughout the network (May et al. 2008; Gai and Kapadia 2010). And third, the type of connection makes a difference, as I will discuss in chapters 2 and 3. For instance, foreign direct investment, which is relatively sticky, contributes to the stability of the network, while foreign portfolio investment, because of its "footloose" character, can lead to the diffusion of shocks during periods of crisis (Bhagwati 1998). The interplay between shock diffusion and absorption dynamics is a central theme of chapter 6 on the European sovereign debt crisis.

It is crucial to underline at this point the main difference between the model of system-wide shock absorption and diffusion proposed in this book and mainstream models of diffusion of disease in the field of epidemiology. "In most epidemiological models, higher connectivity simply creates more channels of contact through which infection could spread, increasing the potential for contagion." In modelling other types of diffusion processes, by contrast, complexity creates buffers and may provide for stability. For instance, in the financial system "greater connectivity also provides counteracting risk-sharing benefits as exposures are diversified across a wider set of institutions" (Gai and Kapadia 2010:2405). Besides the pattern of network complexity, I also take into consideration node complexity, which is a far broader concept than the mere susceptibility of infection because a complex node can act as a firewall or circuit breaker, as discussed in chapters 5 and 7.

It is also important to note that the analysis in this book differs sharply from the one advanced by Ian Goldin and Mike Mariathasan in *The Butterfly Effect: How Globalization Creates Systemic Risks, and What to Do about It* (2014). While for them connectivity between nodes in the global network leads to global complexity and ultimately to enhanced global risks, I argue that complexity by itself is not necessarily conducive to higher risk, and can be shock absorbing (Allen and Gale 2010; May et al. 2008; Gai and Kapadia 2010). Following Perrow's (1984) logic, it is the combination of complexity and tight coupling that leads to higher risk, not complexity alone (see also Guillén and Suárez 2010). I do agree that urbanization, trade in intermediates, and inequality enhance global risks, as Goldin and Mariathasan argue (2014:29, 70–99, 168–97), but not because they increase complexity.

Those are indicators of coupling, as I argue in chapter 3. In addition to this important departure from their work, the analysis in this book rests on the analytical distinction between complexity and coupling at the level of both the network and the node.

Plan for the Book

The chapters that follow provide ample empirical evidence to the effect that complexity and coupling are on the increase in the contemporary global system at different levels of analysis. Chapter 2 focuses on complexity, exploring the sources of increased levels of interaction among countries in the world as well as within countries. Chapter 3 documents the staggering levels of coupling that have resulted from structural changes in the global landscape over the last 30 years, both within and across countries. I will demonstrate that the dynamics of complexity and coupling unfold not only at the level of the global system as a whole, but also within subcomponents such as industries and subsystems such as regional trade blocs. Chapter 4 dives deep into one specific crisis—the Great Recession—to show how interactive complexity and tight coupling at the node level can jointly destabilize a specific country like the U.S, with the crisis spreading to other parts of the world depending on patterns of complexity and coupling at the network level. Chapter 5 examines the relationship between the world's two largest economies—China and the United States—to illustrate the dynamics of complexity and coupling at the dyadic level of analysis, noting how it contributed to the crisis and how it might evolve in the future. Chapter 6 compares two subsystems, the European Union and the Euro Zone, in the context of the acute crisis that started in Europe in 2009. I will argue that the European Union is a complex subsystem but one that is not particularly tightly coupled. By contrast, the Euro Zone is both complex and tightly coupled, and thus extremely sensitive to the disruptions and failures originating even from its smallest countries.

The case studies in chapters 4, 5, and 6 show that the argument about complexity and coupling can be applied at the industry level, at the level of a dyadic relationship between a pair of countries, and at the level of the subsystem of multilateral relationships within a bloc of countries. I will use the interplay between node and network dynamics to analyze why the global system has become so prone to instability and crisis over the last three decades. Finally, chapter 7 takes stock of the evidence presented in the book, and issues specific recommendations as to how to make the global system more predictable, less subject to failure, and safer overall.

2

Complexity

Redundancy of components and pathways, in which one can substitute for another, is also a key element in the robustness of complex systems.

—Robert M. May, Simon A. Levin and George Sugihara, "Complex Systems: Ecology for Bankers." *Nature* (2008:894)

The perception that over the last three decades the global system has become increasingly complex is commonplace. A system is complex to the extent that it has many moving parts in intricate arrangement. In the global system, those parts are countries. Different kinds of economic, political, social, and cultural phenomena unfold both within and across national borders. As a result of complexity, the system can become both more multifaceted and more unwieldy because of non-linear interactions among the interconnected nodes. As I observed in the introductory chapter, complexity can also provide for redundancy and duplication, thus making the system safer. In this chapter I will identify exactly which types of complexity in the global system foster stability and which may have the opposite effect.

It is relatively straightforward to document the increasing complexity of the global system over time from the point of view of both the network and the nodes in the network. I will consider multiple indicators of node complexity and network complexity, and show that they have increased over time in order to demonstrate that the overall global system has become more complex.

Network Complexity

As discussed in the previous chapter, network complexity refers to an intricate pattern of relationships among nodes in the system. I would like to highlight five key indicators associated with increasing network complexity in the contemporary global system; namely the number of countries, trade in goods and services, foreign direct investment, people flows in the forms of tourism and migration, and information flows (see Figure 2.1).

How Many States?

The global system has become increasingly complex from a network perspective simply because there are more nodes in it, i.e. more states. I will use three specific counts to illustrate the trend: membership in the United Nations (UN), the International Monetary Fund (IMF), and the General Agreement on Tariffs and Trade (GATT). Membership in the UN is a relevant indicator because it enables the country to be part of the international community and to interact with other states (Meyer et al. 1997). Membership in the IMF and the GATT (or its successor, the World Trade Organization or WTO) means that the country is part of the global financial and trading communities, respectively.

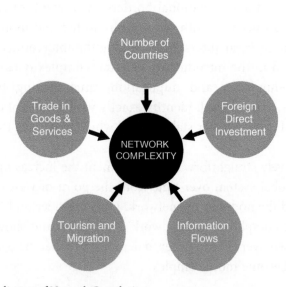

Figure 2.1. Indicators of Network Complexity

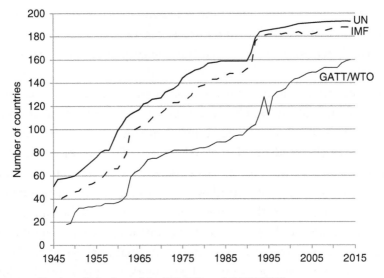

Figure 2.2. Number of Members of the UN, IMF, and GATT/WTO, 1945–2015

Whereas in 1945 there were only 51 member states in the UN and 28 members of the IMF, by the end of 2014 the numbers had risen to 193 and 188, respectively. Similarly, the GATT was founded in 1948 with 18 states as members, a figure that rose to 160 by 2014, with only a temporary decline as the transition was made to the World Trade Organization in 1995 (see Figure 2.2). Clearly, the process of decolonization during the 1960s and 70s, and the unravelling of the Soviet Union and Yugoslavia in the 1990s, are behind the sharp increases in membership during those decades. Thus, the proliferation of states in the world during the second half of the twentieth century was to be expected given the legacy of empire and the long-term unviability of the communist regimes. This trend could continue in the near future due to separatist movements in North America, Africa, Western Europe, Eastern Europe, and the Caucasus, although it could be partially offset if members of the 28-state European Union manage to create a true political union.

An increasing number of countries brings about several consequences, and all of them are associated with complexity. First, there are simply more countries sitting at the table. As a result, multilateral negotiations take longer. For instance, during the 1950s, negotiation rounds at the GATT took less than 10 months to complete, while the Tokyo round of 1973 lasted 74 months, and the Uruguay round of 1986 took 87 months to complete. One consequence of the proliferation of regional trade blocs such as the European Union or the North American Free Trade Agreement is that trade negotiations can be simplified by having fewer actors sitting at the table (Milner and Mansfield 1999). Second, economic and political treaties become more complex and implementation much harder given that individual countries enter into many different overlapping agreements with different sets of countries (Estevadeordal et al. eds. 2009). For instance, the WTO reports that as of the end of 2014 there were more than 270 trade agreements in force in the world, with some countries being signatories to more than 40. And third, global governance per se becomes much harder when an ever larger number of countries seek representation on committees or key executive positions at international agencies (Patrick 2014). Each of these aspects raises the network complexity of the global system.

The Rising Tide of Trade

A second key indicator of network complexity has to do with trade, i.e. with the flow of goods and services across national boundaries. Trade is a pervasive phenomenon, one with implications for virtually every topic of global significance. Figure 2.3 indicates that trade in tangible goods has more than doubled from about 19% of global GDP in 1960 to about 49% in 2013. Trade in services has also expanded at a similar rate, resulting in a combined ratio of 60% of global GDP, slightly more than twice the level back in 1960.

The density of the global trade network has also increased swiftly since the early 1960s. Figure 2.4 shows the dyadic trade density for the entire global economy between 1870 and 2009. It was calculated by taking into account all bilateral (e.g. dyadic) trade flows between pairs of countries for a given year, weighing them by the dollar value of bilateral trade and deflating it to correct for the changing value of the dollar over time. Trade densities grew steadily during the late nineteenth century, and accelerated during the early twentieth century driven by new transportation technologies like the steamship and the railroad, hand in hand with the expansion of manufacturing industry and the diffusion of the second industrial revolution throughout Europe, North America, and Japan. The end of World War I resulted

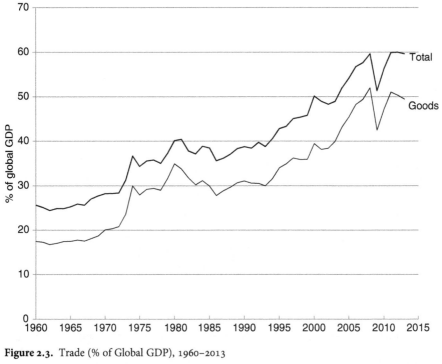

Figure 2.3. Trade (% of Global GDP), 1960–2013

Source: World Development Indicators.

in a sudden decrease. Monetary turmoil and the Great Depression assessed important blows to global trade during the 1920s and 30s. Trade densities did not recover until the beginning of World War II. The postwar period was characterized by a slow increase in trade densities until the 1970s. The fastest rate of increase over the entire period, however, took place beginning at the turn of the twenty-first century, mostly due to the growth of emerging economies and their ever more important role in global trade.

It is important to note that trade contributes to network complexity but not to network coupling. The growth of trade may not only help individual national economies specialize, as Adam Smith observed, but also diversify sources and destinations, as more countries join the global trading system. This is especially true in the case of the type of trade conceptualized by Paul Krugman (1979, 1980), and driven by increasing returns to scale, the presence of monopolistic competition, product differentiation, and network effects. The main corollary of Krugman's theory, compared to Smith's original approach, is that

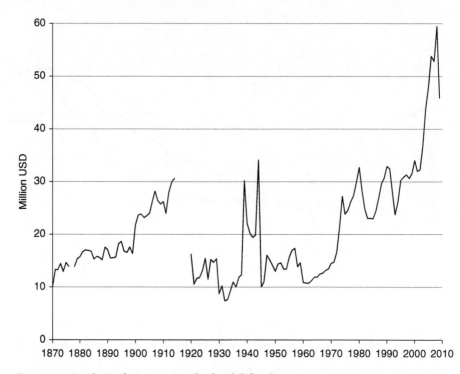

Figure 2.4. Dyadic Trade Density (weighted and deflated), 1870–2009

Sources of data: Dyadic trade data: http://www.correlatesofwar.org/COW2%20Data/Trade/Trade.html
Price index: http://www.minneapolisfed.org/community_education/teacher/calc/hist1800.cfm.

production of a certain good or service may occur in many different locations around the world, leading to complex patterns of trade with multiple suppliers of the same (differentiated) good. Thus, trade flows certainly increase the complexity of the system, but they do not contribute to coupling because they actually offer countries more options whenever there is a disruption or crisis. Moreover, complexity in trade patterns makes more suppliers and more buyers available to choose from, thus contributing to the stability of the overall system. This point can be readily illustrated with a very common current occurrence in the global economy. Whenever a specific source of supply for a raw material, a component, or a final product is disrupted by a political event, a force of nature, or some other cause, companies can readily rearrange their supply chains thus avoiding major long-term consequences (Matsuo 2014; Simchi-Levi et al. 2014).

Under some very specific circumstances, however, trading patterns may contribute to the contagion of shocks. One such situation is when there is a high level of trade with a small number of partners. This situation is known as "trade cohesion" (Guler et al. 2002; Henisz et al. 2005; Polillo and Guillén 2005). Consider country A and country B, which trade intensively with each other but only sparingly with third countries. If A suffers a shock, the disruption is likely to spread from A to B. There are only a few instances of large economies with a high degree of cohesion. Mexico's relationship with the U.S. is very much a cohesive one, although the reverse is not true. Mexico sends 71% of its total exports to the U.S. and receives 51% of its imports from the colossus to the north, while from the U.S. perspective, the percentages are just 14 and 12, respectively. I will analyze in chapter 6 the implications of the high level of trade cohesion within the Euro Zone.

Now consider the situation in which countries A and B export high volumes of goods to country C. If C suffers a shock, both A and B would be affected. This triangular relationship is known as "structural equivalence," i.e. A and B are intertwined because of their triangular trade with C. Lastly, there is the possibility that A and B export high volumes of the same type of goods to country C, i.e. they are "role equivalent" in the sense that A and B play the same role relative to C (Mizruchi 1993; Guler et al. 2002). If a shock related to that type of goods affects C, both A and B would be affected. Role equivalence in trade is a relatively common phenomenon. For instance, oil exporters are generally in a role-equivalent relationship relative to oil importers. Gas exporters, by contrast, are less subject to this effect because gas exports require more extensive and customer-specific investments in pipelines, storage, or in liquefaction and gasification facilities. The economies of East Asia are in a role-equivalent situation because they export to third countries the same types of manufactured products. When the Asian Flu crisis started in Thailand with a devaluation of the baht in 1997, it spread like wildfire throughout the region as countries devalued their currencies in order to remain competitive (Glick and Rose 1999). In chapter 6 we will see that certain countries in Europe are more role equivalent relative to Germany than others, with important implications for their ability to function as part of a monetary union.

Thus, trade contributes to complexity, but depending on the pattern of trade, it can be shock-diffusing or shock-absorbing.

The Blessings of Foreign Direct Investment

Foreign direct investment (FDI) represents a third way in which network complexity has increased over the last decades. FDI involves investment in an asset or company by an individual or company from another country with the purpose of controlling and managing the invested entity (Hymer 1974). Most frequently, FDI is associated with the activities of multinational corporations, which make investments in extractive, manufacturing, distribution, and other types of activities in foreign countries. For the purposes of official statistics, a capital flow across borders is assumed to be direct investment if it represents 10% or more of the voting stock of the target company. Below that threshold, it is considered to be portfolio investment, which I will analyze in chapter 3. One important characteristic of FDI is that it is intended to support a company's competitive strategy, and thus it is not easily reversible.

Several theories of development have considered FDI to be a curse because it tends to perpetuate hierarchical relationships of dependency between the countries at the origin and the destination of the flow (Wallerstein 1974; Evans 1979). Over the last 30 years, however, governments around the world, even in the most developed regions, have worked hard and gone out of their way to attract as much FDI as possible (UNCTAD 2012). In many countries around the world, actors historically opposed to FDI—such as nationalist politicians, leftist parties, or labor unions—have come around to welcome this type of investment (Haggard 1990; Guillén 2001). This reversal has happened because, relative to other types of capital flows, FDI brings about many potential benefits and fewer problems, as I will note later in this section.

Figure 2.5 shows three maps indicating the origin, destination, and magnitude of flows of FDI at three points in time. It is quite clear that in 1914, the global network of FDI was relatively simple. The United Kingdom was the most important source of FDI, and the flows of capital were not particularly convoluted. By 1967 the global network of FDI had become much more complex. The relative importance of the UK and other European countries paled by comparison with the

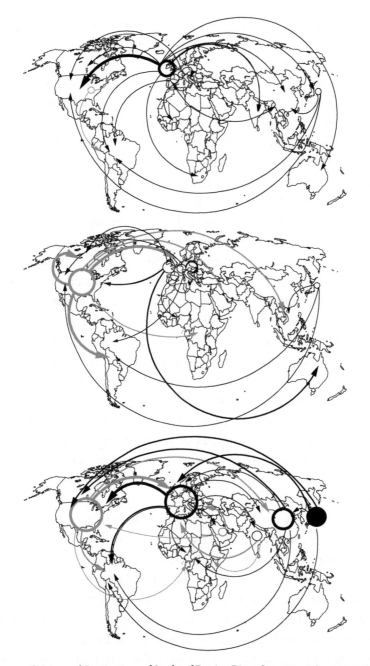

Figure 2.5. Origins and Destinations of Stocks of Foreign Direct Investment, in 1914, 1967, and 2012

Sources of the data: Woodruff (1966); *World Investment Report* (several years); *World Investment Directory* (several years).

dominant position of the United States. Meanwhile, new important destinations had been added, resulting in a more intricate global pattern of FDI flows.

Fast forward another half century to the year 2012, and the situation is radically different. There are four equally large sources of FDI, namely, the United States, the European Union, China, and Japan, with the Middle East and India becoming more and more important. In addition, there are more reciprocal flows, meaning that the global economy has become much more interrelated from the point of view of FDI. In other words, the world has become polycentric or multipolar and at the same time interconnected. Therefore, the global network of FDI is much more complex than it was back in 1914 or in 1967.

Like trade, FDI increases complexity but not coupling. The growth of FDI has been frequently touted as beneficial to host countries because it creates not only jobs and economic activity, but also provides them with a more stable and permanent source to finance their current account deficits. By contrast, portfolio investment tends to be footloose, more mobile. If a country is experiencing difficulties and foreign portfolio investors perceive there might be a crisis, currency devaluation and/or debt default, they can more readily take their money out, contributing perhaps to a self-fulfilling prophecy given that the withdrawal of portfolio capital may precipitate a crisis. In other words, portfolio investment tends to be "hot money," while FDI tends not to. Thus, FDI increases complexity but not coupling.

Another way to assess the nature of FDI is to look at it from the perspective of the firm. FDI provides companies with so-called "real options," namely, it gives them the opportunity to learn about how to operate in a specific host country and, more importantly, to expand or contract their operations in that country depending on changing circumstances. Like financial options, real options are more valuable under conditions of uncertainty (Kogut and Kulatilaka 1993). To the extent that FDI creates real options for companies, it increases complexity but not coupling because real options help companies adapt to shocks. Like trade, the complexity of FDI can lead to shock-diffusing or shock-absorbing dynamics, depending on the underlying pattern.

People on the Move

The global system has also become increasingly complex as a result of cross-border people movements, whether permanent (migration) or temporary (tourism). The impact of migration on both the origin and destination countries was perhaps higher in the past than it is today. Examples with major implications for modern economic history include the arrival of European conquerors and settlers to the Americas, the trans-Atlantic slave trade, or the great migrations of the late nineteenth and early twentieth centuries from both Asia and Europe to the Americas. Still, recent decades have seen a rapid growth in the impact of migration (see Figure 2.6). While the number of immigrants as a percentage of the total population of the world has hovered around 3% since 1960, migration levels to the high-income countries have more than doubled from about 5% of the population in those countries to

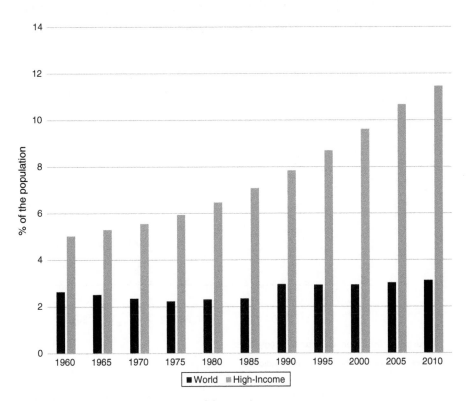

Figure 2.6. Immigrants as a Percentage of the Population, 1960–2010

Source of the data: World Development Indicators.

nearly 12% as of the census year of 2010. As a result of these movements, remittances to friends and family in the home country have also
more than doubled from around 0.3% of global GDP in the 1970s to
0.7% in 2012.

Another kind of movement of people has also increased markedly
due to political and ethnic conflict, namely, refugees. The number of
international refugees in the mid-1960s stood at around six million. By
the late 2000s it had more than doubled to 14 million.[1] To this figure
one could add the 27 million of internally displaced people, i.e. within
their own country. The rise in the number of refugees also makes the
world much more complex.

Tourism has risen quickly over the last few decades as well. Back in
1995 tourism arrivals represented less than 10% of the world's population. By 2012 the ratio had grown to just over 15%. Receipts for
tourism, however, have stagnated at a level of slightly less than 2% of
global GDP, indicating that the average tourist today spends less than
average tourist two decades ago (see Figure 2.7).

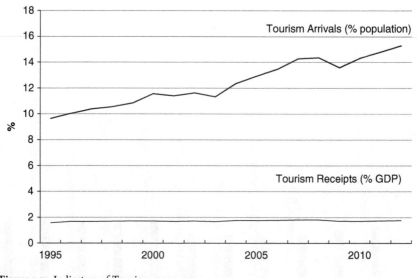

Figure 2.7. Indicators of Tourism, 1995–2012

Source of the data: World Development Indicators.

---

[1] See Center for Systemic Peace, http://www.systemicpeace.org/conflicttrends.html, accessed
June 28, 2014.

Increasing migration and tourism over the last three decades has caused a shift in people's daily lives, expectations, and models of reference to encompass experiences transcending national borders. Every migrant and tourist generates cross-border flows of information and economic resources, and provides new frames of awareness and meaning for his or her own experience, as well as for related others such as family or friends, thus expanding the array of interrelationships in the world (Robertson 1992:8; Albrow 1997:88; Waters 1995:63). It is in this sense that people movements exacerbate network complexity in the global system. Whether this complexity leads to stability through a better understanding of differences in the world or to panic when shocks or crises occur is a difficult issue to tackle, on which there is virtually no research.

Information Flows

Our last, and perhaps most debated, indicator of network complexity has to do with information flows. The rise of the Internet—a medium that did not exist 30 years ago—has greatly expanded within cross-border information exchanges. International telephone traffic has also grown rapidly. According to Telegeography, in 1993 about 50 billion minutes worth of international calls took place. By the end of 2014, the figure had risen to over 320 billion. In addition, calls using Voice over the Internet Protocol (VoIP) have skyrocketed since the turn of the twenty-first century. In 2014, people around the world made VoIP calls worth about 250 billion minutes. Thus, people around the world made that year 570 billion minutes worth of phone calls, up from 50 billion in 1993.[2] Data traffic around the world has grown by nearly a factor of seven, from 29 million to 201 million Mbps in the five years to the end of 2013 (McKinsey Global Institute 2014:13).

The phenomenal increase in cross-border information flows over the last two or three decades has contributed to a much higher degree of network complexity in the global system. The impact of information flows on the rearrangement of economic activity around the world, making possible new forms of economic organization and collaboration

---

[2] See http://www.telegeography.com/research-services/telegeography-report-database/, accessed February 3, 2015.

on a planetary scale, is well documented (Castells 1996; UNCTAD 2013). Political and social change has also taken place in massive proportions. During the 1990s mobile phones and the Internet took global society by storm. The effects on politics of information and telecommunication technologies driven by the marriage of mobility and connectivity at decreasing costs are perhaps as far-reaching as those on business and the economy, and they were felt primarily at the turn of the twenty-first century. For example, mobile phones and the Internet played a key role in the disruptions at the joint IMF–World Bank meetings in Prague in 2000, the demonstrations at the G-8 summit in Genoa in 2001, the anti-government popular uprising leading to the removal from office of the President of the Philippines also in 2001, the cover-up of the SARS epidemic in China during 2003, the Ukrainian Orange Revolution of 2004, the 2004 3/11 terrorist attacks in Madrid, the protests at the Republican convention in New York City in 2004, the anti-Syrian demonstrations in Lebanon in 2005, the anti-Japanese demonstrations in China over the issue of school textbooks also in 2005, the election of Barack Obama in 2008, Iran's "Twitter Revolution" in the wake of the disputed 2009 presidential election, and the posting on the Wikileaks website of documents pertaining to the wars in Iraq and Afghanistan (Bremmer 2010b). In early 2011, popular protests spread like wildfire from Tunisia to Egypt, Bahrain, Yemen, Libya, Morocco, Syria, and other Arab countries. As of the time of writing, several presidents had been removed from power or were on the verge of being ousted, though it was still unclear if the final outcome of the revolts would be a transition to democracy or not.

Rather than changing minds about key political issues or altering votes at elections, the evidence is that information technologies help mobilize people to act politically, which may or may not result in significant political change. It seems as if the twenty-first century will be quite different from the point of view of political mobilization and its effects. Just before the 2004 general election in Spain, text messaging through mobile phones enabled flash demonstrations and the mobilization of young people, who turned out at the polls in great numbers three days after the 3/11 terrorist bombings. The election removed the conservative party from power and ushered in the opposition socialists, who received three million more votes than in the previous election, even though surveys predicted an entirely different outcome, and post-election surveys established that only 0.3% of eligible voters changed their vote in response to the attacks (Suárez 2006, 2011).

As in the case of migration and tourism, the complexity generated by ever higher information flows can be shock-diffusing, as recent financial crises or the spread of the Arab Spring illustrate. The instantaneous availability of information quickened the pace of diffusion in both cases (see chapter 4; Bremmer 2010b). However, improved telecommunications can also foster global stability to the extent that information availability helps individuals and companies adjust to changing circumstances or to disruptions in real time, finding alternative arrangements that enable them to continue operating (Castells 1996).

We thus see that network complexity in the global system has been driven in an upward direction by a battery of economic, political, social, and technological forces. The global system of the early twenty-first century is certainly more complex that the one inherited from the late twentieth century, although there is plenty of room for debate as to whether the present level of complexity is unprecedented in the long-run of history. If we look at node complexity, however, a clearer picture emerges indicating that today's levels are higher than in times past.

Node Complexity

Node complexity has also increased over the last few decades, that is, each individual country in the global system has become internally more complex. The most important indicators of node complexity include the nature of political regimes, the presence of checks and balances on the executive branch of government, the size and capacity of the state apparatus, the problem of state failure, and the degree of industrial diversification (see Figure 2.8).

Democracy and Complexity

The twentieth century witnessed an epic confrontation between dictatorship and democracy, from the start of World War I in 1914 to the end of the Cold War in 1991 (Hobsbawm 1994), and arguably longer. To a certain extent, Francis Fukuyama (1989) was correct in proposing his famous "end of history" thesis in that liberal democracy and free

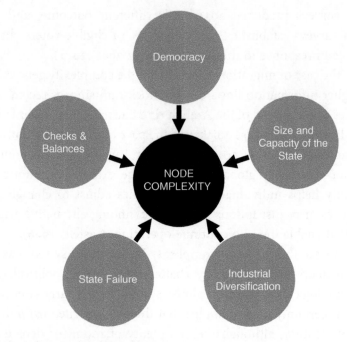

Figure 2.8. Indicators of Node Complexity

markets ultimately won the battle, although many democracies have recently degenerated into failed states or into anocracies, i.e. situations in which elected officials behave in authoritarian ways. I analyze these two types of situations later on. Samuel Huntington's (1993) premonitory analysis of the "clash of civilizations" has also become awfully descriptive of the new politics of identity and conflict in the contemporary global system, in which civil wars are less frequent than during the Cold War period, inter-state wars are even rarer, and the most dangerous and lethal conflict takes the form of ethnic or religious clashes and terrorism.

Democracies are more complex political systems than authoritarian, totalitarian, or sultanistic regimes (those in which members of an extended family control the government). Democracies have multiple points of entry for interest groups to influence the political process (Suárez 2000). As a result, democracies generate more intricate patterns of socio-political organization within each country. Whereas in other types of regimes a single party, individual, or family makes all important decisions, in democracies there are multiple influencers, societal actors such as business and labor are key participants, and public opinion and the press can have overwhelming impact on political processes and outcomes. Democracies are not only "messy" but also complex, with many moving actors, parts, and interest groups influencing the policymaking process. Thus, democratic countries are more complex nodes in the global system than dictatorships.

As of 1900, only parts of Western Europe, some former British colonies such as the United States, and the oligarchical states of Latin America were democracies, at least in form. In addition, not everyone could vote—women, for instance, enjoyed no political rights of their own until decades later. World War I was highly contradictory in its political effects, triggering revolutions that eventually led to totalitarian states like the Soviet Union, while giving democracy a fugacious chance in Germany and Eastern Europe. The rise of fascism in the 1920s and 30s posed the greatest challenge to democracy, one that would be effectively overcome with World War II. The postwar period was also two-sided. In some parts of the world, most notably Western Europe and some newly independent countries in Africa and Asia, democracy took hold. The cases of Germany, Japan, and India are especially important (Moore 1966). But the Cold War led to the proliferation of both totalitarian communist regimes in Eastern Europe and East Asia, and authoritarian regimes supported by Europe and the United States in an attempt to curb communist takeovers of power in Latin America, Africa, the Middle East, and parts of Asia.

Even before the end of the Cold War, however, a third wave of transitions from dictatorship to democracy took place during the 1970s and 80s in Southern Europe (e.g. Greece, Portugal, Spain), Latin America (Argentina, Brazil, Chile, and other countries), and East Asia (South Korea, Taiwan). In many of these countries the transition to democracy took place after social and economic development had made strides (Lipset 1959; Boix 2011), a new class of business owners or professionals grew influential (Moore 1966), and labor movements gained strength and demanded political freedoms (Rueschemeyer et al. 1992). The fourth wave of democratization started in 1989 with the collapse of the Soviet Union and its satellite regimes, with democracy spreading throughout Eastern Europe, the Caucasus, and Central Asia.

Thus, the twentieth century taken as a whole was characterized by the spread of democracy, albeit with notable setbacks. The year

1989 was a milestone, perhaps a culmination, but not an unprecedented turning point. As a result of the four waves of democratization, at the beginning of the twenty-first century there were just 20 countries ruled by dictators while more than 90 enjoyed democratic freedoms (see Figure 2.9). The first year since World War II in which there were more democracies than dictatorships in the world was 1991.

The popular uprisings in North Africa and the Middle East that started in early 2011 represent another step towards democratization, although a complex and complicated one at that. "The revolutions unfolding across the Middle East represent the breakdown of increasingly corrupt sultanistic regimes," Jack Goldstone, a key expert on political revolutions, has argued. "Although economies across the region have grown in recent years, the gains have bypassed the majority of the population, being amassed instead by a wealthy few. [Former Egyptian President Hosni] Mubarak and his family reportedly built up a fortune of between $40 billion and $70 billion, and 39 officials and businessmen close to Mubarak's son Gamal are alleged to have made fortunes averaging more than $1 billion each.... Fast-growing and urbanizing populations in the Middle East have been hurt by low

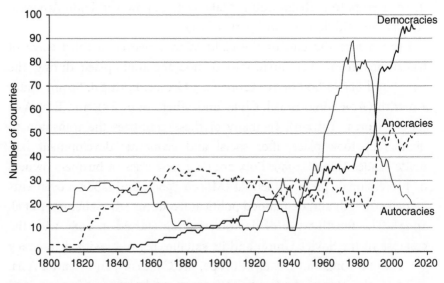

Figure 2.9. Prevalence of Political Regimes (number of countries), 1800–2013

Source of the data: Marshall (2013).

wages and by food prices that rose by 32 percent in the last year alone" (Goldstone 2011:11).

The third type of political regime in Figure 2.9—anocracies—refers to incoherent polities in which a mix of autocratic and democratic authority patterns coexist (Epstein and Converse 2008).[3] Elected officials, especially those in the executive branch, behave in authoritarian ways after assuming office, and tend to perpetuate themselves in power. There are 50 countries presently classified as anocracies, up from fewer than 20 in 1970. Examples include Algeria, Angola, Armenia, Bhutan, Cambodia, Chad, Guinea, Madagascar, Mauritania, Morocco, and Zimbabwe. Perhaps the two that most frequently make the headlines are Russia and Venezuela. Anocracies are also complex political systems, even more so than democracies, with unresolved underlying socio-political conflicts, and unpredictable policies. Thus, the proliferation of democracies and anocracies at the expense of dictatorships has tended to increase node complexity in the global system from a political point of view.

The question of whether the complexities of democratic government are shock-diffusing or shock-absorbing is not straightforward to answer. Consolidated democracies tend to have stable governments, but new democracies tend not to (Haggard and Kaufman 1995). Thus, the external economic and financial shocks that rocked Latin America in 1995-6, East Asia in 1997 or Eastern Europe during the late 1990s spread like wildfire throughout each region at a time when democratic regimes were still young and political actors inexperienced. Western European countries suffered from similar external shocks during the 1970s and 80s, but the economies in that part of the world did not suffer as much. Thus, consolidated democracies tend to be shock-absorbing, while young democracies tend to be shock-diffusing. Given this argument, it is not surprising to see that economic, financial, and political turmoil escalated during the 1980s and 90s (see Figure 1.1; Reinhardt and Rogoff 2009), precisely at a time when the number of democratic countries in the world doubled from 41 in 1980 to 80 in 2000 (see Figure 2.9).

---

[3] See the data on anocracies at http://www.systemicpeace.org/conflicttrends.html, accessed June 28, 2014.

The Witty Idea of Checks and Balances

One of the most distinctive characteristics of democracy as a political regime is the presence of checks and balances on the decision-making power of the executive branch of government. Political checks and balances represent veto points, and tend to provide the political system with more stability and predictability (Henisz 2000). The idea of checks and balances, which dates back to Montesquieu and the American revolutionaries, is a witty constitutional solution to the problem of tyranny. Not only may the different branches of government be controlled by different parties, but the legislative branch can be more or less fractionalized. As the argument goes, the more veto points in the political system, the more stable it is.

Not all democracies, though, have the same level of checks and balances built into their law-making and policymaking procedures, and those levels have changed over time. Figure 2.10 shows that the average degree of checks and balances in the world's political systems has grown quite rapidly since the 1970s. The measure depicted in the

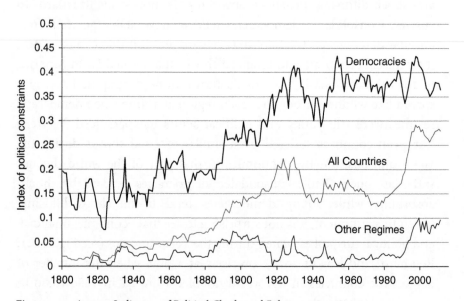

Figure 2.10. Average Indicators of Political Checks and Balances, 1800–2011

Notes:

Based on Witold Henisz's polconiii measure.

Democracies are defined as countries scoring 6–10 on the Polity scale (Marshall 2013).

Source of the data: Henisz (2014).

chart is based on Henisz's (2000) concept of political constraints. Two important messages stem from this chart. The first is that democracies tend to have more political checks and balances in place, hence their higher degree of complexity. The second is that other types of regimes—especially anocracies—have also adopted more checks and balances over the last two or three decades. As a result, the global system has seen a generalized increase in node complexity from this point of view.

Checks and balances contribute to the stability of the political system, making unpredictable changes more difficult. As a consequence, a country with more checks and balances is likely able to sustain the harmful effects of an external shock better than others. Thus, checks and balances are for the most part shock-absorbing. The counterargument, however, is that under conditions of duress veto points can lead to political paralysis given that every interest group may attempt to shift the burden of adjusting to the shock to another interest group. If checks and balances result in gridlock, then they can become shock-diffusing. It is interesting to note that, during the Great Recession, the U.S. political system did not act as swiftly as the Federal Reserve, which is shielded from political pressure (see chapter 4).

The Size and Capacity of the State Apparatus, and the Specter of Indebtedness

In addition to the nature of the political regime and the presence of checks and balances, larger state bureaucracies and government activity also contribute to node complexity. The sociology of organizations has long established that larger organizations tend to have more complex internal structures, higher degrees of specialization and differentiation, and more characteristics commonly associated with the bureaucratic model (Perrow 1986; Blau and Scott 1962; Blau and Schoenherr 1971). For its part, the field of political economy has argued that a bigger role of the state through taxation and spending provides economies with protection against changes in the business cycle and external shocks (Katzenstein 1985; Rodrik 1998).

Figure 2.11 displays two indicators of state size, namely, taxation and spending. Over the last 30 years tax revenue as a percentage of GDP has increased in many countries around the world while in others it has tended to decline (see the upper panel). The largest increases have taken place in low-and middle-income countries, especially China. In Europe and the United States, taxation has grown less rapidly than the economy, although with several ups and downs, especially in the U.S. This has resulted in a similar level of taxation nowadays when compared to 30 years ago. Public spending, as measured by general government consumption, has tended to increase (see the lower panel in Figure 2.11), from about 13.5% of global GDP in 1960 to nearly 18% in 2013. The increase has been most acute in high-income countries, especially the Euro Zone (see chapter 6).

It is important to note that the relative magnitude of fiscal revenue compared to fiscal spending has implications not only for complexity but also for coupling. The fact that spending has grown faster than taxation has resulted in higher levels of indebtedness, a factor that reduces the government's ability to act (Lauder Global TrendLab 2014). The size of the state—as captured by taxation and spending—contributes to node complexity in the global system, while the level of government debt, as I will argue in the next chapter, increases coupling.

An even more important contributor to node complexity is state *capacity*, or the administrative and organizational ability of the state to identify, evaluate, formulate, and implement policies, which requires competent officials with decision-making authority who can insulate themselves from undue political pressures and are in a position to align interest groups in support of their policies (Guillén and Capron 2016). It is important to distinguish between state capacity and state goals or policy priorities (Levi 1988; North 1981). State capacity is "the ability of state institutions to effectively implement official goals" (Hanson and Sigman 2013:2), or "the institutional capacity of a central state, despotic or not, to penetrate its territories and logistically implement decisions" (Mann 1993:59). In other words, state capacity is the administrative infrastructure that enables states to pursue certain goals or priorities, to implement policy, to get things done (Mann 1984; Tilly 1990). As Skocpol (1985:17) put it in an influential essay, states have "capacities" related to their "territorial integrity, financial means, and staffing," and these capacities enable them to incorporate new models or practices. State capacities can also be conceptualized in terms of the extent to which state structures exhibit the characteristics of the Weberian

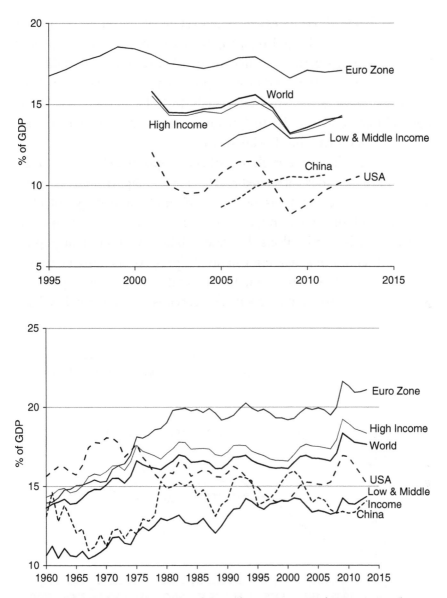

Figure 2.11. Tax Revenue (top panel) and General Government Final Consumption (bottom panel), as a Percentage of GDP

Note: General government consumption excludes investment.

Source of the data: World Development Indicators.

ideal-type of legal-rational, or bureaucratic, rule (Evans and Rauch 1999). In this vein, "sheer sovereign integrity and the stable administrative-military control of a given territory are preconditions for any state's ability to implement policies. [...] Loyal and skilled officials and plentiful financial resources are basic to state effectiveness in attaining all sorts of goals" (Skocpol 1979:16). State capacity ultimately involves "the ability of the permanent machinery of government to implement policies, deliver services and provide policy advice to decision-makers" (Polidano 2000: 805). The state needs to "allocate resources in an optimal manner," in order to "guarantee an effective implementation of policies" (Weaver and Rockman 1993).

Figure 2.12 shows the evolution of state capacity between 1960 and 2009, using the index calculated by Hanson and Sigman (2013), which focuses on "core functions of the state" underpinned by "plentiful resources, administrative-military control of a territory, and loyal and skilled officials," and reflects the state's ability to "reach their populations, collect and manage information," "preserve its borders, protect against external threats, maintain internal order," "develop policy, produce and deliver public goods and services," "enforce policy," and

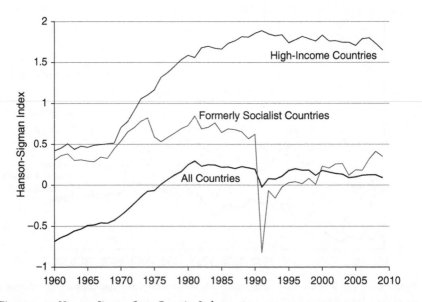

Figure 2.12. Hanson-Sigman State Capacity Index, 1960–2009

Note: Calculated by Hanson and Sigman (2013) as the "capacity1" measure, which is the result of latent-variable analysis on 24 indicators: administration and civil service count, administrative efficiency, anocracy, bureaucratic quality, census frequency, civil service confidence, contract-intensive money, effective implementation of government decisions, efficiency of revenue mobilization, fractal borders, military personnel, military spending, monopoly on the use of force, mountainous terrain, political terror scale, quality of budgetary and financial management, quality of public administration, relative political capacity, statistical capacity, tax evasion, taxes on income, taxes on international trade, total tax revenue, and index of "Weberianness."

Source of the data: State Capacity Dataset version 0.9 (Hanson and Sigman 2013).

"regulate commercial activity" (Hanson and Sigman 2013:2–9). In the world as a whole, one observes an increase in state capacity until the year 1981, with a gradual decline since then. However, in the case of the high-income countries, the peak occurred in 1992, and the overall level of capacity is much higher throughout the period. Finally, the formerly socialist countries are a special category in that they appeared to have levels of state capacity comparable to those among the high-income countries until the mid-1970s. The transition to the market and the creation of new states in Eastern Europe, the Caucasus, and Central Asia during the early 1990s led to a decline in average levels of state capacity, which have only recovered slightly over the past two decades.

The node complexity associated with greater state size and with greater state capacity is clearly shock-absorbing as opposed to shock-diffusing. As I will analyze in chapters 4 and 5, the U.S., Japan, several European countries, and China resorted to fiscal spending in order to buffer themselves from some of the ill effects of the Great Recession. As noted above, government spending is an effective tool when it comes to shielding the economy from the vagaries of downturns and external shocks, especially when the country is heavily interconnected with the rest of the world (Katzenstein 1985; Rodrik 1998). Financial resources, however, are only a necessary condition to smooth out the business cycle through fiscal policy. State capacity is needed to identify the best ways of spending the money, and to avoid mismanagement and corruption. More generally, state capacity is fundamental to dealing with disruptions of all sorts, including natural catastrophes and humanitarian disasters as well as economic or financial crises. Unfortunately, both the fiscal capacity of the state and average levels of state capacity have dropped in most parts of the world over the last two decades, reducing the complexity and resilience of nodes, and thus imperiling the overall global system.

State Failure and Complexity
Another way of looking at the phenomenon of node complexity in the contemporary world is to examine the phenomenon of state failure, which involves the breakdown of centralized state authority, resulting in anarchy, chaos, and lawlessness, i.e. an extremely low level of state

capacity. While well-established and internally differentiated states increase node complexity, failed states exhibit little complexity in the sense that they lack an elaborate state apparatus. The number of failed states in the world has declined from 78 in 1995 to 49 in 2013 (see Figure 2.13). This is a welcome trend, and it means that node complexity is increasing. The geography of state failure is relatively straightforward, and can be summarized in terms of the so-called long arc of geopolitical instability. It starts at relatively mild levels of state failure in some parts of Latin America, becomes more prevalent and intense in Sub-Saharan Africa, the Middle East, and sections of South Asia, and then starts to vanish as one reaches the Asia-Pacific region (Marshall 2013).

It could be argued that state failure contributes to coupling and not to complexity. However, that is only true if the affected country is connected to the global economy or occupies an important geo-strategic location. For instance, state failure in central Africa does not increase coupling in the world as much as state failure in Somalia does. This is due to the fact that Somalia is strategically located at the cross-roads of several key shipping routes. In 1977 war broke out between Somalia and Ethiopia after Somali dictator Mohamed Siad Barre invaded a Somali-populated area in Ethiopia. Cuban and Soviet

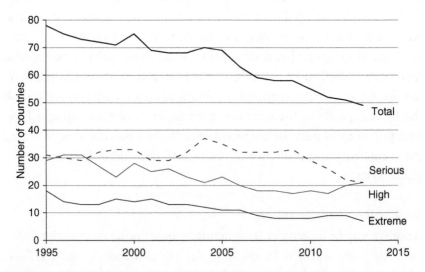

Figure 2.13. Number of Failed States at Different Levels of State Fragility, 1995–2013
Source of the data: Marshall (2013).

support for Ethiopia tilted the military balance against Barre, who had to turn to the U.S. for help. His regime finally collapsed in 1991, and Somalia plunged into chaotic internal conflict. As is often the case, political dislocation led to widespread deprivation and poverty, with more than 25% of children under the age of five being underweight, and more than 75% of the population below the poverty line. Unemployment was reported to be above 50%.

Meanwhile, fishermen became vigilantes in an attempt to defend Somali territorial waters from European and Asian ships, which were dumping toxic waste or illegally harvesting fish, a practice that threatened their livelihoods. In the midst of civil war, they had no trouble securing pistols, automatic weapons, and even rocket-propelled grenades. Eventually, they discovered the lucrative potential of piracy and hostage taking. Gradually, piracy became a way of life. By 2010, over 50 vessels and 1,000 hostages were being held. That year 44 ransoms were paid worth $176 million dollars, according to Oceans Beyond Piracy. Piracy around the Horn of Africa declined thereafter due to massive patrolling efforts by a coalition of countries, which are spending in excess of $5 billion annually to contain the problem. At the present time, the Somali piracy threat to global shipping has subsided, while attacks in other locations like the Gulf of Guinea are on the increase. The global attention paid to piracy clearly indicates that it contributes to coupling, forcing governments to react and shipping companies to re-route ships.

In sum, the recent decline in state failure around the world has increased node complexity. This trend helps countries absorb external shocks and contain them because, as noted above, stronger states act as buffers in the global system. Both the size of the state and the reduction in the degree of state fragility foster stability on a global scale.

Industrial Diversification and Complexity

The last indicator of node complexity has to do with the degree of industrial diversification. As nodes in the global system, countries like Chile or Venezuela are less complex from economic and political points of view because very large proportions of their economies and their external trade are accounted for by one single commodity, copper and oil, respectively. Countries with a more diversified industrial structure

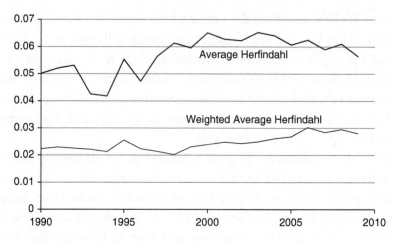

Figure 2.14. Herfindahl Index of Industrial Diversification, 1990–2009

Note: At the four-digit level of the UNIDO industrial classification. Weighted index calculated using size of industrial sector in each country.

Source of the data: UNIDO Industrial Statistics.

like Argentina or Brazil are more complex, let alone the United States, China, or Germany, to name but a few examples.

Figure 2.14 shows two indicators of industrial diversification. Both are based on the Herfindahl-Hirschmann index, which increases as diversification grows. The top line uses information about production at the four-digit level in the international industrial classification, without taking into consideration the size of each economy. The bottom line calculates the index similarly, except that it is weighted by the size of different economies. This indicator displays an upward trend between 1990 and 2006, and a slight decline thereafter, while the unweighted indicator starts to decline around the year 2000, mainly because of the proliferation of new small countries during the previous decade. Over the last three decades, the general trend is towards greater node complexity due to industrial diversification.

The complexity generated by industrial diversification is unambiguously shock-absorbing. External shocks of an economic, political, or technological nature, tend to have a greater impact on countries whose industry structure is not diversified. If the shock is beneficial to the specific industry that dominates the country's economy, a boom follows. If the opposite is true, it can have devastating consequences. The classic example of this dynamic involves the fortunes of commodity-producing countries, which tend to be at the mercy of global economic forces. Another important angle to this argument is that more diversified economies rely on broader and more heterogeneous knowledge foundations, which tend to benefit economic performance over the long run (Hausman et al. 2014).

The Implications of Network and Node Complexity

With only a couple of exceptions (tourism receipts and tax revenue), the indicators shown in this chapter unequivocally point in the direction of increasing complexity in the global system at the level of both the node and the network over the last three decades. It is important to keep in mind that complexity is not by itself conducive to disruption, crises, and their spread around the world. In fact, many manifestations of complexity tend to be shock-absorbing.

Node complexity makes the country more impervious to global isomorphic forces, thus reducing the potential for contagion in the system as a whole. Previous research proposed that practices and disruptions diffuse more easily within, as opposed to across, national boundaries. The "impermeability" of national borders has the effect of slowing down diffusion across countries (Kogut 1991). Shock-absorbing imperviousness is a broader concept than the impermeability of borders because it operates both within and across national borders. For instance, the size and capacity of the state apparatus shields the country from both external and internal coercive influences.

Node complexity also has implications for coercive effects in the global system. Powerful external actors, such as the IMF, do not simply force governments to enact new policies. Rather, they manage to influence countries because their intervention tilts the domestic political balance among interest groups in favor of their preferred policies or reforms (Henisz et al. 2005). In this context, state size places limits on the extent to which external actors exerting their influence through domestic interest groups can coercively impose new models and practices. State size reduces the probability of state capture by special interest groups, and shields the country from external pressure (Evans and Rauch 1999; Rodrik 1998).

Unlike node complexity, network complexity can lead to shock-diffusing dynamics, depending on the specific pattern of trade, foreign direct investment, migration or information flows. While it is important to examine in detail those patterns, I will argue in subsequent chapters that it is even more momentous to assess if network complexity interacts with network coupling to produce highly unstable situations. The Great Recession and the crisis in the Euro Zone will help us visualize why the explosive combination of network complexity and network coupling can be particularly problematic (see chapters 4 and 6).

3

Coupling

The idea and the ideology of free trade and its benefits ... have, in effect, been hijacked by the proponents of capital mobility. They have been used to bamboozle us into celebrating the new world of trillions of dollars moving about daily in a borderless world, creating gigantic economic gains, rewarding virtue and punishing profligacy. The pretty face presented to us is, in fact, a mask that hides the warts and wrinkles underneath.

—Jagdish Bhagwati, "The Capital Myth." *Foreign Affairs* (1998)

Coupling is a very different concept than complexity, and it creates a vastly different reality frequently characterized by risk, disruption, and even catastrophe. It involves the extent to which the nodes (countries) in the global system are internally structured with few degrees of freedom, and the extent to which relationships between pairs of nodes reduce or even eliminate buffers or cushions. In most situations, coupling becomes tighter as individuals, companies, and governments seek to increase efficiency or to multiply the opportunities for profit-making. Unfortunately, it is often the case in today's global system that more profitable or more competitive also means more risky. This is true of financial assets, banks, and even manufacturing firms, as the examples in this chapter illustrate. As in the case of complexity, I propose five indicators of network coupling and five indicators of node coupling to demonstrate that the trend towards a more tightly-coupled global system is robust to the choice of indicator. Moreover, the fact that so many indicators of coupling are trending upwards adds to the problem by creating even more intricate patterns of exposure to risk.

Network Coupling

The most obvious manifestations of coupling in the global system have to do with the nature and structure of relationships between of pairs of countries. Most of the literature on international political economy (Gilpin 1987, 2000), the world-system (Wallerstein 1974), and the world-society (Meyer et al. 1997; Guler et al. 2002; Henisz et al. 2005; Polillo and Guillén 2005) emphasizes the increasing density and tightness of cross-national relationships as a hallmark of the contemporary world.

As shown in Figure 3.1, I will focus the attention on five canonical indicators of network coupling. The first, current account imbalances, captures the consequences of economic exchange among countries in terms of the mutually interdependent and tightly coupled relationship between surplus and deficit countries. The second, trade in intermediates, speaks to the breaking down of the value chain of productive activities by location, a phenomenon that has gathered speed over the last two or three decades. The third indicator deals with the classic topic of foreign portfolio investment, which differs

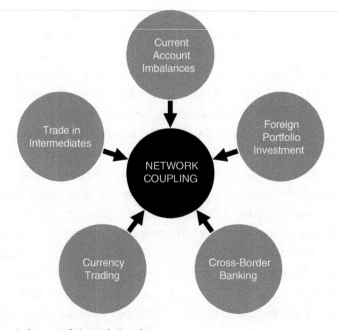

Figure 3.1. Indicators of Network Coupling

from FDI in that it contributes to coupling rather than complexity. The fourth is currency trading, one of the largest markets in the world in terms of volume. Lastly, the fifth indicator is cross-border banking, another phenomenon that has increased markedly in recent decades.

Growing Current Account Imbalances

The global economy is fundamentally one in which countries engage in economic exchange with one another (Gilpin 1987). One of the most important outcomes of that exchange is that some countries end up being in deficit, largely because they import more than what they export, while others end up being in surplus, mainly for the opposite reason. One important corollary of global economic exchange is that if there is a country in the world that enjoys a surplus, it must necessarily be the case that at least one other country is running a deficit, assuming that there is no inter-planetary trade. In other words, global economic exchange is a zero-sum game.[1]

Countries engage in different types of transactions with one another. They trade in goods and services, their capital and labor earn income in foreign locations, and their households and governments transfer funds to other countries. These three types of transactions are part of the so-called "current account." When a country runs a deficit in the current account, it must secure capital from abroad in order to bridge the gap. This may happen either in the form of investments made by foreign households, companies or governments in any type of financial asset, or in the equity of domestic companies. These transactions are registered in each country's "capital account." Conversely, when a country runs a surplus in the current account, it can fund deficit countries, and those transactions get recorded in its capital account. The combined balance of the current and capital accounts for any given country, known as the "balance of payments," is typically zero for a sufficiently long period of time, i.e. one year. Simply put, deficit and surplus countries are mirror images of each other, and they need each other for the global economy to work.

---

[1] In a creative piece, Paul Krugman (1978) considered the consequences of interstellar trade, i.e. when goods travel at nearly the speed of light.

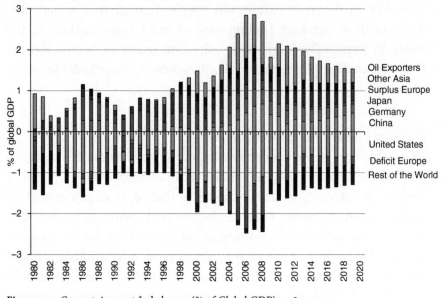

Figure 3.2. Current Account Imbalances (% of Global GDP), 1980–2019

Note: Actual data until 2013; projections starting in 2014.

Source of the data: IMF, *Global Economic Outlook.*

Figure 3.2 shows the evolution of current account surpluses and deficits in the global economy, with actual data running from 1980 until 2013, and projections thereafter. The source of the data is the IMF. The IMF has a keen interest in tracking current account imbalances because it must intervene if a deficit country runs into trouble for failing to secure enough capital to cover a current account deficit, i.e. it faces a balance-of-payments crisis. The vertical scale in Figure 3.2 is percentage points of global GDP, meaning that the numbers involved are quite large. Above the zero horizontal line we find the surplus countries, including Germany, Japan, China, several other economies in East and Southeast Asia like South Korea or Taiwan, and the oil exporters. Below that line, we see the deficit countries, including most of Western Europe, Canada, Australia, Brazil, and, most notably, the United States.

It is important to note that the aggregate current account surpluses in the world do not exactly match the aggregate deficits in magnitude. This is due to the so-called "statistical discrepancy," i.e. errors and omissions in global trade statistics, and differences in valuation methods. Save for the discrepancy, the deficits and the surpluses must be equal in size.

The main message of Figure 3.2 is not that there are surplus countries and deficit countries. That has always been the case since the dawn of the age of trade between national economies. What is truly striking about the recent evolution of current account surpluses and deficits is that their magnitude has increased considerably over the last two decades. While during the 1980s and 90s the size of the imbalances very rarely exceeded one percentage point of global GDP, and it remained lower than half a percentage point during several years, by the mid-2000s the magnitude had grown to a level of more than two percent. The global financial crisis of 2008 had a large negative impact on trade, and thus the imbalances dropped, but to a level still larger than 20 or 30 years ago.

There are two key implications stemming from larger current account imbalances, and both of them increase coupling in the global system. The first consequence is that deficit countries need ever bigger amounts of capital in order to continue operating. Conversely, the surplus countries are increasing their net-asset positions very rapidly. For instance, China went from just a few hundred million to nearly four trillion dollars in net assets vis-à-vis other countries over a period of just 15 years. These net-asset positions are also referred to as foreign reserves, which are usually managed by the central bank or by a sovereign wealth fund.

The second implication is that the world has more of a need for a reserve currency today than 20 or 30 years ago, simply because the size of the imbalances has grown so much. When countries run a current account surplus, they tend to buy assets denominated in the world's safest currencies, such as the dollar, the euro, the yen, pound sterling, or the Swiss franc. The greater the imbalances, the greater the amount of assets denominated in reserve currencies that are needed to keep the global economy in business.

As the so-called net-asset economies continue to grow their stockpiles of reserves, the global economy is becoming more tightly coupled. This is because the imbalances increase the interdependency between surplus and deficit countries. Let me illustrate this important point. During 2013 Germany ran the largest current account surplus, equivalent to 18.4% of the aggregate surpluses in the world, and China ran the second-largest at 13.2%, followed by Saudi Arabia's 9.6% and

Switzerland's 7.0% (in part the result of the ceiling on the value of the franc imposed by the central bank, which ended in January 2015). These countries are the largest accumulators of reserve assets, and their economies have become addicted to exports, i.e. they create jobs for their populations primarily by selling goods and services to other countries. Essentially, their economic model could not possibly work without massive amounts of exports. But for these countries to enjoy current account surpluses, there must be other countries that are running deficits: every exporter needs an importer, and vice versa. In the year 2013, the United States was by far the biggest deficit country, accounting for 28.8% of aggregate deficits in the world (down from 40.4% in 2012, largely due to increased exports), followed at a large distance by the UK (8.2), Brazil (5.8), Turkey (4.7), and Canada (4.2), all of them large economies that import more than what they export.

Increasingly big current account imbalances pose a serious threat to the global economy. They make countries more interdependent, creating jobs in certain parts of the world while destroying employment in others. They exacerbate the need for ever larger quantities of assets denominated in reserve currencies. They have the potential to generate economic and political tensions as countries succumb to the temptation of manipulating their currencies in order to redress the imbalances, as China, the U.S., Japan, Switzerland, and Brazil did between 2011 and 2014. Most importantly, when imbalances are very large, a disturbance in trade or in the capital markets needed to support trade deficits spells trouble for the entire global system. This is a sign of tight coupling, which is a shock-diffusing phenomenon.

The role that reserve currencies play in the global system is of utmost importance, given that surplus countries tend to use them in order to help deficit countries keep going. I will analyze in chapter 5 the role that the dollar plays in the global economy in general, and especially in the context of the dyadic relationship between China and the United States, the world's two largest economies and traders. In chapter 6, I will turn to the euro, noting that the European Union of 28 countries is a complex arrangement while the Euro Zone of 19 countries (a subset of the former) is a tightly-coupled scheme, with momentous consequences for its internal stability and effects on the rest of the global economy.

Trade in Intermediates

In addition to the aggregate patterns of trade discussed in the preceding chapter, the composition of trade also has the potential for increasing coupling. In particular, the phenomenon of trade in intermediates creates new opportunities and also some important challenges. The concept of an intermediate good is closely related to that of the value chain. In order to produce a final good or service ready for consumption or investment, companies must either buy or make intermediate goods and services such as different parts or components. A global value chain is one that involves production of intermediate goods and services in different parts of the world in order to arrive at a final good (Gereffi and Sturgeon 2005; UNCTAD 2013). New transportation and telecommunications technologies such as container shipping and the Internet have greatly expanded the universe of global value chains, leading economists to write about "trade in tasks" (Grossman and Rossi-Hansberg 2006). Today's global trade landscape cannot be understood without taking intermediate goods and services into account.

Figure 3.3 shows, however, that the increase in total trade in intermediates has been relatively modest since the turn of the twenty-first century, from about 8% of GDP in 2002 to 11% in 2012. Most importantly, trade in intermediates has grown at a slower pace than trade in

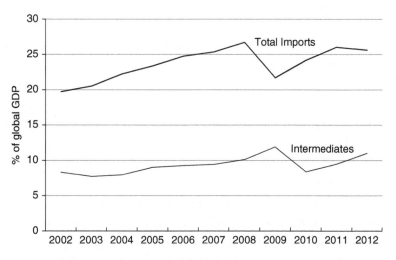

Figure 3.3. Trade in Intermediates (% of Global GDP), 2002–12

Source of the data: WTO.

final consumer and capital goods. However, in the case of emerging economies and developing countries, trade in intermediates has expanded faster than total trade. This is especially true of trade in electronics and automobiles. In the case of countries such as China, Mexico, Malaysia, Thailand, and Vietnam, trade in intermediates has grown at double-digit rates (Sturgeon and Memedovic 2010).

The importance of trade in intermediates can be readily illustrated with the case of the iPhone. The company asserts that this product is "designed by Apple in California, assembled in China." This phrase, inscribed on the back of all iPhones, must be taken literally, i.e. the product is *assembled* in China, not made in China. Of the total value added to an iPhone before it reaches U.S. shores, about 4% originates from China and the rest from South Korea, Taiwan, Germany, and other countries, although some of the parts inside the components sourced from these countries may have originated from China (Maurer n.d.; OECD-WTO 2013; Sposi and Koech 2013; UNCTAD 2013). The iPhone is far from being unique in terms of the trade in intermediates that it generates. The final assembly of most electronic devices and automobiles exhibits a similar pattern of trade in intermediate components (Timmer et al. 2014; Dedrick et al. 2010).

In spite of assembled products like the iPhone, it would be a mistake to assume that an economy such as China's contributes little domestic value to its exports. In fact, about 70% of the value of China's exports is added domestically. Among the top 25 exporters, only India (90%), the U.S. (89%), Australia (87%), Brazil (87%), Japan (82%), Italy (73%), Spain (72%), Switzerland (71%), and Taiwan (71%) surpass China, with Canada also at 70%. Australia and Brazil have high ratios because they export primary or semi-transformed commodities. Germany (63%) and South Korea (56%) have lower ratios (UNCTAD 2013:129).

Global value chains and trade in intermediates are efficient to the extent that they produce each component in the lowest-cost location, adjusting for coordination and transportation costs. They are a clear manifestation of the coordinated global economy described by Manuel Castells (2000). They are, however, vulnerable to disruptions to the extent that they push the principle of specialization by location to the extreme of relying on just a few global sources for each component.

If there is a production problem, a strike or a natural disaster in one or several of them, global supplies would be interrupted.

This negative effect of tight coupling is exacerbated by the practice of just-in-time supply, whereby components are produced and shipped just as they are needed for final assembly in order to reduce the costs associated with holding inventory, including storage, working capital, and obsolescence. Under this system, pioneered by Japanese firms in the 1950s, assembly plants hold very small or no backup inventories of parts and components (Goldin and Mariathasan 2014:70–99). When a powerful earthquake and tsunami struck Japan in 2011, global supplies for a number of important components where temporarily disrupted, idling factories several thousand miles away (Matsuo 2014; Simchi-Levi et al. 2014). For instance, the U.S. affiliates of Japanese multinationals suffered losses in output of as much as 60% in the wake of the tsunami relative to other firms with similar characteristics that did not rely as much on imported inputs from Japan. These declines were commensurate with the proportion of inputs sourced from Japan and the ability of the firms to find alternative sources of supply (Boehm et al. 2015:65). The researchers further noted that "global supply chains are sufficiently rigid to play an important role in the cross-country transmission of shocks," and that "such rigid production networks will also play a substantial role in aggregate volatility, productivity growth and dispersion, and the international ownership structure of production" (Boehm et al. 2015:1, 34). Under the older "just-in-case" system,[2] manufacturing value chains had many buffers and cushions in the form of stockpiles of parts and components. This was an inefficient practice for sure, but it provided the overall system with protection against unforeseen circumstances.

Another interesting instance of tight coupling in intermediates has to do with the global food supply chain. Fertilizers, animal feed, and food ingredients are increasingly produced in different parts of the world and shipped to far-flung destinations in order to produce food for final human consumption. A disruption in this chain could be especially catastrophic given the seasonal lags in food production. If the required

---

[2] Unfortunately, this term of mine has not caught on.

inputs are not available when needed, one cycle of food production might be lost.

Tight coupling in global value chains can be managed, but it still produces a qualitative change in the structure and interconnectedness of the global system, creating multiple shock-diffusing dynamics. It is also possible that new technological breakthroughs might lessen the system's exposure to the consequences of this type of tight coupling. For instance, 3D printing technologies have the potential of freeing assemblers, as well as consumers, from the shackles of global supply chains (De Jong and de Bruijn 2013).

The Uncontrolled Growth of Foreign Portfolio Investment

In chapter 2 I analyzed the growth of FDI, i.e. cross-border flows of capital aimed at managerially controlling the invested company located in a foreign country. FDI increases network complexity in the global system, but does not contribute to coupling because it offers both the receiving country and the investing firm more degrees of freedom and real options.

Foreign portfolio investment, which lacks that goal of control and typically involves owning less than 10% of the equity of the invested firm, is an entirely different matter. Here we are not dealing with a capital flow intended to support some kind of production, distribution, or sale activity. It is purely an investment, a money flow in search of a return. I will argue that it is a phenomenon associated with an increasing degree of tight coupling in the global system. For instance, countries that rely on foreign portfolio investment to compensate for a large current account deficit often find themselves in a vulnerable situation because those inflows of portfolio capital could be reversed in a moment's notice if financial conditions change and/or if investors lose trust in the country. Many balance-of-payments and external debt crises have been precipitated by swift reversals in foreign portfolio investment flows, as illustrated by the episodes of crisis throughout the emerging world during the 1990s (Reinhardt and Rogoff 2009).

Perhaps nobody has grasped the potential impact of free portfolio flows on network coupling across countries better than the Columbia University economist Jagdish Bhagwati. In the wake of the Asian

Flu crisis of 1997, during which several East and Southeast Asian economies suffered from the effects of the withdrawal of portfolio investment, he cogently argued:

> When we penetrate the fog of implausible assertions that surrounds the case for free capital mobility, we realize that the idea and the ideology of free trade and its benefits [...] have, in effect, been hijacked by the proponents of capital mobility. They have been used to bamboozle us into celebrating the new world of trillions of dollars moving about daily in a borderless world, creating gigantic economic gains, rewarding virtue and punishing profligacy. The pretty face presented to us is, in fact, a mask that hides the warts and wrinkles underneath. (Bhagwati 1998)

Reinhardt and Rogoff (2009) have also argued that cross-border capital flows make it more likely for domestic banks to go bust when portfolio investment suddenly deserts the country in anticipation of a currency realignment, changes in monetary policies, or simply poor economic conditions. Using data on 66 countries since 1800, they show that banking crises were rare during periods of low cross-border capital mobility (1800–80 and 1945–80), while they were quite frequent during periods of high capital mobility (1880–1940 and 1980 to the present time). During the latter periods, up to one-third of all countries experienced systemic banking crises with a significant number of defaults (see Figure 1.1). Thus, unlike foreign direct investment, foreign portfolio investment is shock-diffusing.

Figure 3.4 indicates that foreign portfolio assets grew from 25% of global GDP in 1997 to 70% in 2007, declined with the crisis to a low of 50% in 2008, and then recovered to 62% by the end of 2013, a level more than twice as high as that in 1997. This is a remarkable increase over two decades. Figure 3.5 shows the density of dyadic foreign port-folio investments between pairs of countries. The density measure, weighted by the magnitude of each dyadic flow and adjusted for inflation, grew from $189 million in 1997 to $699 million by the end of 2013, after declining during the crisis. This is, again, a phenomenal growth rate. The global system has clearly become more tightly coupled in terms of foreign portfolio investment, to levels three times greater than during the historical peak of the early twentieth century (Taylor

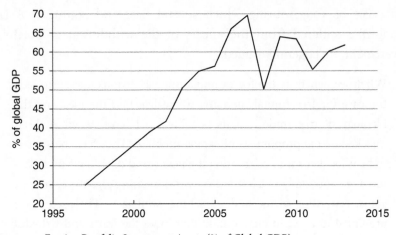

Figure 3.4. Foreign Portfolio Investment Assets (% of Global GDP), 1997–2013

Note: Data for 80 reporting economies.

Source of the data: IMF, Coordinated Portfolio Investment Survey.

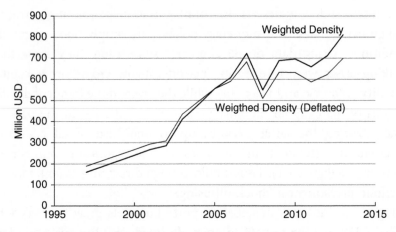

Figure 3.5. Density of Dyadic Foreign Portfolio Investments, 1997–2013

Note: Data for 80 reporting economies.

Source of the data: IMF, Coordinated Portfolio Investment Survey.

2014). I will ascertain in chapter 6 the extent to which this variable played a role during the European sovereign debt crisis.

The Joys and Consequences of Currency Trading

Currency trading is another phenomenon that contributes to network coupling. Currencies are not just money used to make payments. They are also units of account and stores of value. The different magnitudes in a country's balance of payments are affected by the relative value of currencies, known as exchange rates. Securities are denominated in a specific currency, or possibly in a basket of currencies. Fluctuations in exchange rates may affect flows of trade and investment. Most importantly, countries may experience currency crises when their current account deficits prove unsustainable, which tends to occur episodically, affecting clusters of countries. For instance, there was a spur in the occurrence of currency crises in 1919–22, 1931–3, 1946–50, and most notably since 1975 (Reinhardt and Rogoff 2009). When a country runs a large current account deficit or has accumulated too much debt, or both, the markets exert an enormous amount of downward pressure on the value of the currency.

Examples of this phenomenon abound. Currency crises tend to diffuse regionally, affecting countries that are either very integrated or that compete against one another for exports to third markets, i.e. are role-equivalent. Regional currency crises proliferated during the 1970s and 90s due to the combination of free cross-border capital flows and currency speculation (Glick and Rose 1999). The latter is a prime mechanism through which balance-of-payments difficulties translate into major currency realignments. Thus, the increase in currency exchange trading tends to result in a shock-diffusing dynamic.

Currency markets are easily the largest and most liquid of all financial markets. Each *day* over five million currency transactions take place, totaling over $5.3 trillion in value. Currency markets have become much bigger over the last two decades, and the speed at which a currency can be the subject of speculation and lose value has also increased. Figure 3.6 shows that daily currency exchange turnover in the world has grown from 3% of global GDP in 1989 to nearly 9% by 2013, with a decline between 1998 and 2001 due to the introduction of the single currency in Europe. Currency futures and options have grown by a factor of four over the same time period.

In spite of their rapid growth, currency markets did not melt down in 2008 along with the rest of the financial sector of the rich economies. They are relatively safe thanks to an institution called the Continuous Linked Settlement system (CLS), a bank-owned platform launched in

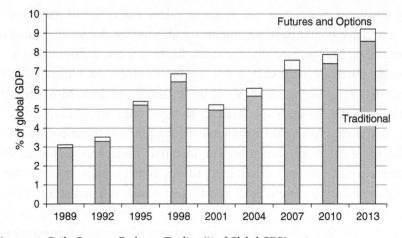

Figure 3.6. Daily Currency Exchange Trading (% of Global GDP), 1989–2013

Source of the data: Triennial Central Bank Survey, Bank for International Settlements.

2002 that settles transactions instantaneously as "payment-versus-payment," thus minimizing counterparty risk. CLS has 63 members. It has some limitations, however. First, it only settles about two-thirds of all currency exchange transactions. Second, it serves 17 currencies accounting for 95% of total transactions,[3] but excluding others likely to play an important role in the near future, namely, the renminbi and the rouble. Third, it is U.S.-centric and regulated by the New York Fed. And fourth, there is a built-in incentive for banks to settle bilaterally in order to avoid fees. In sum, while the CLS system has prevented a systemic failure, problems could occur in the future as economic and financial activity continues to shift towards the emerging world.

Did Cross-Border Banking Contribute to the Spread of the Crisis?
One last indicator of rapidly increasing network coupling in the global system has to do with cross-border banking activity. Banks engage in all sorts of financial activities across borders, and they also create their own subsidiaries in foreign countries. As they do business across borders and in

---

[3] AUD, CAD, DKK, EUR, HKD, ILS, JPY, MXN, NZD, NOK, SGD, ZAR, KRW, SEK, CHF, GBP, and USD.

many locations, banks accumulate financial positions in different countries and currencies. During the recent financial crisis, it became readily apparent to regulators and policymakers that such cross-border activity created risks that no single national authority could entirely detect and understand (Gorton 2012; Rajan 2010; Roubini and Mihm 2010).

The upper panel of Figure 3.7 shows the staggering tenfold increase in external bank positions from less than $3 trillion in the late 1970s to nearly $27 trillion in 2014, adjusted for inflation (2010=100), after peaking at almost $36 trillion in the first quarter of 2008. According to several analyses, these high levels of external bank positions probably made the global financial crisis more viral, allowing the problem to spread more easily across the Atlantic (Minoiu and Reyes 2011; IMF 2010c). Thus, cross-border banking positions tend to be shock-diffusing. The top panel of Figure 3.7 also shows that cross-banking activity was more important for banks with residence in the Euro Zone. We will explore in chapter 6 the implications of this fact. The lower panel of Figure 3.7, displaying the evolution of consolidated positions since the mid-1980s, shows a similarly fast rate of increase, peaking just before the financial crisis as well. We can also measure the increasing cross-border banking interconnections in terms of density. Figure 3.8 displays the weighted and deflated densities, which exhibit a sharp increase before the crisis and somewhat of a decline after 2008. Thus, different indicators of cross-border banking activity show a strikingly similar pattern over time.

It is no coincidence that, in the presence of such formidable levels of network coupling, the Great Recession triggered by the 2008 financial implosion of U.S. financial markets affected so many countries. In fact, during two quarters in the year 2009 all member economies of the Organization for Economic Cooperation and Development (OECD) were in recession, compared to just 40% of them during the mid-1970s, 30% during the early 1980s, and nearly 40% in 1993 (see figure 2.2 in Guillén and Ontiveros 2012). Emerging economies weathered the perfect storm relatively unscathed by substituting aggressive government spending for some of their exports, although they too started to suffer from reduced growth by 2013.

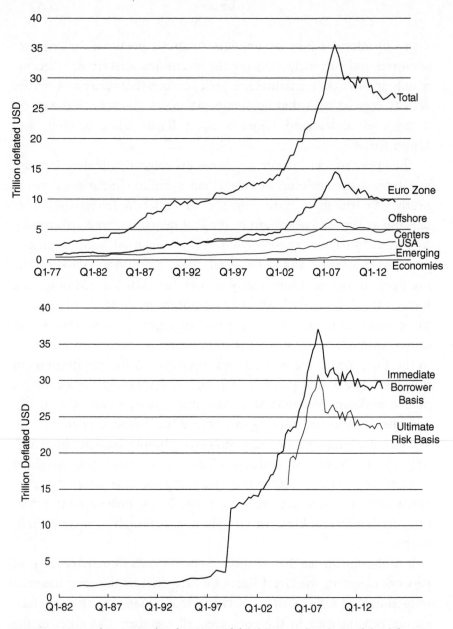

Figure 3.7. External Positions of Banks, Unconsolidated (top panel) and Consolidated (bottom panel)

Notes: Upper panel: Using the residence criterion for banks, i.e. without consolidating at the banking group level. Data range from Q4-1977 to Q3-2014. The Euro Zone includes Austria, Belgium, Cyprus, Finland, France, Germany, Greece, Ireland, Italy, Luxembourg, the Netherlands, Portugal, Spain, and Sweden. Offshore centers include Bahamas, Bahrain, Bermuda, Cayman Islands, Curacao, Guernsey, Hong Kong, Isle of Man, Jersey, Macao, the Netherlands Antilles, Panama, Singapore, U.S. banks in Panama, U.S. branches in offshore centers, and Switzerland. Emerging economies includes Brazil, Chile, India, Indonesia, Malaysia, Mexico, South Africa, South Korea, Taiwan, and Turkey.

Lower panel: Consolidated basis. Data range from Q4-83 to Q3-14 for immediate borrower basis, and from Q1-05 to Q3-14 for ultimate risk basis.

Deflated figures using CPI index for all times in the United States, 2010=100 (Federal Reserve Bank of St. Louis).

Source of the data: Bank for International Settlements.

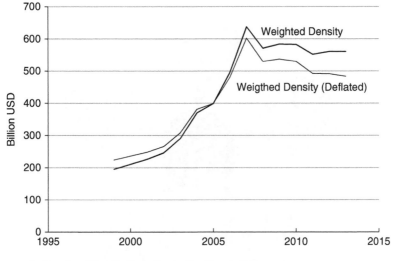

Figure 3.8. Density of Dyadic Cross-Border Banking Activity, 1999–2013

Note: Immediate Borrower Basis.

Source of the data: Bank for International Settlements.

Node Coupling

While network coupling in the global system refers to the absence of buffers in the relationships between pairs of countries, node coupling operates inside countries and entails the extent to which individual countries lack such buffers or cushions. Long-standing trends in population aging, urbanization, public debt, income inequality, and wealth inequality have pushed many societies to the limit, leaving governments with very few degrees of freedom with which to implement policies (Figure 3.9).

More Grandparents than Grandchildren

The decline in fertility rates around the world, from about five children per woman in 1950 to 2.5 in 2012, with projected rates approaching two by the mid-twenty-first century, is bringing about an abrupt process of population aging. In the more developed parts of the world, fertility fell below the standard replacement rate of 2.1 children per woman in the early 1970s. In the emerging economies, fertility has also declined precipitously since the 1970s driven not only by China's one-child policy but also by broader social changes similar to the ones taking

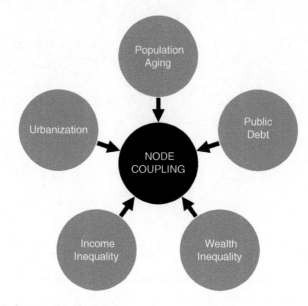

Figure 3.9. Indicators of Node Coupling

place in the richest countries, especially those related to women's increased access to education, job opportunities, and contraception. In the least developed countries, fertility started to decline in the 1970s, driven as well by women's changing roles in society and in the economy.[4]

At the same time, people around the world now live much longer than in previous generations. While in 1950 life expectancy at birth stood at less than 50 years, by 2012 the figure had increased to nearly 70. The increase in life expectancy—mainly driven by improvements in living standards, education, nutrition, disease prevention, and healthcare—is a veritable global phenomenon, with the least developed parts of the world catching up very quickly. While in 1950 life expectancy at birth was 30 years higher in the more developed than in the least developed countries, by 2012 the difference had narrowed to less than 20 years, and the projection was that by the end of the twenty-first century it would fall further to about 10 years.[5]

The simultaneous decline in fertility and increase in life expectancy cannot bring about anything but a greying of the population (Dorius

---

[4] United Nations Population Division, *World Population Prospects: The 2012 Revision.*
[5] United Nations Population Division, *World Population Prospects: The 2012 Revision.*

2008; Wilson 2011). Rich countries are already entering a phase in which there are more grandparents than grandchildren. As a result, serious doubts are being cast on the viability of not just pay-as-you-go pension systems but the economy as a whole. Consumer and financial markets will also be transformed as spending, saving, and investing patterns shift. Older people do not spend as much on durable goods and housing as younger people, two major drivers of the economy.

Most importantly, population aging puts countries and their governments in a situation in which they have little room to maneuver. Taxes cannot be increased indefinitely on the younger generations to pay for the pensions and healthcare of retirees. Labor scarcity sends wages higher, undermining international competitiveness. And the political landscape is transformed, making policy change to adapt to new circumstances unlikely as retirees seek to protect their hard-won benefits by being the most politically engaged age group in terms of voting and lobbying. Population aging makes nodes in the global system more tightly coupled, unwilling and unable to change course, limited in their options, and ultimately sclerotic.

The Growth of Cities
At the same time that population aging progresses, the distribution of people across space is also undergoing massive change as a result of migration from the countryside to the city. While in 1950 less than 30% of the world's population was urban, by 2010 more than 50% was, and by the end of the twenty-first century nearly 70% will be. In 1960 only two cities had more than 10 million people, New York City and Tokyo. By 2030 as many as 39 cities will exceed that threshold, most of them in India and China. At the present time, the number of urban dwellers swells by 1.5 million each week.[6]

The growth of cities is in many ways a welcome change. Cities are dynamic and vibrant, offering their residents a wide array of economic and cultural opportunities. But cities are also limiting future options for many countries around the world, and placing enormous pressure on resources. The provision of food and water becomes a challenge as millions move away from the sources at which they are abundant.

---

[6] United Nations Population Division, *World Urbanization Prospects, the 2014 Revision.*

Cities pose a major distribution and logistical problem, one that can only be addressed by massive investments in infrastructure.

Most importantly, rapid urbanization leads to social dislocation, inequality, and duality. There are two different dualities driven by the growth of cities. The first is the gulf that develops between the countryside and the city in terms of income and opportunity. The second has to do with the often extreme economic disparities that tend to develop within cities, especially rapidly-growing cities. Both types of duality put enormous pressure on the economy and on the political system, which has always had a hard time coping with massive change.

Most importantly, urbanization increases tight coupling. Cities require supplies of almost everything, which must be delivered in a timely way. Throughout modern history, food riots in cities have been a major source of instability. From medieval France to the Arab Spring, food shortages have driven political history (Tilly 1997). During the Middle Ages, cities became melting pots and disease pools, with enormous consequences for the extension of European power around the world (McNeill 1978; Diamond 1997). And cities are, above all, fragile ecosystems in which water contamination and air pollution can get out of control, especially in the developing world. Urban societies have been known to collapse more swiftly than traditional societies (Diamond 2005). Simply put, cities are tightly coupled, and they make nodes in the global system more so.

The Indebted State

Historically, governments have had a tendency to spend more than the revenues they raise, especially as a result of inter-state competition and war (Tilly 1992; Mann 1992; Centeno 2003). Government debt can become a binding constraint because, on the one hand, the population's expectations as to services and benefits tend to increase as government spending rises, often leading to a self-reinforcing spiral, and on the other, as governments accumulate debt a larger proportion of the budget needs to be allocated to servicing it. These two forces can become mutually reinforcing, and put enormous political pressure on the state. As a result, its options become more limited.

The global system in the early twenty-first century is characterized by a sharp increase in the level of government indebtedness among the

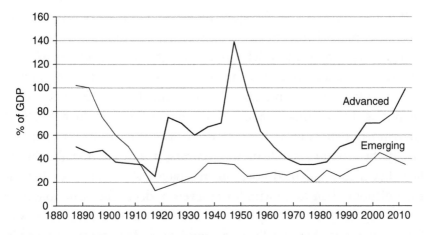

Figure 3.10. Government Debt as % of GDP, 1885–2010
Advanced: Australia, Canada, France, Germany, Italy, Japan, Korea, the United Kingdom, and the United States.
Emerging: Argentina, Brazil, China, India, Indonesia, Mexico, Russia, Saudi Arabia, South Africa, and Turkey.

Source of the data: IMF.

rich countries, accompanied by a decline in the emerging economies. This may sound paradoxical, but it actually is not. Figure 3.10 shows the evolution of government debt as a percentage of GDP from the late nineteenth century to the present time. Emerging economies used to be deeper into debt than the rich countries, but the latter surpassed the former first as a result of the two world wars and more recently as a consequence of certain promises made to rapidly aging populations.

Ultimately, government indebtedness makes nodes in the global system very tightly coupled internally because of the dynamics of taxation and spending. Economically, the state can be a source of stability and help alleviate the negative consequences of downturns in the business cycle. But a heavily-indebted government may end up imposing too much of a burden on the private sector, stifling entrepreneurship and economic dynamism. Politically, an increasing public debt triggers a series of conflicts between savers and borrowers, between the young and the old, and among competing conceptions of policy. Very high levels of public debt make societies and economies more tightly coupled because governments need to operate at the limit of their ability to sustain services for citizens using the base of available resources.

It is important to note that government spending has a very important role to play when it comes to overcoming economic problems such as high unemployment or deflation, although the effectiveness of stop-and-go, Keynesian-style policymaking can be undermined by supply-side rigidities and by free cross-border capital flows, as analyzed in chapter 4. My argument about tight coupling due to high levels of government debt is in no way a diatribe against government intervention in the economy. Quite on the contrary, it is meant to highlight the fact that highly-indebted governments have more limited options at their disposal than those with lower levels of debt. They can no longer borrow aggressively to help out the economy during recessions, and they may not be able to deliver on promises made to specific groups in society. Simply put, a country that is deeply into debt is a more tightly-coupled node in the global system. Nodes characterized by indebted governments can contribute to shock-diffusing dynamics due to their limited ability to react.

Income Inequality Drags Down the Economy

Another feature of contemporary societies that make them more tightly-coupled nodes in the global system has to do with the distribution of income. In *The Great Transformation*, the social scientist Karl Polanyi (1944) famously argued that on the one hand inequality laid the foundations for the dynamism of the market, but on the other it could undermine the "substance of society." Excessive inequality in the distribution of the economy's rewards ultimately undermines the incentives for people to invest in human capital and to work hard (Easterly 2007). Most importantly, high levels of income inequality reduce the ability and degrees of freedom of governments when it comes to raising additional resources in order to overcome recessions or other types of crises. Inequality reduces middle-class consumption, and thus dampens aggregate demand.

Recent trends in inequality over the last three decades are heterogeneous. In most of Europe, the United States, Russia, and China, income inequality is on the increase. Meanwhile, it is on the decline in Brazil, Sweden, and Mexico, to name but a few countries (see Figure 3.11). A wide array of changes are causing inequality to rise, including technological change, the disruptive impact of trade in certain

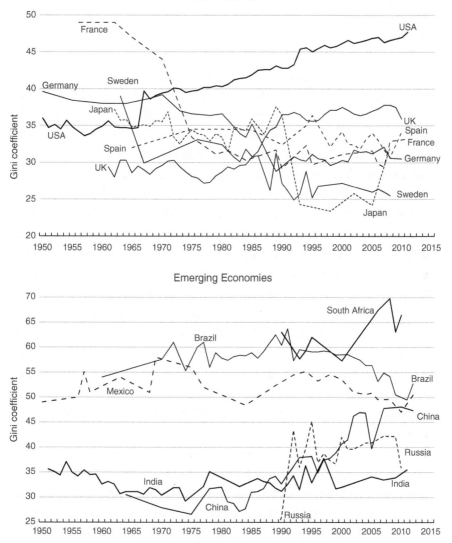

Figure 3.11. Income Inequality within Countries (Gini Coefficients), 1950–2012
Source of the data: All the Ginis Dataset (April 2014 Update), World Bank.

industries and locations to the benefit of others, the growth of the service sector (which employs both highly-skilled and unskilled workers), changes in taxation, and welfare state retrenchment, among others (Milanovic 2009). As MIT economist Paul Osterman has cogently argued, "the migration of manufacturing jobs to other parts of the world has generated a decline in the share of income accounted for by labor. Meanwhile, jobs created in the service sector have proved to be much more heterogeneous in terms of skill level, stability, and pay than those in manufacturing" (Lauder Global TrendLab 2013).

The growth of emerging economies is also game-changing from the point of view of inequality because hundreds of millions of people are joining the new global middle class. By the year 2022, and for the first time in human history, there will be more middle-class people in the world than poor people, defined as individuals with at least $10 per day to spend but no more than $100. Moreover, the center of gravity of middle-class consumption will shift towards India and China, which combined will represent more than half of the global middle-class market (Kharas 2010). In Africa, the middle class is also expanding, albeit from a very low base (AFD 2011). Interestingly, the rise of the middle class in China and India has so far widened inequality within cities and between the city and the countryside, whereas in Brazil it has led to a large decline in inequality, although starting from very high levels and thanks to a government program involving income redistribution (Chen et al. 2010; Cain et al. 2008). Chinese policymakers, for instance, are much more constrained in terms of what policies they can pursue in the wake of rising inequality because poor people in the cities, and especially, the countryside, are becoming impatient with the pace at which their lot is improving. Thus, China has become a more tightly-coupled node in the global system because of rising income inequality.

One clear negative consequence of rising inequality has to do with the muted role of domestic consumption in economic recoveries. In the U.S., inequality has squeezed the middle class. As a result, the recovery from the Great Recession triggered by the 2008 crisis has been relatively slow, taking the economy more than 20 months to become 5% bigger than it was at the official start date of the economic contraction, compared to an average of eight months for previous recessions. Thus, excessive inequality is constraining to the economy as a whole as well as painful to those suffering from it (Temin and Vines 2013:132).

Wealth Inequality and Its Effects
While the middle class expands in some countries and shrinks in others, the proportion of income going to the top 1% is growing rapidly to levels not seen since the 1920s (see Figure 3.12). In the U.S., the top

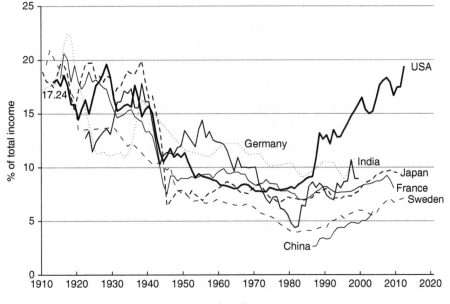

Figure 3.12. Income of the Top 1 Percent (% of Total Income), 1910–2012

Source of the data: World Top Incomes Database (February 2014 Update).

1% accounts for nearly 20% of total income. Wealth concentration at the top has become even more pronounced than income. The world's top 1% will soon own more wealth than the rest combined, i.e. more than 50% of total wealth (Credit Suisse 2014). Lower taxes on capital gains and other munificent conditions for the rich, have resulted in a sharp rise in the number of millionaires during the early years of the twenty-first century (Alvaredo et al. 2014). While the crisis brought about a fugacious decline, the number of millionaires—technically referred to as high-net-worth individuals—has grown to 12 million around the world, who collectively own $46 trillion in investable assets, excluding their primary residence, collectibles, consumables and consumer durables, a truly staggering figure (Capgemini and RBC Wealth Management 2013). The countries topping the ranking of millionaires are the United States, Japan, Germany, China, the UK, France, Canada, Switzerland, Australia, Italy, Brazil, and South Korea.

Wealth inequality tightens coupling in a different way than income inequality. Wealth inequality results in part from income inequality, but acquires a dynamic of its own as individuals and households with wealth accumulate it and invest it, leading to higher rates of social reproduction. Wealth inequality tends to be more skewed than income inequality, although the dynamics of accumulation are driven by complex forces having to do with the returns to capital and labor. While income inequality has risen to the levels of a century ago, wealth inequality is still below historical levels, especially in Europe (Picketty 2014; Picketty and Saez 2014). The growth in wealth inequality over the last few decades, however, perpetuates the prevailing pattern of social stratification and leads to node coupling in the sense that it ossifies the social structure and makes the political economy more rigid by entrenching powerful interest groups (Olson 1965, 1982). The wealthy have the ability and the resources to shape policymaking, especially in certain countries where spending on lobbying and political campaigns is unrestricted.

The Potentially Devastating Consequences of Network and Node Coupling

The increasing degree of coupling in the global system poses serious threats to the ability of governments to steer their countries out of trouble. Coupling also makes global governance so much more problematic. Under conditions of tight coupling every problem, every deviation from normal circumstances, and every calamitous event becomes difficult to overcome because of the lack of buffers, cushions, and degrees of freedom. Thus, both node and network coupling tend to be shock-diffusing. We will analyze in the next chapters three specific situations to assess whether the increasingly complex and tightly coupled nature of the global system makes the world more prone to disruptions and crises. I begin in the next chapter by assessing if the crisis of 2008 and the resulting Great Recession had anything to do with complexity and coupling. In chapter 5, I examine the effects of the increasingly complex and tightly coupled relationship between China and the United States, the world's two largest economies. In chapter 6, I will compare the European Union and the Euro Zone with a view to assessing their future viability.

4

Complexity, Coupling, and the Great Recession

with Sandra L. Suárez

For European banks, the American model of minimizing capital and using high levels of leverage was something to be emulated, not scorned. Ultimately, common global tendencies produced a common global crisis.

—Barry Eichengreen, *Exorbitant Privilege* (2011:101)

The global financial and economic crisis that exploded in 2008 brought about the Great Recession, the worst economic crisis since the 1930s. It was triggered by the implosion of the U.S. real-estate market, whose effects were magnified by the securitization of mortgages and other financial assets, and by the high degree of leverage of financial companies, two key indicators of tight coupling at the organization and industry levels of analysis. The crisis spread very quickly to other developed and developing markets through a variety of tightly-coupled channels, including investment, trade, cross-border banking assets, and the breakdown of trust and confidence more generally. Ultimately, the crisis brought about the loss of tens of millions of jobs worldwide, trillions of dollars in financial wealth, and the disappearance of some of the most storied financial institutions.

The swiftness and gravity of the crisis elicited a massive government response in the forms of liquidity injections, bailouts, and economic stimulus efforts on a scale not seen since the 1930s. It was also a crisis that reopened a series of important intellectual debates, especially those between Keynesians and monetarists, and those between the believers in the so-called "efficient market hypothesis" and those who proposed to approach economic phenomena from a behavioral perspective (Cassidy 2010; Lo 2012).

The crisis is also unique because of its political edges. No account of the crisis would be complete without examining the politics of financial regulation, or lack thereof, and the ways in which politics shaped the choice of government actions to contain and overcome its effects. In this chapter, I consider evidence from several economies around the world to assess the extent to which complexity and coupling contributed to the crisis and its spread.[1]

The Financial Crisis in the United States, 2007–8

On February 7, 2007 one of the world's largest banks, HSBC, announced losses related to U.S. subprime mortgage loans. A couple of months later, on April 3, New Century Financial, a subprime specialist, filed for Chapter 11 bankruptcy. In June, Bear Stearns told an incredulous financial community that two of its hedge funds suffered large losses related to subprime mortgages. Other Wall Street standard-bearers also started reeling from bad investments, including Merrill Lynch, JP Morgan Chase, Citigroup, and Goldman Sachs. Before the end of August the problems had spread to some French and German banks, and prompted the Federal Reserve and the European Central Bank to pump liquidity into the banking system and to reconsider their interest-rate policies. Thus, evidence of the gathering storm was piling up months prior to the epochal collapse of Lehman Brothers in September 2008.

The financial and economic crisis of 2008 marked the end of one of the greatest financial expansions in history (Philippon and Reshef 2013). The recession in the U.S. officially started in December 2007. By mid-2009, the crisis had brought to their knees major bank and

---

[1] This chapter relies heavily on Guillén and Suárez (2000). Note that, in response to Perrow's (2010) critique, we clarify that we do not see the crisis as a pure form of a "normal accident," but rather as the outcome of ideologies of deregulation and irresponsible behaviors made worse by a situation of high complexity and tight coupling, as we recognized in our original statement of the argument (Guillén and Suárez 2000:261).

non-bank financial institutions, causing several to collapse, leading to a severe economic contraction, plummeting trade, rising unemployment, and price deflation. The crisis quickly acquired global proportions after hitting Western and Eastern Europe, Japan, Latin America, the rest of Asia, and parts of Africa, although several of the most vibrant emerging economies sailed through it relatively unscathed thanks to aggressive fiscal spending.

The chain of interrelated trends and events leading to the crisis in the United States is complex. At the core lay the problem of asset-price inflation, especially in the stock and housing markets (Akerlof and Shiller 2009; Gorton 2012:182–99; Mishkin 2011; Shiller 2008; Stiglitz 2010; Temin and Vines 2013:141–50). The belief that prices would go up indefinitely seemed to be deeply ingrained in the minds of market participants. With the benefit of hindsight, we know that the bubbles were largely the result of unusually low interest rates between 2001 and 2006. Out of deflation fears in the wake of the Internet bubble, the Fed lowered the federal funds rate from 6.25 to 1.75% during 2001, reaching a low of 1% in 2003, well below what the "Taylor rule" of monetary policymaking would prescribe (Eichengreen 2011:111; McKinnon 2013:59). The Federal Reserve could have curbed asset-price inflation. After all, central banks enjoy independence from political power precisely so that such excesses are avoided (Polillo and Guillén 2005).

The Fed's attention, however, was focused on sustaining the economic recovery. It ignored other signs of economic stress and risky behavior by financial institutions. In particular, Greenspan was not as technocratic and independent as everyone assumed. In fact, he had behaved in a rather charismatic way since the early 2000s, becoming a larger public figure than the venerable institution he chaired. Most importantly, it appears that he preferred to downplay the first signs of trouble so as to avoid raising interest rates during the months leading to the 2004 Presidential Election, in a reversal of his policy stand in 1992, when he was accused of undermining George H. W. Bush's reelection chances. Loose monetary policy was, in many ways, a first important background factor leading to the crisis.

A second contributing factor had to do with recent developments in emerging economies, especially China. During the 1990s, emerging economies had witnessed or experienced first-hand what could happen to them in the event of a currency or sovereign debt crisis, or both. Between 1997 and 1999 several East Asian economies, Brazil and Russia fell like dominos to the pressures of short-term currency specu-lators. The International Monetary Fund (IMF) stepped in to provide liquidity, but subject to stringent demands and limitations, including wide-ranging institutional reforms. These "conditionality" clauses became the source of major debates among economists and produced a backlash in emerging economies against the coercive practices of the IMF (Rodrik 2006). In many cases, the policies and reforms mandated by the IMF proved counterproductive (Guillén 2001:190-7; Henisz et al. 2005; Stiglitz 2002). China, in particular, took good note of the situation. It embarked on a frenetic policy of amassing foreign reserves and investing them in securities issued by foreign governments, espe-cially the United States. According to IMF (2009b) data, during 2008 China accounted for 24% of all capital exports in the world, and the United States for 43% of all capital imports. Other big exporters included Germany (nearly 13%), Japan (9), Saudi Arabia (8), and Russia (6). After the United States, the largest recipients of capital were Spain (10% of the world's total), Italy (5), and Greece (3). (The fact that three Southern European countries ranked just behind the U.S. should be kept in mind when analyzing the euro crisis in chapter 6.)

Thus, by 2006 or 2007 the world of international capital flows had become polarized between the exporters and the importers, with China and the United States playing the leading roles, respectively (see chapter 5). Massive inflows of cheap money from abroad helped keep interest rates low in the U.S., thus fuelling the twin asset-price bubbles in the securities and housing markets. Foreign holdings of U.S. corporate and treasury securities soared from between 10 and 20% in the mid-1990s to 25% in the case of corporate bonds and 50% of treasuries on the eve of the crisis (Eichengreen 2011:114–22). One way to reduce the imbalances between the U.S. and China would have been for the latter to allow its currency to float, something that Beijing continued to resist since it would reduce the competitiveness of its exports. Overall, the capital flows and investment positions prevalent in 2008 made the global system increasingly tightly coupled, as I argued in chapter 3.

The crisis, however, would not have reached such massive proportions without the peculiar, and to a large extent unprecedented, developments taking place inside the financial sector, which also contributed
to tight coupling and to shock-diffusing dynamics. During the years
leading up to the crisis, financial institutions, both bank and non-bank,
felt strong pressures to meet growth and profit expectations in order to
prop up their share price. This aspect, in and of itself, was not unique
to the financial services industry. Corporations across the board
were under intense pressure to increase performance, especially at
a time when shareholder wealth maximization dominated debates
about corporate governance (Davis 2009; Fligstein 1990; Guillén and
Capron 2016; O'Sullivan 2000). Low interest rates, however, affected
financial and non-financial companies in sharply different ways.
A manufacturing firm usually benefits from low rates because it can
more cheaply fund its needs for working and fixed capital, and because
its customers also see their access to credit improve. By contrast, low
rates tend to constrain the ability of banks and other financial institutions to make a profit because spreads are minuscule. In more ways
than one, the crisis of 2008 epitomizes the historical divergence of
interests between banking and manufacturing.

And yet, financial industry profits surged during the 2000s from
representing less than 20% of total U.S. corporate profits to more than
40%. During 2007, on the eve of the crisis, 41% of all corporate profits
in the U.S. were accounted for by the financial services industry, at a
time when it represented about 15% of economic activity, as measured
by gross value added. The financial industry came to play a dispropor-
tionate role in the U.S. economy (Eichengreen 2015a; Temin and Vines
2013:130). Although the growth of the financial sector was especially
pronounced in the U.S., it was a global phenomenon (Philippon and
Reshef 2013). These massive profits could not possibly have come from
interest-rate spreads at a time of record-breaking loose monetary
policies. Rather, they came from financial leverage as well as from
fees and commissions collected through the design and sale of new
financial products. While non-financial corporations and the government barely increased their leverage, households and, especially, financial institutions did so at a staggering rate. According to the IMF
(2009a), by the end of 2007 financial institutions had trebled their

leverage when compared to the late 1990s. Entities that are highly leveraged are tightly coupled in the sense that they have little margin for error. Tight coupling means that there are no buffers. Quite on the contrary, both profits and losses get multiplied many times over (Bookstaber 2007:143–5).

At the center of the quest to generate shareholder wealth in financial services through leverage and new financial products were a series of perverse incentives. Bonuses were perhaps the most blatant, especially when they were tied to revenue growth and not profits, or when financial companies could generate fees and commissions without taking responsibility for the risk attached to the products they issued because they changed hands multiple times and were merged into synthetic securities. Concerning top management, stock grants were especially pernicious, as they would perversely reinforce risky behavior so as to meet Wall Street's expectations. Whether they were selling their products to private investors or purchasing their own products with borrowed money, financial institutions were playing with "other people's money," thus widening the divide between risk and responsibility (Eichengreen 2015a; Johnson and Kwak 2010; Rajan 2010; Shiller 2008). Competition for the best traders also proved problematic because they were showered with incentives based on short-term performance, which invited risky behavior as well. Moreover, when compensated in stock, executives and traders borrowed against it in order to maintain a lavish lifestyle. Their own leveraged finances as individuals added to the desire to meet revenue and profit expectations.

Moral hazards are another oft-mentioned cause of the crisis. There is some evidence indicating that after the Savings and Loans bailout of the late 1980s—the largest since the Great Depression—the CEOs of financial institutions came to the realization that the government would not let them collapse. This sense of being ultimately backed up by the taxpayer was probably reinforced by the 1998 bailout of Long Term Capital Management (LTCM). The government did not finance the rescue operation of LTCM, but orchestrated it, reinforcing the belief that financial institutions would be protected if they ran into trouble. The actions of the government thus contributed to the intensification of the risky behavior that it should have sought to discourage.

Ignorance or irresponsibility regarding the costs of risky behavior afflicted not only financial institutions but individual citizens as well. Just like financial institutions, U.S. consumers leveraged themselves lured by lower interest rates and the belief that housing prices would never drop. When the economy is healthy, borrowing allows individuals and families to share in the relative prosperity and to boost their consumption, but it also makes the household sector more vulnerable to changes in interest rates and disposable incomes. In turn, increases in mortgage delinquency and foreclosures further contributed to the losses of financial institutions. From the 1980s, household debt as a percentage of disposable income increased to over 100% in many developed countries. By 2005, household leverage was 159% in the UK, 135% in the U.S., 141% in Ireland, and 107% in Spain and Germany. Leveraged households, however, do not always pose a potential problem. During the 1980s and 90s, the majority of household debt was held by higher-income families with the means to pay it down. The pressure for profits and the relaxation of financing rules, however, allowed credit to be extended to households with a much smaller capacity of paying it back, especially if variable interest rates on the loans reset to higher levels (Girouard et al. 2007; Lauder Global TrendLab 2011).

Initially, the concept of debt securitization and the slicing of mortgages was thought to shield financial institutions from the risk of extending credit to subprime borrowers. But as debt securitization became more popular, the risk actually became more concentrated within U.S. banks. We now know that most holders of securitized debt were highly-leveraged financial institutions. Clearly, leverage was making the entire financial system more tightly coupled.

Finally, the financial crisis that exploded in 2008 brought to the surface the massive information asymmetries among the various actors involved in the activities of complex financial institutions, including top executives, traders, directors, shareholders, bondholders, raters, insurers, regulators, and so on. Clearly, employees were not telling top executives every detail of their doings, as the bizarre episode of renegade trader Jérôme Kerviel at the French bank Société Générale illustrates. Top executives, whether out of ignorance or not, failed to give board directors a clear picture of the situation. Shareholders and bondholders were in the dark, in part because raters and insurers were saying that everything was fine. And even as rating agencies began issuing downgrades and subprime delinquencies started to spike, the IMF (2007) reported that financial institutions were "sufficiently capitalized, diversified and profitable to absorb direct losses." Regulators, for reasons to be analyzed later in this chapter, were even more in the dark due to their lack of resources and the fragmentation of the regulatory structure.

Who's Afraid of Financial Innovation?

Innovation lies at the heart of the capitalist economy. Financial innovations, however, are peculiar because it is very difficult to protect them from imitation by competitors. Financial institutions quickly learned that innovations such as derivatives could be the source of sustainable profits if novel products or structures were designed, new types of underlying assets became available as raw material, technology or expertise barriers could be created, mass production was possible, and at least some of the assets could be taken off the books in order to maximize the use of the available capital base. The pressure to innovate and engage in increasingly risky behavior in order to secure above-average returns was also used as justification for the exuberant bonuses, which could no longer be earned by selling the idea of a "mere" 10% return on investment. The pursuit of above-average returns for investors resulted in greater risk-taking through financial innovation. The early successes of JP Morgan and Goldman Sachs in derivatives innovation attracted myriad imitators, including commercial and investment banks, and insurance companies, both domestic and foreign. A key issue in this respect was that the imitators often misunderstood the risks and the limits of the innovations (Fligstein and Goldstein 2010; Johnson and Kwak 2010; Lauder Global TrendLab 2011; Mishkin 2011; Rajan 2005; Tett 2009; Lerner and Tufano 2011; Bookstaber 2007). Then IMF Chief Economist Raghuram Rajan (2005:332) presciently argued that regulatory and market changes had not "marginalized traditional institutions like banks.... The changes have allowed such institutions to focus on their core business of customization and financial innovation, as well as risk management. As a consequence, the risks borne by traditional institutions have not become any lower." Or as Paul Krugman put it in the *New York Times* (December 3, 2007), the year before Lehman Brothers collapsed,

> the innovations of recent years—the alphabet soup of CDOs and SIVs, RMBS and ABCP—were sold on false pretenses. They were promoted as ways to spread risk, making investment safer. What they did instead—aside from making their creators a lot of money, which they didn't have to repay when it all went bust—was to spread confusion, luring investors into taking on more risk than they realized.

Financial innovations come under three categories, namely, those that allow to transfer value over time, contract on future values, and enable the negotiability of claims (Lerner and Tufano 2011:7). The most important innovation in securitization was collateralized debt obligations (CDOs). In essence, they involve putting a large number of income-generating assets such as bonds, mortgages or other types of debt into a pool and then issuing securities for sale to investors. CDOs could also be made from other CDOs, and they were called CDOs squared. Yet another type was synthetic CDOs, made from credit derivatives. The issues with CDOs and other securitizations were three fold. First, originators cared about volume, not quality. Second, in order to calculate the risk you would need to have historical data on how the underlying assets performed over several business cycles. This was certainly possible with bonds issued by major corporations, but not with residential mortgages, simply because there had never been a truly devastating mortgage crisis in the past and the quality of many of the new borrowers was not known, at least not to every financial institution or division. In general, default probabilities for CDOs were grossly underestimated. In addition, increasingly complex and unreliable computer models had to be used in order to calculate default probabilities when the underlying assets were sliced and diced multiple times. And third, in order to maximize profits, originators needed to mass produce the securities, move assets off balance to free up capital, and obtain the highest possible rating for a given return level. Among other tactics, they engaged in "ratings arbitrage," whereby originators exploited loopholes in the rating agencies' computer models (Carruthers 2010; Eichengreen 2011:98–100; Rona-Tas and Hiss 2010; Roubini and Mihm 2010; Tett 2009).

Credit derivatives were the other important financial innovation of the time, and the one that brought AIG down, which required a $180 billion bailout (Mishkin 2011). In the classic credit default swap (CDS), the buyer makes a periodic payment and receives a payoff from the seller if an underlying debt instrument such as a loan or bond defaults. CDSs had certain peculiarities that are important to note. First, the buyer need not own the underlying instrument. Second, the seller need neither be a regulated insurer nor set aside enough capital to cover potential losses. Third, the seller often misunderstood the risk inherent to the underlying instrument. And fourth, the buyer might be fooled by a false sense of security and take on more risk, thus exacerbating moral hazard.

The mounting pile of mortgage debt from the credit expansion of the 2000s provided excellent raw material for derivatives. Subprime loans were especially attractive to originators because of their high interest rates; all they needed to do was persuade the rating agencies and the investors that the slicing and dicing reduced the risk while preserving the return. Moreover, CDOs and CDSs were over-the-counter instruments, meaning that there was no central clearinghouse or market. The result was a lack of transparency concerning the risk-return profile of the innovative products (Gorton 2012). Barry Eichengreen described the situation as follows:

> This securitization machine, itself almost as complex as the securities it spit out, had a voracious appetite for fuel. With leverage rising, portfolios expanding, and investors stretching for yield, it required extensive inputs of high-yielding securities. This need in turn encouraged the creation of more CDOs and residential-mortgage-backed securities, which in turn encouraged the origination of more mortgages. Banks loosened their credit and documentation standards. Mortgage brokers moved down the credit-quality spectrum in search of borrowers. It was an elaborate dance, although not one in which all participants were fully in touch with their partners. (Eichengreen 2011:101)

Deregulation Galore

The rapidly changing regulatory landscape of the 1990s and 2000s contributed to the financial meltdown by allowing—even encouraging—the system to become more complex and tightly coupled. The overall trend since the 1980s was one of removal of obstacles to the free unfolding of market forces and to the introduction of sophisticated financial innovations, under the assumption that markets could self-regulate. In 1986, Margaret Thatcher set into motion a major revolution in financial services with the so-called London Big Bang. This reform should be seen in the context of a package of "neo-liberal" reforms (Babb and Fourcade-Gourinchas 2002; Campbell 2010). Fixed trading commissions were eliminated, electronic trading introduced, and the cozy club of City insiders was effectively dismantled. Over the next two decades, London regained its long-gone status as the world's leading financial center, attracting the likes of JP Morgan, Lehman, and AIG. The fact that regulatory oversight was less stringent in London than in New York made it a magnet for U.S. financial institutions as a location in which to experiment with new financial products (Eichengreen 2015a:204–5).

Meanwhile, regulatory developments in the U.S. were creating a more fertile ground for financial innovation and risk-taking, and making the financial system both more complex and more tightly coupled. In the early 1990s regulators and Congress considered several initiatives and bills to monitor and oversee the expanding universe of derivatives products. Intense industry lobbying caused these initiatives to be shelved. In 1996, with Alan Greenspan at the helm, the Federal Reserve made the astonishing and reckless decision to allow financial institutions to reduce required reserves if they used credit derivatives to curb risks. Perhaps the most prominent piece of legislation from the 1990s was the Financial Services Modernization Act of 1999, which repealed the even more famous Glass-Steagall Act of 1933 and amended the Bank Holding Company Act of 1954 to permit commercial banks to enter the securities and insurance business and vice versa. Then Treasury Secretary Lawrence Summers explained that "at the end of the 20th century we will at last be replacing an archaic set of restrictions [on financial activity] with a legislative foundation for a 21st century financial system." He asserted that the legislation "would provide significant benefits to the national economy" (as quoted in Labaton 1999). As commercial banks entered the securities business, investment banks felt competitive pressure, triggering a race to the bottom in terms of risk assessment standards (Eichengreen

2011:108–9; Rajan 2010). Investment banking was becoming more like gambling than a traditional financial activity.

Greenspan, Summers, and Robert Rubin—a former manager of Goldman's fixed-income division—opposed new regulations on derivatives which could have made the system safer. The modest recommendation of the Commodity Futures Trading Commission in 1998 to regulate derivatives, including disclosure rules and capital cushions, was ignored. Then Treasury Secretary Summers argued that derivatives "serve an important purpose in allocating risk by letting each person take as much of whatever kind of risk he wants." He made the following statement at the U.S. Senate:

> derivatives facilitate domestic and international commerce and support a more efficient allocation of capital across the economy. They can also improve the functioning of financial markets themselves by potentially raising liquidity and narrowing the bid-asked spreads in the underlying cash markets. Thus OTC [over-the-counter] derivatives directly and indirectly support higher investment and growth in living standards in the United States and around the world. (Quoted in Eichengreen 2011:103)

There are many factors that contributed to the dismantling of the Depression-era regulations, among them, international competition, the ideological convergence of the Republican and Democratic parties when it came to economic and financial matters, and changes in the marketplace resulting in a merging of interests among commercial banks, securities firms, and insurance companies (Suárez and Kolodny 2011). For many years after the Great Depression, American commercial banks operated differently from European banks. Since the early 1980s, financial interests argued that Glass-Steagall should be repealed to enable American banks to enter the securities business so as to level the playing field. Though initially the argument emphasized the banks' loss of business to other domestic financial institutions, eventually U.S. banks argued that they could not compete with Japanese banks, which had become among the largest in the world and were able to operate securities firms in the U.S. Then in 1986, Margaret Thatcher's decision to revolutionize the financial services sector with the London Big Bang put additional international competitive pressure on U.S.

policymakers. In 1987, the Reagan Administration announced that Treasury had concluded that American banks should be allowed to merge with other financial institutions if they were going to be able to compete in the international arena (Nash 1987). In 1989, the Bush White House was also explicit in that international competition was a motivating factor for advocating regulatory change. The argument made at this time was not that U.S. banks could not compete with British banks, but that the City of London had taken over New York as the financial capital of the world (Choi, Park and Tschoegl 2002). These competitive pressures coincided with the ideological convergence of the Republican and Democratic parties on a deregulation agenda (Suárez and Kolodny 2011).

The repeal of Glass-Steagall and amendments to the Bank Holding Company Act occurred with a Republican Congress and a Democratic President. Democrats in Congress had opposed the integration of banking, securities, and insurance businesses in the mid-1980s, but would eventually reverse their position and follow the lead of the Clinton Administration. In 1992 Bill Clinton captured the White House after 12 years of Republican administrations by claiming to be the leader of a new Democratic party, one that would embrace private sector growth vs. the government sector. Clinton's margin of victory over the other contenders for the Democratic Party nomination had allowed him to set a more pro-business agenda than the one advocated by the more traditionally liberal Democratic constituencies (Borrelli 2001; Suárez and Kolodny 2011). The Clinton Administration supported financial deregulation from the outset. Then when in the 1994 mid-term elections the Republican Party won a majority in both the House and Senate, the stage was set for a major overhaul of the Depression-era regulations long advocated by the large commercial banks.

The evolution of business interests with regards to the dismantling of regulations dating back to the 1930s was the result of important changes in the financial markets. During the 1960s and early 70s, large commercial banks had very little interest in expanding into other areas of finance because they were able to make money from interest-free or low interest deposits, safe government securities, and commercial loans. By the mid-1970s, their profitably started to erode in part because bank customers were looking for more profitable investments such as mutual funds and money market accounts, and borrowers were able to secure loans from other sources such as commercial paper and junk bonds (Wilmarth 2002). From the point of view of the banks, the fact that *their* customers were no longer using their services meant that their territory was being invaded by securities firms. Thus, commercial banks complained to Washington that the playing field should be leveled and they should be permitted to enter the securities business. Commercial banks did take advantage of the removal of restrictions to intra-state and inter-state mergers and bank operations and responded to the reduced profits by acquiring competitors.

During the 1980s and 90s there was a big wave of commercial bank consolidations. After literally thousands of mergers, what emerged was a completely transformed banking sector dominated by large banks. There was significant consolidation in Europe as well. Banks on both sides of the Atlantic took advantage of financial deregulation in the U.K. and also acquired a number of investment banks (Wilmarth 2009). Lobbying, and the accompanying campaign contributions, by commercial banks did not let up. Their efforts were thwarted by the securities and insurance industries, which did not want competition from commercial banks. Legislators were also wary of allowing federally insured commercial banks to merge with other financial firms whose profitability was more volatile. Eventually, the securities industry decided that they end their long-standing opposition to the repeal of Glass-Steagall. In exchange, securities firms wanted to be allowed to expand into commercial banking and have access to the Fed's emergency borrowing, while commercial banks wanted entry into the insurance industry as well and continued to pressure Congress for across-the-board integration of financial services.

By the mid-1990s, however, the insurance industry was making noises in a way suggesting that they also wanted Congress to permit them entry into commercial banking. Theirs was also a defensive move in reaction to the 1996 Supreme Court ruling that permitted national banks to sell insurance in towns with 5,000 or fewer residents. In July 1997, State Farm Mutual Automobile and Casualty Insurance, at the time the largest property and casualty insurance company in the U.S., announced that it had filed an application with the Office of Thrift

Supervision to form a commercial banking subsidiary (*New York Times* 1997).[2] A few months later, the Travelers Group, which was amongst the largest U.S. commercial and property insurers and also owned Smith Barney, a brokerage firm, announced its acquisition of Salomon Brothers, an investment house. By all accounts, Travelers had wanted to merge with a large commercial bank but suspected regulators would likely block the acquisition; it decided to shop for an investment firm instead. When Travelers failed in its efforts to acquire Goldman Sachs, it opted for Salomon Brothers. Reflecting the trend towards the consolidation of financial services, the *New York Times* remarked that "after combining with Salomon Inc., Travelers will rival the likes of Merrill Lynch & Company, the American Express Company and Citicorp, as well as the biggest financial companies in Europe and Japan" (Truell 1997). State Farm's decision to enter the banking industry and the Travelers Group's being public about its desire to merge with a large bank illustrates how the interests of insurance firms had changed. Along with securities firms, insurance companies would now pressure Congress to legislate a repeal of Glass-Steagall and the Banking Act to enable them entry into the commercial banking and securities business (Lauder Global TrendLab 2011).

In 1998 Citicorp announced that it was merging with Travelers, creating the world's largest financial services company, one combining commercial banking, securities trading, and insurance services. The announced merger was a complete turnaround; the Chairman of Citibank had been known for his dislike of the securities business. But it was the Chairman of Travelers who first approached Citibank. The new entity now known as Citigroup, along with other large commercial banks, securities firms, and insurance companies, would become a major supporter of a legislative overhaul of the Depression-era regulations because without changes federal regulators would have no choice but to force it to break up within two to five years. The passage of the Financial Modernization Act of 1999 thus signaled the end of an era when the fear that financial entities could become "too big to fail" had kept financial deregulators at bay.

---

[2] *New York Times* (1997).

The removal of restrictions per se did not necessarily have to spell trouble. After all, at this time, many countries around the world allowed integrated and diversified financial firms to operate. Unlike in other countries, however, the U.S. regulatory structure was not overhauled in order to guarantee the stability of this radically transformed financial system. This was arguably the key mistake made by the Clinton Administration, later compounded by the lack of oversight during the Bush years. Commercial banks continued to be supervised by the Federal Reserve, the Office of the Comptroller of the Currency, the FDIC, and individual states. Securities firms were primarily under the watch of the Securities and Exchange Commission (SEC). Insurance companies were regulated by individual states and by the Department of Labor. After 1999, a diversified financial services company was allowed to choose the regulator for each of its businesses, leading to a situation in which no single government body had a 360-degree view of the entire portfolio of each company and the associated systemic interactions. The Commodity Futures Modernization Act of 2000 also added to the problem by treating swaps as distinct from futures or securities. This essentially meant that neither the SEC nor the Commodity Futures Trading Commission (which is overseen by the U.S. Congress Agriculture committee and was explicitly barred by Congress from regulating the over-the-counter derivatives market shortly after LTCM!) could supervise these new, and potentially lethal, financial products. Industry lobbying was very effective at obtaining a favorable ruling on the part of the SEC concerning leverage ratios. In 2004 the agency voted to raise them. Not surprisingly, Lehman Brothers, Bear Stearns and Morgan Stanley increased their asset-to-equity ratios above 3,000%, and Merrill Lynch and Goldman Sachs above 2,500%. The Basel Committee on Banking Supervision also agreed to lower capital ratios. "For European banks, the American model of minimizing capital and using high levels of leverage was something to be emulated, not scorned. Ultimately, common global tendencies produced a common global crisis" (Eichengreen 2011:101).

The case of AIG — by far the largest and most costly bailout of the crisis—illustrates the effects of deregulation and fragmented supervision. Before the end of 1999, the ink on the Modernization Act still fresh, AIG acquired the status of thrift holding company, when the

Office of Thrift Supervision (OTS) approved its application to charter AIG Bank. It also received approval to buy a small savings and loans bank in Delaware. The OTS had been created in the wake of the savings and loans crisis to replace the Federal Home Loan Bank Board, and had virtually no expertise in credit derivatives. Still, AIG's infamous financial products division (based in London)—as well as the thrifts at General Motors, General Electric and some divisions of Lehman Brothers, Merrill Lynch, and Morgan Stanley—came under the supervision of the OTS, primarily because these firms chose it as their regulator. After lobbying European regulators, the OTS was conferred equivalency for supervising AIG between 2004 and 2007, which meant that it was the only agency supervising the company's London operation and its growing portfolio of derivatives, which eventually reached $1.5 trillion (Gerth 2008). In early 2007, the Government Accountability Office issued a bruising report documenting the lack of expertise at several of the regulatory agencies, including OTS, when it came to supervising derivative products (GAO 2007). On March 3, 2009, Ben Bernanke summarized the situation at a Senate Hearing when he stated that AIG "exploited a huge gap in the regulatory system," and that "there was no oversight of the [AIG] Financial Products division" (Gerth 2008). AIG could not be allowed to fail, however, because its credit default swaps were used to insure the mortgaged-backed holdings of FDIC-insured commercial banks as well as of other financial institutions. Among AIG counterparties that were perceived as "too big to fail" and received 100 cents on the dollar on their insured mortgage-backed securities were not only U.S. companies such as Goldman Sachs, Merrill Lynch, Bank of America, Citigroup and Wachovia, but also many European banks such as Société Générale, Deutsch Bank, UBS, and The Royal Bank of Scotland.

The trend towards deregulation was driven by lobbying and outright regulatory "capture" (Johnson and Kwak 2010). Commercial banks, investment banks, insurance companies, and financial intermediaries of all sorts had come to influence the political process to the point they could ask for the regulation they desired. But as Mark Mizruchi (2010) has argued, the fragmentation of the financial elite led to a patchwork of regulations that greatly enhanced the potential for a meltdown.

Complexity and Coupling

From an organizational point of view, the financial crisis of 2007–9 was a rather unique event because, while it was not a "normal accident" in the strictest sense of the term due to the role of ideologies, greed, and deception (Campbell 2010; Perrow 2010), it was fueled and exacerbated by complexity and coupling at different levels of analysis. Since the late 1990s, the financial system of the United States became both far more complex and more tightly coupled than in the past, and thus prone to systemic failure. Its increasing complexity stemmed from the rise of large, diversified financial institutions, often with operations spanning the globe (see point 1 in Figure 4.1). These organizations created specialized entities to pursue new products and markets. In many cases they located the divisions far away from corporate headquarters, in places friendly to innovation. This was the case for JP Morgan, Lehman Brothers, and AIG, whose financial products divisions were located in London, taking advantage of less restrictive regulations. These divisions operated with a high degree of autonomy, and often without direct supervision from the CEO's office thousands of miles away. They innovated in new financial products involving securitization of certain income-producing assets (CDOs) and credit derivatives (CDSs). The so-called quantitative wunderkinds or *quants* developed the products and the computer models to price them, while the managers made the decisions as to how to allocate billions of dollars across different products and activities. This specialization of roles meant that neither the CEO nor the regulators had a coherent view of the rising complexity of the overall set of activities in which each financial institution was engaged.

The new products had a number of characteristics that increased complexity (point 2 in Figure 4.1). They exposed a large number of financial institutions to risks that they did not fully understand because the underlying assets were sliced and diced multiple times (Tett 2009). While the innovators had a reasonably good understanding of the characteristics and risks of the new products, the imitators did not. Another tricky aspect was that profitability depended on charging fees and commissions, which encouraged the mass production and sale of the products to other market participants, further complicating risk

Complexity :	Tight Coupling :
1. Rise of large, diversified financial institutions with: • A high degree of internal organizational specialization and differentiation, including new financial product departments enjoying a high degree of autonomy. • An increasing division of roles and responsibilities (*quants*, managers, traders, etc.). As a consequence, few if any people inside large, diversified financial institutions had an overall understanding of the various activities conducted by separate departments and individuals.	3. Leverage: • Given thin margins, financial leverage used to squeeze returns from the available capital base. As a consequence, financial institutions were operating close to the edge, with little room for making corrections, and subject to enormous pressure if the predicted profits turned into losses. The liquidity crunch exacerbated this problem.
2. New financial products (asset-backed securities, credit default swaps): • Given thin margins, mass production is necessary to generate sizable profits. • Imitators do not fully understand the risks. • Innovators were hard-pressed to design new products in order to stay ahead of the imitators. • Profitability of fees and commissions resulted in new products changing hands quickly. • A tendency to use sophisticated mathematical models to overcome issues and difficulties with the pricing of risk, and to feed the models with derivative prices as opposed to historical default data. As a consequence, financial institutions exposed themselves, and each other, to risks they did not fully understand and could not calculate accurately.	4. Lack of a clearinghouse or market for many of the new financial products, especially those tailor-made for specific clients and traded over the counter: • Exposure to counterparty risk vastly increased. As a consequence, domino-like effects from one financial institution to another became likely and potentially catastrophic for the financial system as a whole. The liquidity crunch aggravated the problems faced by counterparties because they found it harder to meet their contractual obligations.
5. The above factors were fueled and aggravated by the fragmented regulatory structure inherited from the 1930s, the practice of regulator-shopping, and the lax enforcement of existing regulations. In a complex and tightly-coupled system, regulators must have: (1) a 360-degree view of the system to identify problems; and (2) the authority necessary to deal with problems that could imperil the system.	

Figure 4.1. Factors Contributing to the Complexity and Tight Coupling of the Financial System

Adapted from Guillén and Suárez (2010).

assessment. Moreover, newly developed models and techniques such as the Gaussian copula function were used since approximately 2000 by Wall Street banks to calculate CDO risks based on CDS prices instead of historical default data, under the assumption that the market was pricing correctly (Salmon 2009). Mathematical models built on very specific simplifying assumptions were stretched and used in ways that were unwarranted: "Banks, confident that they had reduced their risks to a single number, became confident of their ability to shoulder more" (Eichengreen 2011:107). As of December 2007, there were $3 to $4 trillion worth of outstanding CDOs, and a staggering $35 to $45 trillion of CDSs. Literally, millions of counterparties were involved in an exceedingly complex web of interconnections. When Lehman went bankrupt in September 2008, for instance, more than 700,000 counterparties were affected.

In addition to its increasing complexity, the U.S. financial system also became far more tightly coupled than in the past. This was due to two key causes. First, financial institutions increased their leverage in order to extract the highest possible returns from their capital base, thus reducing the slack in the system (point 3 in Figure 4.1). Increased leverage reduced the buffer against adverse events or wrong bets, thus making the system more rigid, leaving very little margin for error. Financial institutions simply found it hard to absorb shocks or unexpected events because they lacked an appropriate capital base to cope with unforeseen deviations in the performance of their supposedly finely-tuned bets and investments.

Second, the new securities and credit derivatives were mostly tailor-made for specific buyers, and transacted over the counter, i.e. there was no clearinghouse or market for them (point 4 in Figure 4.1). This meant that it was difficult to exit investments when conditions took a turn for the worse. Not surprisingly, one of the earliest symptoms of the gravity of the crisis had to do with the inability of banks to price the products in their portfolios. This was due to the lack of a market for transacting them. The twin problems caused by the lack of a clearinghouse or market and by excessive leverage became exacerbated with the liquidity crunch that started in the summer of 2007. In a related event, the collapse of the commercial paper market also wreaked havoc with another innovation, structured investment vehicles (SIVs). They had been pioneered by Citigroup in the late 1980s. These funds made money by issuing short-term securities at relatively low interest rates and lending the proceeds in the form of long-term securities at higher rates, some of them asset-backed. In the summer and fall of 2007 Bank of America and Northern Rock, the British bank, both suffered substantial losses from SIVs essentially because they managed themselves into a corner of the financial system so tightly coupled that a disruption in the rollover scheme produced billions of dollars in losses.

Although not new, another factor that contributed to the tight coupling of the financial system was advances in computer technology. During the crash of 1987, known as "Black Monday," the U.S. stock market suffered a one-day decline of 22.6%, the largest since 1914. Another sudden drop occurred in 1997, commonly referred to as "Black Friday." On both occasions, program trading was seen as a factor. Program trading occurs when computer models determine the time to execute buy and sell orders. With the advent of what is referred to as "high-frequency program trading," the trade occurs in nanoseconds (Adler 2012; Lewis 2014). Program trading makes the markets highly interconnected and tightly coupled as it enables financial institutions to profit from small discrepancies in price across exchanges. It can also trigger a domino effect that results in wild price swings during a single day. In the U.S., exchanges estimate that between 30 and 50% of all of their trades are executed by a small group of high-frequency traders, among them Goldman Sachs. The month of October 2008 saw "Bloody Friday," and several markets halted trading after experiencing some of their worst downturns on record. Program trading likely played a role in the unfolding of the crisis that needs to be further investigated. Faster computers and the 2000 switch from eighths and sixteenths of a dollar to decimal pricing likely increased the coupling of financial markets (*Economist* 2009).

The U.S. financial system might have withstood the bursting of the real-estate bubble and the subprime meltdown if financial companies had been less leveraged and a clearinghouse or market had been available, that is, if the system—however complex—had not been as tightly coupled as it was. After years of daring financial innovations and rising financial leverage, the system lacked appropriate cushions and buffers, bells and whistles. When trust among financial institutions evaporated in the summer and fall of 2007, the liquidity crunch pushed this tightly-coupled system to the brink of collapse. Only massive liquidity and capital injections by the Fed, the European Central Bank, and other monetary authorities prevented a full-blown catastrophe. It was the combination of rising complexity and tight coupling that created the conditions for a meltdown of epic proportions to occur, driven by the reckless actions of many different types of actors, one that required hundreds of billions of dollars to repair, and transformed the industry for years to come.

Contagion

The problems in the U.S. spread quickly around the world due not to the complexity of trade or investment patterns, but rather because of the tight coupling in the global financial and trading system. In fact, during the 1980s and 90s, the entire global economy had become a complex and tightly-coupled system itself, making it much easier for the problems in the U.S. to contaminate other economies (see Figure 4.2). The global economic and financial system became much more complex

Complexity:	Tight Coupling:
1. Increase in trade in goods, which made the global economy more complex and interconnected.	3. Growth of global imbalances stemming from the rise of the United States as the consumer of last resort, and China as the leading exporter of capital.
	As a consequence, U.S. securities showed up on the balance sheets of banks around the world.
2. Increase in foreign direct investment, which in turn raised the number and size of multinational corporations and their subsidiaries worldwide.	4. Fragmentation of value chains across borders as a result of restructuring, outsourcing, and offshoring.
As a consequence, more decisions about investment and job creation made by transnational actors.	As a consequence, more intricate patterns of cross-border trade not only in finished goods but especially in intermediate inputs, subassemblies, and services meant that problems or disruptions in one part of the global trading system would affect other parts almost instantaneously. The increasing prevalence of just-in-time supply chains also contributed to the sharp increase in the degree of tight coupling.
	5. Liberalization of trade in services and of portfolio flows lead to the rise in global portfolio and currency trading.
	As a consequence, money be brought in and pulled out of countries more easily, eroding policymakers' ability to influence market developments.

Figure 4.2. Factors Contributing to the Complexity and Tight Coupling of the Global Economic and Financial System during the 1990s and 2000s

Adapted from Guillén and Suárez (2010).

Note: Please notice that, following the theoretical framework laid out in chapter 1, global imbalances contribute to coupling, not to complexity, as Guillén and Suárez (2010) had originally argued.

during the 1990s and 2000s for two reasons. First, trade continued to rise around the world, as documented in chapter 2. And second, there was a pronounced increase in the number and size of multinational firms and their subsidiaries. This important change meant that more decisions about investments and job creation were being made by transnational actors. While in 1980 the cumulative stock of foreign investment by multinational firms amounted to 6.7% of global GDP, by 2007 the figure had risen to 27.9% (UNCTAD 2009).

At the same time the global economic and financial system was becoming more complex, it was also turning more tightly coupled, for three reasons. First, the growth of global imbalances stemming from the rise of the United States as the consumer of last resort, and China as the leading exporter of capital, meant that U.S. securities, both public and private, were purchased by investors from around the world and showed up on the balance sheets of banks in Asia and Europe (IMF 2009b). According to the Bank for International Settlements, cross-border banking external assets stood at 54.0% of global GDP in 2005 up from 13.7% in 1980. Second, all sorts of companies, not just multi-national ones, engaged in restructuring, outsourcing, and offshoring as ways to reduce costs and increase operational flexibility, thus increasing coupling through trade in intermediates, as we analyzed in chapter 3. The value chain of product development-production-distribution was broken down into its various constituent activities and located in different parts of the world in a breadth-taking quest for lower costs (Gereffi 2005). As a consequence, more intricate patterns of cross-border trade not only in finished goods but especially in intermediate inputs, subassemblies, and services meant that problems or disruptions in one part of the global trading system would affect other parts almost instantaneously. The increasing prevalence of just-in-time supply chains also contributed to the sharp increase in the degree of tight coupling because they eliminated the buffer or cushion afforded by inventories of intermediate inputs and finished goods.

The liberalization of trade in services and of capital flows during the 1990s was the third factor behind the tight coupling of the global economic and financial system. Trade negotiations during the early 1990s yielded an unprecedented commitment to free trade in services and the creation of the WTO in 1995. China's entry into the WTO in

2001 represented a key milestone in the integration of the global trading system. The liberalization of cross-border capital flows was an even more important process, including trading of foreign stocks and bonds, borrowing in foreign currencies, listing shares abroad, and currency trading (Abdelal 2007; Davis 2009). For instance, capital flows amounted to about 21% of global GDP in 2007, up from 6% in 1996 (Blanchard and Milesi-Ferretti 2009). While in 1980 *daily* currency exchange turnover amounted to about 0.7% of global GDP, as of April 2007 it had increased more than ninefold to 6.6%, according to the Bank for International Settlements. The greater ease and volume of cross-border capital flows had the consequence of constraining policymakers' ability to influence market developments, especially during times of crisis. Governments lost autonomy as market participants could move money from one country to another at dizzying speed.

Given this background of increasing complexity and tight coupling in the global economic and financial system, it is no surprise that one of the key characteristics of the crisis was its blistering spread around the world in terms of reduced economic growth and rising unemployment. Except for the Great Depression of the 1930s, previous financial crises had been regional in scope, affecting just a few countries (Glick and Rose 1999). For instance, the economic and monetary crises of the early 1970s affected the most developed economies in the world, but not the developing world. In 1992, a new episode of monetary turmoil unfolded in Western Europe alone. In late 1994 the Mexican crisis spread to other emerging and developing countries, mostly in Latin America, but not to the developed world. In 1997 the so-called Asian Flu diffused throughout East Asia and parts of Latin America like wildfire, but spared other parts of the world, except for South Africa and two or three Eastern European countries. Thus, as of 2007, the possibility of a truly global economic and financial crisis was not something that most policymakers were contemplating, even after the first signs of serious trouble became readily apparent.

Channels of Contagion

The crisis of 2007–9 was different from those of the 1970s, 80s and 90s primarily because of the very different ways in which it spread globally (Reinhardt and Rogoff 2009). In most countries, the causal chain leading to contagion did not primarily involve a direct impact from

U.S. toxic financial products, although some banks in Germany and Switzerland reported heavy subprime losses as early as August and October 2007, respectively. In the United Kingdom and Ireland, the contagion channel started, like in the U.S., with the bursting of the domestic real-estate bubble infecting the financial sector and in turn bringing about a severe economic recession.

In a second group of countries, the problems started in the financial sector and then spilled over into the real economy. In the dramatic case of Iceland, the problems originated in dubious financial investments and cross-border arbitrage bets. In Switzerland, bad financial investments by UBS and other banks (and falling trade volumes) hit the real economy hard. In most Eastern European countries, growth was based on foreign borrowing, which largely evaporated as a result of global financial turmoil. The ensuing credit contraction brought these economies to a standstill. Persistent currency depreciations made matters worse in Hungary, Poland, and the Czech Republic. Meanwhile, countries with fixed exchange rates (Bulgaria, the Baltics) ran the risk of a sudden devaluation.

A third contagion channel started with a drastic fall in construction and real-estate activity that infected the real economy, and would eventually affect the financial sector (e.g. Spain, Dubai). Construction had been a major engine of economic growth and employment in both countries. The quick reversal of fortune in that sector spilled over into the real economy very fast, causing growth to slow down and unemployment to soar. These countries also suffered from plummeting tourist arrivals and, in Dubai's case, reduced global trade. Continuing economic stagnation severely affected the financial system as non-performing loans proliferated.

A fourth contagion channel involved the decline in trade and its potentially devastating effects on industrial production and employment in export-oriented economies such as China, Mexico, Japan, Germany, and, as noted above, Switzerland. The smaller, export-oriented Eastern European countries also suffered from the decline in trade. China responded by orchestrating a large investment program to boost the economy, while Germany buffered the shock by incentivizing companies to keep workers until the economy turned around. Finally, exporters of commodities were hurt by the sudden drop in prices, including Russia and several Middle Eastern, South American and African countries, as well as Canada and Australia.

These contagion channels indicate that the crisis diffused from the U.S. to export-oriented economies through the trade channel, especially in a situation in which proportionally speaking more trade is destroyed as GDP growth slows down as a result of the offshoring of so many business functions and intermediate goods. A second group of countries experienced economic difficulties when their domestic construction, real-estate, and/or financial sectors got into trouble. Very few countries were directly and significantly affected by U.S. toxic financial products. As the IMF noted, "the United States is grappling with the financial core of the crisis" (IMF 2009b:63). The complexity and tight coupling of the global economy and financial markets paved the way for the spread of the crisis worldwide.

Politics, Ideology, and the Responses to the Crisis

Government officials and central bankers responded with different degrees of urgency to the crisis, due not only to the lags in its spread around the world but also because of the different ways in which each country entered the crisis, political preferences and ideologies, and the power of the various interest groups. Most of the early policy responses had to do with a strategy of containment, especially in terms of interest-rate reductions, emergency liquidity support, and enhanced guarantees for bank deposits. These measures sought to provide the buffers and cushions that the tightly coupled financial system lacked. Other more extreme measures, like a suspension of the convertibility of bank deposits and regulatory capital forbearance, were avoided for their politically costly or even counterproductive effects, although they had been used in other recent banking crises around the world (Laeven and Valencia 2008).

Policymakers then turned to resolution strategies. The repertoire of potential measures included workout programs of bad loans, government insurance of bad debt, the transfer of bad debts to a government asset management company (i.e. a "bad bank"), sales of financial institutions to new owners, government intervention and recapitalization of banks, and bank liquidations (Laeven and Valencia 2008).

In the two large countries with the most severely damaged financial systems—the U.S. and the UK—the government and the central bank followed different approaches. The British government moved swiftly to nationalize the first victim (Northern Rock) in February of 2008, as well as other smaller institutions, including Bradford & Bingley, and to stage major recapitalizations through state ownership of the country's major banks, such as Lloyds and Royal Bank of Scotland. By contrast, American policymakers engaged in a haphazard series of actions, in part driven by pressures from the banks themselves, and by the difficulty of selling to the Congress and the public massive government intervention in the financial sector.

Thus, during the crucial year of 2008, U.S. policymakers implemented a breadth-taking variety of responses (Eichengreen 2015a; Stewart 2009): in March they orchestrated the takeover of Bear Stearns by JP Morgan; in July regulators seized IndyMac; in September mortgage giants Freddie Mac and Fannie Mae were brought under government conservatorship; in September Lehman Brothers was allowed to go bankrupt, in a decision that sent the markets into a tailspin; shortly thereafter, a lifeline was established for AIG, Bank of America took over Merrill Lynch, JP Morgan acquired Washington Mutual, and Citigroup was slated to purchase Wachovia, although Wells Fargo finally got the prize a month later; in early October Congress passed a $700 billion Troubled Assets Relief Program (TARP), subsequently used to recapitalize Citibank ($25 billion), JP Morgan Chase ($25 bn.), Bank of America ($20 bn.), Wells Fargo ($20 bn.), and, after converting themselves into bank holding companies, Goldman Sachs ($10 bn.) and Morgan Stanley ($10 bn.); in November AIG became practically owned by the government while Citigroup received a lifeline potentially worth $306 billion and a further capital injection of $20 billion, leaving the government with a one-third equity stake; and in December GM and Chrysler received approval for bailout funds of up to $18 billion. The Obama Administration, for its part, passed through Congress a stimulus packet worth $787 billion and a modified Troubled Asset Relief Program (known as TARP II). Meanwhile, the largest banks went out of their way to return bailout money in order to free themselves from government impositions, especially those having to do with executive compensation (Suárez 2012, 2014).

Given the Fed's policy of offering free funds to the banks upon request, and the government's implicit guarantee of banking activities as the lender of last resort, it is not surprising that banks could make profits during the second half of 2009, even though they had not unloaded the toxic assets that threatened to bring them down in the fall of 2008.

Other countries did not have to deal with massive problems in the financial sector, but with a major economic downturn or the potential for one. As a result, they did not engage in major financial bailouts and reengineering, but in fiscal stimulus to prop up the real economy. A noteworthy case is China, which approved a vast stimulus packet worth 5.5% of GDP in 2009 and 6.5% in 2010, three times larger than the U.S. stimulus. India also announced a similarly large packet. In both cases, up to 90% of the money was spent on physical infrastructure projects, compared to only 10% in the U.S., where the rest went into tax credits for families, education, science and technology, renewable energy, Medicaid, unemployment benefits, and healthcare information technologies. Clearly, the political process—rather than the counter-cyclical impact of the spending—shaped the allocation of funds. Europe appeared to be divided, also for ideological and political reasons. The UK approved a fiscal stimulus as big as the U.S.'s relative to the size of the economy, and France implemented an infrastructure program, but Germany was much more reluctant to spend its way out of the recession. For historical and ideological reasons, the Germans felt they could live with high unemployment but wanted to avoid inflation at all costs, while the French had the reverse preferences. But after first attempting to survive the crisis with a limited stimulus package in 2008, earning Chancellor Merkel the nickname of "Frau Nein," the German government announced a much larger second package ($63 billion) in early 2009. Meanwhile, researchers at the IMF demonstrated that a coordinated global stimulus would be somewhat more effective at turning the global economy around than individual efforts by different countries, in large measure because the spending from any stimulus packet leaks or spills over into other countries due to trade and other interconnections (Freedman et al. 2009). In other words, the IMF recognized the complexity of the global system at the time.

What did we learn?

As far as the implosion of U.S. financial markets in 2008 is concerned, there are two paramount global factors that played a decisive role in the crisis. First, the loose monetary policy that paved the way to the bubbles in the markets for equity and for housing was made possible by the massive accumulation of trade surpluses and savings in emerging economies, especially China (see chapter 5). Second, financial deregulation in the U.S. was driven by a combination of economic and political changes, in part fueled by London's earlier deregulation drive and its implications for New York's supremacy as the leading financial center in the world. High leverage ratios were the other important background factor, one that made the financial system in the U.S. tightly coupled in addition to complex.

Problems in the U.S. financial system diffused globally like wildfire through tightly-coupled financial and trade circuits. One could also argue that plummeting confidence in financial markets and institutions provided the right kind of context in which even countries with relatively strong banks suffered the consequences. The rapidly evolving sovereign debt meltdown that started in 2010 provides yet another example of globalization and tight coupling at work. Starting with problems in relatively small and peripheral economies in Europe, sovereign debt concerns rattled the markets, and posed a fresh challenge to the incipient economic recovery in various parts of the world (see chapter 6).

The financial and economic crisis has thus reminded us about the increasingly complex and tightly-coupled nature of the global system. It is reasonable to argue that, while the world has historically seen other periods of intense economic and financial integration, the crisis has put on the agenda the need for reexamining certain aspects of economic and financial globalization as well as the urgency of building a strong framework of collaboration among governments to prevent crises from spiraling out of control. Globalization has not only made us keenly aware of global interdependencies, but also brought about a system of tightly-coupled markets in which confidence is essential but easily undermined. In the next chapter, I examine the various ways in which the U.S./China relationship contributes to complexity and coupling.

5

The U.S./China Relationship

The U.S. and China "suffer similar maladies: They are the most unbalanced major economies in the world today."

—Stephen Roach, *Unbalanced: The Codependency of America and China* (2014:213)

The world dollar standard is an accident of history that greatly facilitates international trade and exchange.... Erratic U.S. monetary and exchange policies since the late 1960s have made, and still make, foreigners unhappy.... It is a remarkable survivor that is too valuable to lose and too difficult to replace.

—Ronald I. McKinnon, *The Unloved Dollar Standard* (2013:3). By permission of Oxford University Press, USA

The relationship between the world's two largest economies is complex but not particularly coupled. The complexity primarily stems from the close economic ties that have developed between the two countries over the last three decades. China is the United States' second-largest trading partner after Canada, and the U.S. is China's number one. When it comes to foreign direct investment, the relationship is not as strong. China is not a top 10 destination for U.S. outward investment, although from the Chinese standpoint, the U.S. is the second-largest destination of foreign direct investment after Australia.

The U.S./China relationship scores lower in network coupling than in network complexity. First, while China is not the United States' most important trading partner it is the country with which the U.S. runs its largest deficit. Still, China accounts for less than half of the United States' total deficit. For China, the U.S. is the country with which it enjoys the largest trade surplus, although it is also less than half of its total surplus. Moreover, the local content of Chinese exports to the U.S. is lower than the local content of U.S. exports to China, meaning that the U.S. trade deficit with China would be cut by about one-third if value-added measures were used, and reallocated to the U.S. trade balance with other economies that sell intermediate goods to China such as Germany, Japan, South Korea, and Taiwan. For example, the U.S. deficit with China generated by trade in iPhones amounted to about $1.9 billion during 2009. However, if one decomposes the deficit in terms of the country of ultimate origin of the components, it breaks down as follows: $685 million from Japan, $341 million from Germany, $259 million from South Korea, $543 million from several other countries, and just $73.5 million from China (Maurer n.d.; UNCTAD 2013: 129; OECD-WTO 2013). Thus, the U.S./China relationship is somewhat tightly coupled in terms of the current account but less so than that between Germany and the rest of the European Union (see chapter 6). Second, more specifically, the two economies are intertwined in terms of manufacturing value chains, with 70% of U.S. exports to China being intermediate goods, and 75% of Chinese exports to the U.S. being final goods (Sposi and Koech 2013:2). This combination of trade in intermediates in one direction and trade in final goods in the other direction generates tight coupling. And third, the two countries have an intense relationship in terms of portfolio investment. China is the single largest foreign holder of U.S. Federal government bonds, to the tune of nearly $1.3 trillion, or 23% of the net debt owed to non-U.S. agencies or investors, though only 11% of total net debt, and 8% of total gross debt. Japan is the second with $1.2 trillion (Prasad 2014:91–3).

From the point of view of currency trading and cross-border banking, however, the U.S./China relationship is not significant. For starters, the Chinese currency is not convertible and freely tradable, an issue that I shall analyze in depth later in this chapter. And from the perspective of cross-border banking assets, the U.S./China relationship pales by comparison with the U.S. relationship with other parts of the world. For instance, the U.S. has greater consolidated bank claims on an immediate borrower basis with Australia, Brazil, Germany, France, UK, Japan, South Korea, Mexico, and the Cayman Islands than with China, which accounts for just 2.5% of the total.[1]

In sum, the U.S./China relationship has become more complex over time, although less tightly coupled, especially when compared to the Euro Zone (see chapter 6). It is certainly a dyadic relationship characterized by a certain degree of economic and financial interdependency (Roach 2014). China needs to trade with the U.S., while the U.S. needs China's continued investments in treasuries, although both countries have alternatives. What are the consequences of the highly complex and somewhat coupled relationship between the two economies for each of them and for the world? Are the global economy and geopolitical system more dangerous or more stable because of the mutual interdependency between the U.S. and China? How is it likely to evolve in the next few decades?

The Evolution of the Major Economies

In order to assess the implications and future evolution of the U.S./China relationship, it is useful to adopt a historical perspective. During much of the nineteenth century, the UK was the leading economy in terms of development and trade. It was not the largest economy, however, because China, while poor, was the largest until about 1888, when the U.S. became the number one economy. France was the second-largest economy until 1820, and then the UK became the second largest until 1872, the year in which the U.S. surpassed it in size. Germany was not bigger than the UK until 1908. Western Europe as a bloc was the largest economic region between 1840 and 1942 (Maddison 2012).

The UK was only second in economic output, but it was the largest trader and had both the largest navy and the most important reserve currency, pound sterling. During the Victorian era and until World War I, the UK was the most important economy in the world. Its status was reflected in its preeminent position in the global network of capital flows, as we saw in Figure 2.5 for the year 1914. No other country came even close in terms of global financial influence.

---

[1] Q3 of 2013. Bank for International Settlements, International Bank Claims dataset.

Fast forward half a century to the mid-1960s, and the situation had radically changed after two world wars and the dismantling of the British Empire. At that time the United States was the largest economy and trading nation. It was the only one with the ability to project force throughout the world thanks to its massive navy and sprawling network of military bases and facilities. And it was the country that issued the most important reserve currency, at the time convertible into gold.

Half a century later, in the year 2012, the global network of capital flows looks very different. The United States will be the world's largest economy for a few more years, and China already is the world's largest trader. The U.S., however, continues to be the only country capable of enforcing rules of behavior around the world, albeit with some limitations, and the dollar is still the most important reserve currency, although not as dominant as it once was. The world is multipolar, one in which the U.S., Europe, China, and Japan share the global economic and financial stage. India, and possibly Brazil and Indonesia, could join the club of the world's most important economic powers (World Bank 2011).

In this multipolar world, however, the largest economies are playing very dissimilar roles. From the point of view of currency reserves, for instance, there are reserve issuers and reserve accumulators. The main reserve issuers nowadays are the United States and the Euro Zone, while the main reserve accumulators are the largest emerging economies, the oil-exporting countries, and Germany and Japan. Figure 5.1 shows the rapid increase in reserve asset accumulation in the world, from less than $2 trillion in 1995 to nearly $12 trillion at the end of 2013. Most strikingly, the emerging economies surpassed the advanced economies in 2005, and presently hold twice as many reserve assets as the rich countries. Figure 5.2 displays the main reserve accumulators above the horizontal line. According to the IMF, only Japan is projected to reduce its holdings of foreign assets. The United States is projected to plunge deeper into a negative net foreign asset position, while the deficit countries in Europe will also see their position deteriorate as they recover from the crisis, which has temporarily generated current account surpluses due to increased exports and reduced imports.

The bifurcating paths of reserve accumulators and reserve issuers became the subject of global debate in 2005 when Federal Reserve

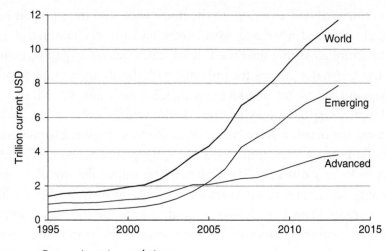

Figure 5.1. Reserve Asset Accumulation, 1995–2013

Source: IMF COFER database.

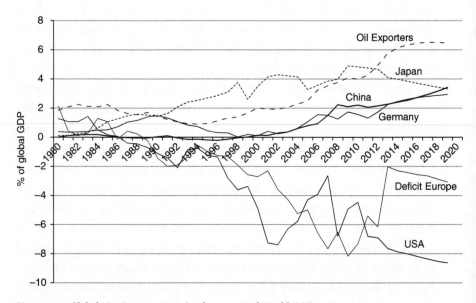

Figure 5.2. Global Net Foreign Asset Stocks, as a % of World GDP, 1980–2019

Note: Projections from 2014 onwards.
Source: IMF, *Global Economic Outlook* (2014).

Chairman Ben Bernanke commented on the "global savings glut," whereby current account surpluses in emerging economies created a huge demand for U.S. assets. The issue has polarized opinions. "One side views the current global imbalances as a natural result of economic fundamentals, savings surpluses, on one side, and savings deficits on the other," argues Kenneth Austin (2014:609–10), an economist with the U.S. Treasury Department. He continues:

> The global effects, particularly the effects on reserve issuing countries like the United States and the Euro Zone, are either benign, unimportant, or the result of poor policies and low savings rates. The other side views the effects of Chinese exchange rate policies and external deficits on other countries as being less benign: intended to promote economic growth even at the expense of trading partners.

Other observers, like Peking University's Michael Pettis (2013:136), put the ensuing dynamic in stark terms:

> Exporting capital means importing demand, and except in a few restricted and very specific cases, importing capital, especially for rich countries, will mean slower growth and rising unemployment. The "currency wars" that have been much in the news recently are simply "wars" in which countries try desperately to export their unwanted savings to each other.

The phenomenal increase in reserve accumulation is mainly the result of the large current account imbalances that have made the entire global economy more tightly coupled (see chapter 3). "Unlike the gold standard or the original Bretton Woods system, these reserve flows have not been fettered by the physical availability of gold; the resulting imbalances are clearly larger and more persistent," mainly because they are driven by the twin decisions of many emerging economies, especially China, "to set the value of their own currencies low enough to engineer large current account surpluses," and to purchase reserve assets from deficit countries (Austin 2014:632). These flows of capital do not seem to respond to market incentives because they go to richer countries with lower interest rates and slacking aggregate demand (Austin 2014:629). The *Financial Times* columnist Martin Wolf (2014:166) has framed the issue in even starker terms when arguing that "the global market for the U.S. dollar is rigged. It is one in which governments are prepared to buy massively, to prevent prices from reaching natural market clearing levels." It is hard to estimate the exact quantitative impact of such distortions. "We do not know how much lower the dollar would have been if there had been no such intervention, but surely it would have been substantially weaker and US monetary policy would have consequently needed to be less expansionary."

Why are International Currencies so Important?
Money plays three roles in the economy, namely, medium of exchange, unit of account, and store of value. An international currency can also play those three roles. From the point of view of private actors, an international currency serves as a medium of exchange in trade invoicing and financial transactions, it can also become a unit of account when it comes to denominating trade and financial transactions, and investors can use it as a store of value. From the point of view of governments, an international currency can be a medium of exchange if it is used to intervene in currency exchange markets, a unit of account if it becomes an anchor for pegging the local currency, or a store of value for keeping foreign reserves.

The wheels of cross-border trade and investment need international currencies to support payments and, most importantly, deficits and surpluses. International currencies have existed for a very long time. From the first century BCE to the fourth century AC, the Roman *aureus* was the perhaps the currency that came closest to playing the role of an international currency. The Byzantine *solidus* was widely used in international trade from the fourth to the twelfth centuries. During the Renaissance it was the Florentine *fiorino* that played this essential role, and later came the Dutch *gulden* (seventeenth–eighteenth centuries), and the Spanish *real de a ocho*, dubbed as the "Spanish dollar" (eighteenth–nineteenth centuries). In the contemporary period, the world has seen two main international currencies, pound sterling and the U.S. dollar.

The importance of the U.S. dollar to the global economy cannot be exaggerated. The dollar is the only currency accepted all over the world, i.e. a truly international medium of exchange for private actors and governments alike. It is the unit of account used for valuing many commodities and the dominant currency for trade invoicing. It is also the currency used by many governments to anchor their own local currency, and the most widely used reserve currency. The dollar has geopolitical and symbolic value as well, enabling the projection of

American influence around the world. Although the U.S. financial sector has a long history of recurrent panics and crises (Kinddleberger 1978; see chapter 4), the world continues to trust the dollar more than any other currency.

And yet, the dollar and the country whose government issues it, and stands by it, is showing clear signs of fatigue. One such symptom is the decline in the dollar's share of total allocated reserves, from close to the total in the 1950s to about 60% today. The dollar is also becoming less important as an anchor for other currencies. Out of 191 countries, 23% used the dollar as an anchor in April 2014, down from 33% in 2008. The euro has remained stable at around 14%. Meanwhile, other types of arrangements such as targeting a monetary aggregate or simply no nominal anchor have become more popular (IMF 2014:6).[2] Another sign of the dollar's declining importance is the increasingly introspective, inward-looking posture of the American public and of its Federal government, distracted as both of them are by domestic issues and controversies, ranging from taxes and spending to state rights and the culture wars. The stability provided by the two-party system is also in doubt.

International Currencies, Convenience, and Trust

In order to fully grasp the importance of reserve currencies to the global economy, and the institutions underpinning them, let us use a hypothetical example. Assume that the author of this book owes you one U.S. dollar, and that he offers you two ways of paying you back. The first is to give you a one-dollar bill, i.e. a greenback, and the other to give you a personal check written to the order of cash for one U.S. dollar and drawn on a bank located in the United States. The question is which of the two you should take. Let us not forget that the U.S. dollar is no longer convertible into gold. President Nixon made that decision in 1971, intriguingly one month after he announced that the U.S. was in talks with China and had accepted an invitation to visit the country.

---

[2] While which currency is an anchor matters, the specific type of exchange rate regime does not seem to. According to Rose (2011), similar countries make very different choices and they do not seem to matter when it comes to real outcomes like GDP growth or unemployment.

Compared to a personal check, the greenback has the advantage of convenience. You can use it virtually anywhere around the world. By contrast, the personal check has to be cashed or deposited at a bank in the United States. In fact, if I were to give you my personal check, you should immediately go to my bank to ensure that there are funds in my account. If you were to deposit it in your own account at a different bank than mine, you would not be able to dispose of the money until a few days later and only after your bank had verified that I have enough money in my account. Alternatively, you could discount the check by passing it on to someone else, but that would entail a loss of a certain percentage of its face value. While most people have a considerable amount of trust in the issuer of the dollar bill, i.e. the U.S. government, trust in a check drawn on a personal checking account is not as high. Thus, it all boils down to trust as well as convenience.

Now let us consider a different situation. The surrealist painter Salvador Dalí is one of the most famous artists of the twentieth century. Back in the 1960s, he went to a restaurant in New York with a bunch of friends. They had a very nice meal. Upon receiving the bill, Dalí would normally write a personal check for the full amount, sign it, and hand it over to the waiter, who in turn would give it to the manager. The manager would proceed to endorse the check by turning it on its back and signing it. The check would then be sent to the bank for deposit.

One day, Dalí decided to run a small experiment. Before giving his personal check to the waiter, he turned it on its back, drew a little surrealist sketch, and signed it. Then he passed the check on to the waiter, who gave it to the manager. After turning the check on its back in order to endorse it, the manager noted the sketch and paused for a moment, realizing that the check had become an original Dalí drawing. The manager decided to frame it and hang it on the wall of the dining room. Remember that Dalí was a living legend at the time and one of the most famous artists of the twentieth century. His oil paintings routinely sold for millions of dollars.

Days later, Dalí verified that the check had not been deposited. "This is very interesting," he probably thought, "I can print my own money." In the following weeks and months, he proceeded in the same fashion, and restaurant managers continued to frame and hang the checks on the wall instead of depositing them.

The key question raised in this true story is, until when was Dalí able to get away with a free lunch? Well, the answer is rather obvious, but it has little to do with whether the restaurant already had a Dalí check-drawing hanging from the wall. Like art museums, restaurants might want to exhibit several works by the same artist. Rather, the manager would deposit the check if the market value of the drawing on the back of the check were smaller than the face value of the check. That point was reached rather quickly because of the inflation in Dalí check-drawings stemming from his proclivity to print money. I would like to refer to the lesson from this true story as the Dalí principle: If too much money is printed, trust in it will decline.

Now back to the dollar. The U.S. government issues currency that is not backed by gold or any other real asset. Instead, people accept it as a form of payment or medium of exchange in international transactions, and in trade invoicing and settlement, because of the trust they have in Uncle Sam. Central banks around the world use it as an exchange rate anchor, an intervention currency or a store of value for exactly the same reason. The issue is, how long will that trust last, especially in the wake of the rise of the emerging economies and the fiscal woes in the U.S.? For how long will the U.S. be able to write checks that are not deposited? When will the Dalí principle kick in?

Institutions Supporting a Reserve Currency

It is important to take notice of the institutions that generate the trust needed for a currency to be widely accepted and to perform the function of a store of value. This issue is especially important because the country that issues a widely-used reserve currency obtains certain important benefits, including lower transaction costs in trade, lower interest rates, international prestige, and power and influence over global affairs (Eichengreen 2010). In the 1960s, then French Finance Minister, later President of the Republic, Valéry Giscard d'Estaing famously referred to these benefits as the "exorbitant privilege." Even if the dollar's value were to plummet, the U.S. would benefit, not lose:

> But what would happen if foreign investors were to pull their money
> out of the U.S., leading to a sharp fall in the exchange rate of the dollar
> relative to other currencies? The value of U.S. liabilities would not fall.

> But the value of its assets would go up in dollar terms. Thus, the
> U.S. would make a one-time windfall gain from the fall in its cur-
> rency's value. Such is the benefit of the exorbitant privilege enjoyed by
> the world's dominant reserve currency. (Prasad 2014:114)

A reserve currency can only be solid and trustworthy in the presence of
eight kinds of institutions. First, full convertibility, i.e. its price must be
determined in free markets in which the currency is traded relative to
all other currencies. Second, there must be free capital flows between
the country that issues the reserve currency and the rest of the world.
Third, the banking system must be strong and sophisticated enough to
thrive under conditions of full convertibility and free capital flows.
Fourth, the rule of law must be fully guaranteed through a solid and
transparent legal system. Fifth, in order for foreigners to hold and
dispose of the reserve currency, there must be a large and liquid market
for securities denominated in the currency, including government
bonds. Sixth, the government's policies must be predictable. Seventh,
the government must exercise a considerable degree of fiscal responsibility. And eighth, an international language like English must
be widely spoken so as to reassure foreign investors that they will be
able to communicate easily. Without solid institutions, trust in the
reserve currency will not be possible (Eichengreen 2013; Prasad
2014). In other words, issuing a reserve currency brings benefits, to
be sure, but it can only be sustainable if certain basic responsibilities are
met. This is what I call the Spiderman principle: "with great power
comes great responsibility."

Enter China

There is little doubt that in the near future the Chinese currency must
play an important role in the global financial architecture due to
China's size and increasing wealth. "Chinese officials see renminbi
internationalization as advantageous for their banks and firms, as
part of the broader process of rebalancing the Chinese economy, and
as a way of reducing their dependence on the dollar," argues Barry
Eichengreen (2013:364), a leading expert on the global financial architecture. "In addition, renminbi internationalization is integral to their
vision for reforming the international monetary system." Putting in

place the institutions needed to fully internationalize the renminbi, however will take politics and time:

> China faces significant challenges as it pursues renminbi internationalization. While China may be a large economy, it remains a poor one. Its financial markets lack depth and liquidity. Encouraging international use of the renminbi will require substantial liberalization of the current account, in the course of which many things can go wrong. As growth slows, China will face economic, political and social tensions. There may then be pressure for officials to slow or reverse the external financial liberalization. [...] Finally, China's political system may be an obstacle to renminbi internationalization. Foreigners will feel comfortable holding financial instruments in China only if they believe that their investments are secure. (Eichengreen 2013:372–3; see also 2011:143–7)

For instance, it took one decade for the U.S. to turn the dollar into an international currency from being a purely national currency with virtually no international use prior to 1914. At that time, the U.S. had no central bank, no reserves were held in dollars, and no domestic banks could open foreign branches. By the mid-1920s, however, the dollar was more important than pound sterling as a reserve currency (Eichengreen and Kawai 2015:355). Nevertheless, China has a different kind of economic, political, and legal system, one that will be harder to reform and prepare for taking such a step.

The practical problems surrounding a transition of the renminbi to full international use are staggering. In the short run, it is just not feasible for China to simply float its currency. An appreciation of the renminbi will not by itself reduce the gap between China's savings and investment. If a stronger renminbi reduces the willingness to install productive capacity in China, then investment may start to fall, thus widening, not reducing, the gap (McKinnon 2013:162–3; Yang 2012). Therefore, domestic savings must decrease in favor of domestic consumption, something that could be facilitated by a stronger currency both because domestic sales of domestic goods would be relatively more profitable, and because imported goods would be less expensive. In addition, government spending and the allocation of credit by state-owned financial institutions must shift towards research and education, and Chinese firms should engage in more foreign direct investment (Yang 2012). Population policies also ought to change in order to rebalance the age structure, and eliminate the strong effect on savings that the gender imbalance is causing due to competition by the disproportionately high number of households with a single son to find marriageable women (Wei and Zhang 2011). Making these changes actually happen is far from easy.

Thus, the main issue confronting the global financial architecture in the early twenty-first century is that, unlike during most of the nineteenth century or the post-World War II period, the provider of the dominant international and reserve currency is not in a position to continue doing so by itself for a much longer period of time. After World War II, the U.S. accounted for half of world GDP, more than half of exports, and the overwhelming majority of foreign direct investment. It made a great deal of sense for the U.S. dollar to be the world's reserve currency. Moreover, the U.S. was committed to sell as much gold as needed at a fixed price of $35 an ounce.

Fast forward to the second decade of the twenty-first century. The U.S. represents less than 20% of the global economy, and even less of global trade. The dollar–gold peg was abandoned in 1971 because the amount of dollars in circulation exceeded by a wide margin the dollar value of gold in the vault. The country does not have its fiscal house in order, and population aging will further aggravate the problem (Eichengreen 2011:162–7). It has adopted a loose monetary policy so as to stimulate growth and employment, income inequality is growing fast, and trust in the greenback has been eroding since the 1970s. In turn, a declining dollar will make a global military presence so much more expensive to sustain (Eichengreen 2011:175–6). Some experts note that these problems are thrown in stark relief when considering the simultaneous rise of the emerging economies, especially China. "The United States cannot escape the inherent logic of demography and convergence," asserts Arvind Subramanian, an economist with experience at the IMF and the GATT. In order for the inevitable dominance of China to be derailed, "not just will the United States have to grow substantially faster than the long-run trend but it must be seen as strong fiscally and, above all, able to reverse the pall of economic and social stagnation that has enveloped its middle class" (Subramanian 2011:190–5).

Ronald McKinnon has put it best when he recently wrote that "the world dollar standard is an accident of history that greatly facilitates international trade and exchange.... Although the strong network effects of the dollar standard," he continues, "greatly increase the financial efficiency of multilateral trade, nobody loves it. Erratic U.S. monetary and exchange policies since the late 1960s have made, and still make, foreigners unhappy." In spite of all the crises and vicissitudes of the last half century, the dollar "is a remarkable survivor that is too valuable to lose and too difficult to replace" (2013:3–4). As the economist Edwar Prasad asks, "if not the dollar, then what?" And he continues: "This is not a story about American exceptionalism. Rather, it is one about weaknesses in the rest of the world and deep problems in the structure of the global monetary system" (Prasad 2014:11, 13).

The situation is unprecedented because capital is flowing to the country that seeks to influence global affairs, and not the other way around. "The excess capital of the world has, after all, flowed to the United States to maintain its high standard of living rather than, as hegemonic stability theory would suggest, to aid in development else-where," observe sociologists John Campbell and John Hall (2015:38). "One might take indebtedness as a sign of weakness, but then one might see it as something rather different—an extraction from other national economies made all the more attractive given the hegemon's ability to diminish its debt by printing money. [...] One is tempted at times to describe such behavior as predatory, but it is perhaps best to diminish emotions by continuing to speak of seigniorage." It is also worth noting that the ability of the U.S. to benefit from the dollar-based global economy is limited in scale and scope by the health of its own economy and political system.

Meanwhile, the country that already is the largest trading nation, and will soon become the largest economy, is not ready to issue a reserve currency because it has none of the eight necessary institutions mentioned above. This situation is problematic for two reasons. First, the annual demand for reserve assets is nowadays three times greater than in the late twentieth century, judging from the size of the current account imbalances in the world (see Figure 3.2; Prasad 2014:12). And second, only large economies can offer enough assets for foreigners to buy. The larger the Chinese economy becomes, the more its currency should play an important role in the global financial architecture. The situation is also unusual because China cannot be a *net* provider of reserve assets to the rest of the world if it continues to have both a current account surplus (largely due to its trade surplus) and a capital account surplus (Yu 2015). To the extent that China remains a net reserve accumulator, other countries will need to step up to the plate, although they may not be willing or able to do so.

In spite of its institutional shortcomings, the Chinese currency is playing a growing role internationally in at least four respects. The first is that China has concluded swap arrangements with more than 20 countries, which essentially entail bypassing the U.S. dollar when it comes to bilateral trade and financial transactions. The European Union has signed an agreement worth €45 billion. China and Russia began trading in their own currencies in November of 2010 after doing away with the dollar in bilateral trade. As of 2014, nearly one-third of China's trade was being settled in renminbi, although 80% of it had to do with Hong Kong. The proportion of foreign direct investment settled in renminbi has skyrocketed in recent years to over 80% (Eichengreen and Kawai 2015:133, 218, 261). The second is that other countries are starting to track the renminbi as opposed to the dollar. In the wake of the financial crisis of 2008, the currencies of Malaysia, the Philippines, Singapore, and Thailand have parted ways with the world's leading reserve currency (Subramanian and Kessler 2013; McKinnon 2013:176–80). Third, the renminbi became in 2013 the second most important currency for trade finance after the dollar, with an 8.7% share of letters of credit and collections compared to 81.1% for the dollar (*Bloomberg*, December 3, 2013). And fourth, the dim-sum bond market for renminbi-denominated bonds issued outside China has grown considerably since its inception in 2007, although it is still an "offshore" operation (Eichengreen 2011:146–7). While the renminbi is the seventh most widely used currency for international payments, it represents only 1.4% of the total, and much of it has to do with the transactions between Chinese companies and their Hong Kong subsidiaries. In spite of the dim-sum bonds, China has only made about $300 billion of renminbi-denominated assets available to foreign investors, compared to the $56 trillion denominated in U.S. dollars, $29 trillion in euros, and $17 trillion in yen (*The Economist*, June 21, 2014).

China is in possession of a potentially game-changing card, and it involves the Special Administrative Region of Hong Kong. When the former British colony was handed over in 1999, it was not just territory and population that changed hands. Most crucially, Hong Kong offers China a world-class financial center with all of the desirable institutions that foreigners like to see before investing. The Hong Kong dollar is fully convertible, investors enjoy the benefits of free capital flows, its banking system has long operated under open conditions, the British left behind a sound legal system based on common law, the city is home to a large and vibrant securities market, policymaking is predictable, the government is fiscally responsible, the English language is widely spoken, and there is a large expatriate community working in financial services.

It is impressive to note that Hong Kong's stock market is the sixth largest in the world by market capitalization after the NYSE, Nasdaq, Tokyo, LSE, and Euronext. According to the Global Financial Centers Index published by the Z/Yen Group (2014), Hong Kong is the world's third most competitive center after New York and London in terms of talent, business environment, market access, and infrastructure. In addition, Hong Kong is a major source and destination of FDI, ranking as the fifth-largest outward investor in the world with a cumulative stock of nearly $1.4 trillion as of the end of 2013, up from just $12 billion in 1990, and as the second-largest recipient of FDI, with just above $1.4 trillion in 2013, up from $202 billion in 1990, trailing only the United States (UNCTAD 2014). Most of these large amounts have to do with the activities of companies from mainland China and other countries that use Hong Kong as a financial platform. Thus, Hong Kong is already playing a key role in the internationalization of the Chinese economy, although the duality of domestic and offshore renminbi deposits, assets, and transactions creates distortions and could hinder the modernization of China's domestic financial sector (Cheung 2015).

China's Array of Domestic and Geo-Strategic Constraints

In order for China to play a major role in the global financial architecture, however, it will need to address formidable challenges of both a domestic and a geo-strategic kind, as noted above. Domestically, China is beset by an aging population, lower-cost competition from neighboring countries, rising income inequality, asset-price inflation, a yawning gap between its booming cities and its backward countryside, urban congestion, air pollution, environmental degradation, separatist movements in two-fifths of its territory (Tibet and the Western provinces), and a colossally inefficient and corrupt political system (Hu 2011; Cheng 2011 and Kokubun and Wang eds. 2004). It will take an extraordinarily ambitious and wide-ranging reform effort to tackle these issues successfully. Justin Yifu Lin, the first Chinese national to serve as Senior Vice President and Chief Economist of the World Bank, offered a comprehensive catalogue of China's constraints in his book, *Demystifying the Chinese Economy*. He concluded that "China has great potential to continue the current dynamic growth for another two decades or more. [...] To achieve that, China needs to overcome many intrinsic problems," including income disparities, the rural–urban gap, the inefficient use of resources, environmental imbalances, external imbalances, currency appreciation, corruption, and education focused on quantity rather than quality (Lin 2012:17–19).

Demographically, China is not on the rise but on the decline, and will soon be outnumbered by India (Howe and Jackson 2012). It is germane to note that there is no instance in history of a society with a shrinking population becoming a regional or global leader. The launching of the Spanish, Portuguese, and British empires, for example, came hand in hand with rapid population growth. The United States became an industrial giant thanks to both massive immigration and high fertility, which helped create a large labor force and domestic consumer market.

The Chinese environmental problem is simply massive. In the book, *Collapse: How Societies Choose to Fail or Succeed*, Jared Diamond (2005:358) argued that "China's environmental problems are among the most severe of any major country, and are getting worse," adding that "the list ranges from air pollution, biodiversity losses, cropland losses, desertification, disappearing wetlands, grassland degradation, and increasing scale and frequency of human-induced natural disasters, to invasive species, overgrazing, river flow cessation, salinization, soil erosion, trash accumulation, and water pollution and shortages." In fact, Diamond observed that China's size is not an advantage, but a serious drawback: "China's large population and large growing economy, and its current and historic centralization, mean that China's lurches involve more momentum than those of any other country" (Diamond 2005:377; see also Lauder Global TrendLab 2012).

Unlike the UK and the U.S. in their heyday, China is a country that is geo-strategically constrained, as Paul Kennedy pointed out in his 1987 book, *The Rise and Fall of the Great Powers*. The UK had unimpeded access to the seas, and the U.S. even more so. China simply lacks access to the open ocean, an issue that also limited Germany's ambitions during the late nineteenth and early twentieth centuries. A quick look at Figure 5.3 suffices to realize China's fragile geographical predicament. In order to reach Chinese ports, ships need to negotiate narrow straits when approaching from the West, or two island chains when arriving from the East. The region is dotted by U.S. naval bases and military installations.

Most importantly, China is surrounded by more than 20 countries in every direction, and all of them are deeply suspicious of, if not outright hostile to, it. In combination, these neighboring countries outnumber China one-to-two in terms of population and economic size. To make matters worse, China also has frequently sought

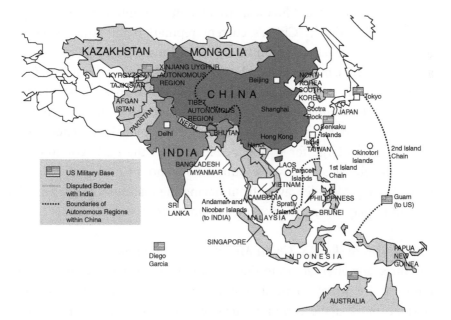

Figure 5.3. China's Geopolitical Location, 2015

dangerous showdowns with its neighbors, including the tensions over the Paracel Islands with Vietnam in 1974 and 2014, the Spratly Islands with both Vietnam in 1988 and the Philippines in 1994, the Okinotori Islands with Japan in 2004, the Socotra Rock with South Korea in 2006, and the Senkaku/Diaoyu Islands with Japan in 2010 and 2013 (Carr 2010:11; Roach 2014). China has active border disputes with no less than India, the other emerging Asian giant. China is increasingly perceived as a neo-colonialist power in Africa, where it has made headway by nurturing ties to corrupt and genocidal governments (Shinn and Eisenman 2012). To the detriment of its international prestige, China has failed to curb North Korea's nuclear ambitions. And for all its financial and economic muscle, China's ability to project force is anemic given that it is militarily outspent by its immediate neighbors taken as a group, and more than sixfold by the United States (Carr 2010). In the eye-opening book, *The Next 100 Years: A Forecast for the 21st Century*, George Friedman (2009:88) put it succinctly: "I don't share the view that China is going to be a major world power. I don't even believe it will hold together as a unified country. But I do agree that we can't discuss the future without first discussing China."

Thus, China's ability to play an important, even dominant role, in the global economy and financial architecture is limited. As Joseph Nye has shrewdly noted, "China's current reputation for power benefits from projections about the future. [...] China does have impressive power resources, but we should be skeptical about projections based on current growth rates and political rhetoric" (Nye 2011:178–9). However, the global financial architecture cannot work properly unless China has a part to play. Its economy and global influence have grown far too large for it not to. Hereby lies the basic conundrum facing the global economy: we cannot do without China, but China is years, perhaps decades, away from having the institutional framework needed to play a constructive role commensurate with its size.

Alternatives to the U.S./China Monetary Cohabitation
Are there any alternatives to the U.S. and China when it comes to the future of the global financial architecture? Certainly the euro—or the German mark if the common currency were to collapse—must continue to play a role. Pound sterling and the Japanese yen can be of some

limited help, but neither country is willing to shoulder the costs in terms of lost competitiveness through an appreciated exchange rate. The Swiss franc, while incredibly safe, will never be a big player given the country's size (Eichengreen 2011:126–7).

Another possibility involves India, a country that will soon have the largest consumer market in the world and already possesses several of the eight institutions needed for issuing a successful reserve currency, especially those related to convertibility, capital flows, the banking system, the legal system, and the English language. However, India ostensibly lacks a large and liquid securities market and a government whose policies foreign investors can trust. While India is frequently billed as the "world's largest democracy," policymaking is far from predictable, especially at the regional and local levels (Stepan et al. 2011), and its track record in terms of women's rights casts a long shadow over the ability of the political and judicial system to protect citizens against abuse. As the Indian economy develops and becomes more outward-oriented, however, it is entirely possible that it could become an attractive option for foreigners seeking to diversify their holdings of reserve assets (Panagariya 2008; Eichengreen 2011:151–2).

The other, perhaps more tantalizing, possibility involves a radical re-thinking of what a reserve currency is and who issues it. Here we encounter two options. The first is SDRs or special drawing rights, a synthetic currency based on a basket of national currencies and issued by the IMF, which as of early 2015 can only be used to settle debts with governments or with the IMF itself. Lacking a private market in which they can be traded, SDRs account for less than 5% of total reserves (Eichengreen 2011:138–42). Still, some economists believe it can play a strong role in the future (e.g. Pettis 2013:150–77).

A more useful alternative may involve the so-called digital currencies. Bitcoin, for instance, is a computer program that creates and manages the supply of its namesake currency, and establishes procedures for processing payments between users. At a series of hearings organized by the U.S. Senate in 2013, officials from the Treasury Department and the Fed displayed a striking degree of comfort with the prospects for digital money (U.S. Senate 2013; Lee 2013). Chairman Ben Bernanke published a letter in anticipation of the hearings to clarify his views about digital currencies, citing former Vice Chairman

Alan Blider, who in 1995 testified at the U.S. House of Representatives on the future of money. "Blinder's testimony at that time made the key point that while these types of innovations may pose risks related to law enforcement and supervisory matters," Bernanke wrote, "there are also areas in which they may hold long-term promise, particularly if the innovations promote a faster, more secure and more efficient payment system."[3] Similar hearings took place in the House of Representatives in early 2014, with witnesses emphasizing the potential for low transaction costs and financial inclusion for the unbanked and underbanked (U.S. House of Representatives 2014).

The Federal Reserve Bank of Chicago has explained in a brief letter the virtues of digital currencies like bitcoin:

> The bitcoin protocol provides an elegant solution to the problem of creating a digital currency—i.e., how to regulate its issue, defeat counterfeiting and double-spending, and ensure that it can be conveyed safely—*without relying on a single authority*. What, in the end, is this new currency? It is a list of authorized transactions, beginning with the creation of the unit by a miner and ending with the current owner. The currency can be exchanged because all potential recipients have the means to verify past transactions and validate new ones, and one's ownership rests on the consensus of the nodes. (Velde 2013:2; emphasis added)

Thanks to an ingenious algorithm, some argue, bitcoin eliminates the need for a state authority. "Bitcoin is free of the power of the state, but it is also outside the protection of the state" (Velde 2013:3). In other words, it is an entirely fiduciary currency that is not monopolized by any one state.

David Schweikert, Republican of Arizona, stated at the hearings his belief that bitcoin could displace the dollar as an international currency, a possibility that conservatives find tantalizing rather than threatening. "What becomes fascinating here in monetary policy is all of a sudden you would have a currency, without intervention from a

---

[3] The full text of the letter is at http://qz.com/148399/ben-bernanke-bitcoin-may-hold-long-term-promise/#148399/ben-bernanke-bitcoin-may-hold-long-term-promise/, accessed June 21, 2014.

central bank," he said. "You would actually have an honest peg of value" (Boring 2014). Back in 1999, the famed Chicago economist Milton Friedman argued that "we don't need a Fed...I have, for many years, been in favor of replacing the Fed with a computer" (quoted in Kozmetsky and Yue 2005:379). Thus, the prospect for a digital currency appeals to conservatives and libertarians for its potential of eliminating what they see as government interference in monetary affairs.

Despite its attractive features, digital currencies remain marginal and their value has proven to be very volatile. While their growth rate is steep, they account for a tiny fraction of all payments. And they still need to earn the trust of those who use it. The field of digital currencies is populated by many competitors, including Bitcoin, Ripple, Litecoin, Auroracoin, Peercoin, Dogecoin, Nxt, Mastercoin, and Namecoin (Andolfatto 2014). To make matters worse, the Internal Revenue Service has ruled that bitcoins are property and not a currency. Therefore, buying or selling them could generate a capital gain or loss.

An entirely different issue is whether digital currencies could become a store of value and even play the role of reserve currency in the global economy. The presumed creator of bitcoin, Satoshi Nakamoto, compared in a blog the advantages of digital (fiduciary) currencies over fiat currencies like the U.S. dollar:

> The root problem with conventional currency is all the trust that's required to make it work. The central bank must be trusted not to debase the currency, but the history of fiat currencies is full of breaches of that trust. Banks must be trusted to hold our money and transfer it electronically, but they lend it out in waves of credit bubbles with barely a fraction in reserve. We have to trust them with our privacy, trust them not to let identity thieves drain our accounts. Their massive overhead costs make micropayments impossible.[4]

Clearly, if digital currencies were a credible alternative to fiat money, they could also become a store of value. In any event, the potential role of bitcoin or other digital currencies as reserve currencies is years, if not decades, away.

---

[4] http://p2pfoundation.net/bitcoin, accessed June 28, 2014.

The Future of the U.S./China Relationship

It is becoming increasingly clear that the global system of the twenty-first century will to a very large extent revolve around the U.S./China axis. As the world's two largest economic, trading, and financial powers, they have developed a largely synergistic relationship in which one is, at least partially, the hostage of the other. China needs continued access to the U.S. consumer market, and the U.S. needs Chinese capital to finance its current account and fiscal deficits. Moreover, a sudden dollar crisis would hurt China immensely given its vast holdings (Eichengreen 2011:159–60). The U.S. and China "suffer similar maladies: They are the most unbalanced major economies in the world today" (Roach 2014:213). In addition, they are the world's biggest contributors to income and wealth inequality. As documented in Figures 3.11 and 3.12, inequality has risen very fast in both China and the U.S., and wealth inequality even faster (Credit Suisse 2014; Alvaredo et al. 2014; Capgemini and RBC Wealth Management 2013). In China, inequality has risen both within the cities and between urban and rural areas (Chen et al. 2010:20).

This type of intense bilateral relationship apparently leaves very little room for error. A major geopolitical event or a domestic crisis in either country could potentially destabilize the relationship and, as a consequence, the entire global system. I would argue, however, that the U.S./China relationship is not as tightly coupled as it appears to be. First, neither country can put unlimited pressure on the other. When compared to the U.S./Japan relationship during the 1930s and the 80s, the U.S. cannot easily bully China because it is a much bigger country than Japan, and it is dependent on it for cheap consumer goods and funding. During the late 1930s, the U.S. put enormous pressure on Japan in response to its expansion throughout Southeast Asia, restricting access to oil supplies, and eventually inviting the hardliners in the government and the bureaucracy to press ahead with a preemptive attack on Pearl Harbor. And during the 1980s, the U.S. imposed "voluntary import restraints" on Japan, meaning quotas, an action that would be unimaginable in the case of China. While it is true that the U.S. has accused China of being a currency manipulator and has filed, and mostly won, numerous suits with the WTO over unfair trade practices and intellectual property transgressions (Bergsten 2015; Hufbauer and Woollacott 2010), the economic and financial relationship between the two countries is fundamentally collaborative.

A second reason is that both countries, and especially the better-off segments of the population within both countries, benefit massively from the current international order, which is essentially based on liberal economic principles regarding both trade and capital flows (Abdelal 2007; Gilpin 2001). China understands that the U.S. will continue to be the dominant cultural force in the world, and that it stands to benefit from U.S. leadership as long as the emphasis on liberalism does not spill over into domestic political matters (Carr 2010; Ikenberry 2006; Nye 2004). Moreover, the U.S. is subsidizing Chinese trade and the globalization of Chinese firms by being the only country with the ability to police shipping lanes and assets critical to global trade and investment. At the present time, China has little to lose, and actually much to gain, from a continued U.S. military presence around the world.

China's transition from an export-driven and investment-oriented economy to one more reliant on the domestic consumer market will undoubtedly usher in changes in its relationship with the United States. But even this change, if gradual and successful, will provide the global system with an even greater degree of stability and flexibility by reducing trade imbalances and currency tensions (Eichengreen 2013; Temin and Vines 2013:236–40). The global system actually needs the Chinese economy to slow down, mature, and evolve towards domestic consumption. The hard-working Chinese population also deserves just that. Whether the political system can lead that change and remain relevant, however, is an entirely different matter.

China's intended future course of action is consistent with a more general desirable transformation in the global economy. Global financial imbalances cannot be worked out unless two developments take place. First, there must be some expenditure switching from deficit to surplus countries. And second, there must be an adjustment of real exchange rates supporting a new equilibrium. This "cooperative outcome" would be the best possible future scenario. Unfortunately, more pessimistic scenarios are also possible, especially one in which the dollar loses value in a sudden way, something that is not in the best interest of anyone in the global economy (Temin and Vines 2013:240–1).

China is also making headway in terms of becoming a more innovative economy. The country is rapidly approaching the average ratio of R&D spending to GDP in the world, already is a top 15 country in terms of patents, and is one of the top producers of scientific and technical research. Most importantly, 74% of its R&D effort is accounted for by companies, about the same as in the U.S. and South Korea. It is by far the most dynamic innovator among the BRIC economies (Thomson Reuters 2013; Breznitz and Murphree 2011).

Still, the U.S. remains the number one country in many respects, even with a resurgent China and a rapidly-growing India. "It retains considerable economic power, both at the higher end of the product cycle and in finance, and its relationship with emerging markets is not necessarily antagonistic." Nevertheless, the issue is that the advantage that the U.S. continues to enjoy in economic and technological development "may yet be undermined through internal political stalemate, through failure to adapt to changing circumstances" (Campbell and Hall 2015:113).

Meanwhile, it is important for the world to make room for the global aspirations of China, India and the other large emerging economies. For instance, "China resembles Wilhelmine Germany" in that its leadership is eager to gain international legitimacy, "and it may yet seek to enhance it by playing the nationalist card" (Campbell and Hall 2015:117). As the historian David Calleo once wrote,

> geography and history conspired to make Germany's rise late, rapid, vulnerable, and aggressive. The rest of the world reacted by crushing the upstart. If, in the process, the German state lost its bearings and was possessed by an evil demon, perhaps the proper conclusion is not so much that civilization was uniquely weak in Germany, but that it is fragile everywhere. And perhaps the proper lesson is not so much the need for vigilance against aggressors, but the ruinous consequences of refusing reasonable accommodation to upstarts. (Calleo 1978:6)

Like Wilhelmine Germany, but definitely unlike Nazi Germany, China appears to be interested in finding a more prominent place at the table rather than in subverting the liberal global order that has served it so well (Campbell and Hall 2015:47; Osterhammel 2014).

In this chapter, I hope I have demonstrated that the global financial architecture is nowadays a "modus vivendi between China and the United States," a G-2 of sorts (McKinnon 2013:203–5). While not tightly coupled, there are some serious concerns about its sustainability. In the next chapter I will show that the Euro Zone is perhaps the most tightly-coupled subsystem of the global economy, with major negative implications for Europe and for the rest of the world. In contrast to the single market known as the European Union, the 18-nation monetary union has shown many signs of its self-destructive character. The consequences of too much coupling are readily apparent, and ultimately translate into mediocre economic performance, high unemployment, mounting political cleavages, and global instability.

6

The Euro Zone as a Complex, Tightly-Coupled System

Europe will be made of money, or it will not be made.

> —Jacques Rueff, French economist and
> Bank of France official, quoted in Eichengreen,
> *Hall of Mirrors: The Great Depression, The Great Recession,
> and the Uses-and-Misuses of History* by Eichengreen
> (2015) 13w from pp. 380–81. By permission
> of Oxford University Press, USA

The whole of Deutschland for Kohl, half the deutsche Mark for Mitterrand.

> —A "wit," quoted in Timothy Garton Ash,
> "The Crisis of Europe," *Foreign Affairs* (2012)

Not all Germans believe in God, but they all believe in the Bundesbank.

> —Jacques Delors, President of the European Commission, 1992 (quoted
> in the *Financial Times* June 8, 2012)

The 19-nation currency union known as the Euro Zone (EZ) is one of the most complex and tightly-coupled systems the world has ever seen, in sharp contrast with the 28-member European Union (EU), which is also a complex arrangement but hardly a tightly-coupled one. In this chapter I will explain how the EZ came into being as a tightly-coupled network, why it is so prone to disruption, crisis, and breakdown, and the ways in which the sovereign debt crisis has been dealt with has transformed network coupling into node coupling.

Was the Euro a Good Idea? Was it Adopted Prematurely?

Imagine Europe at the end of World War II. The continent was ravaged by destruction, famine, and uncertainty about the future.

Cities, transportation systems, factories, and other productive assets lay in ruins. Massive refugee population movements created new tensions and needs as borders were redrawn by the allied powers. The British Empire, the largest the world had ever seen, was on its way to inevitable decline. The Soviet Union, while victorious, had suffered enormous losses, both human and material. The world had just learned about the atrocities committed against various civil populations, and especially about the Holocaust. Hiroshima and Nagasaki changed geopolitics forever. The end of the war was certainly a relief, but another confrontation loomed large, one with the potential of being even more destructive. The Cold War changed Europe by creating an East–West divide, thus encouraging both sides to dig their heels in and build their own economic and political models.

It took massive American aid through the Marshall Plan and a great deal of institutional creativity and political compromise to lay the foundations for re-launching Western European countries as viable economies (Djelic 1998). The magnitude of the success of this effort at institution-building and economic reconstruction went well beyond the wildest dreams of those involved in it. From the mid-1950s to the early 70s, Western Europe enjoyed an exceptional period of growth and prosperity. While during the 1970s and 80s a succession of energy, economic, and monetary crises represented major setbacks, Western Europe entered the twenty-first century as a politically stable and economically wealthy part of the world, boosted by the prospects of further growth and development with the transition of Eastern Europe to the market.

The European Union as a Complex System

There were two essential pillars to Western Europe's postwar success. The first was its partnership with the U.S., which included economic, financial, and military aspects. Most importantly, both sides of the North Atlantic collaborated to create effective institutions for global governance, including such pivotal agencies as the United Nations, the General Agreement on Tariffs and Trade, the International Monetary Fund, the World Bank, and the World Health Organization.

The second pillar was the push towards integration in Western Europe, especially in terms of trade and other economic matters, as a way to overcome the rivalries and conflicts of the past. Driven both by the desire to avoid future wars and by an aspiration to global influence in a super-power world dominated by the U.S. and the Soviet Union, six European countries concluded in the mid-1950s a series of treaties leading to the formation of the European Coal and Steel Community, the European Atomic Energy Community, and the European Economic Community. The Treaty of Rome was signed in 1957 by the three largest economies on the continent (France, Germany, and Italy) along with three smaller ones with historically strong ties to them (Belgium, the Netherlands, and Luxembourg, also known as the Benelux).

This initial scheme evolved in fits and starts over five decades to become the EU, an arrangement that has become ever more complex over time. For instance, it now includes 28 members, compared to the original six. The EU presently extends from the Mediterranean Sea to the Arctic Circle, and from the Atlantic Ocean to the Black Sea (see Figure 6.1).

In addition to growing in size, the EU has also expanded in terms of depth. Member countries progressively agreed to pursue integration in

Figure 6.1. The European Union (EU) and the Euro Zone (EZ), 2015

trade for goods, services, capital, labor, and information. The member countries created a *customs union* with a coordinated trade policy vis-à-vis third countries by the end of the 1960s, a *common market* with capital and labor mobility by 1973, a *single market* with a coordinated value-added tax framework and joint regulatory and competition policies starting in 1993, and many aspects of an *economic union* involving the coordination of macroeconomic policies during the 1990s. Not surprisingly, trade within the EU soared relative to EU trade with other parts of the world, and the same went for foreign direct investment, tourism, migration, and information flows. On every indicator of complexity, the EU scores extremely high after decades of integration.

EU members have also persuaded themselves to become more internally complex. As a condition for membership, countries have had to beef up their democratic credentials, often building checks and balances into their constitutional and political systems. As a rule-based arrangement, the EU has also forced countries to increase the size of the state apparatus and state capacity (Fligstein 2001). In addition, EU membership has raised the public's expectations as to the provision of social services, leading to an expansion of the welfare state (Esping-Andersen 1990). Thus, the EU is complex at both the network and the node level.

Monetary Unions and Tight Coupling
In contrast to trade blocs, monetary unions tend to be tightly-coupled systems. Currencies are a peculiar commodity. Most importantly, they are the main way in which an economy adjusts to external shocks, and are a symbol of a country's stature in the global system. Surrendering monetary authority to the supranational level requires a number of preparatory steps that imply tighter coupling because they involve fundamental political and sovereignty issues. Moreover, monetary unions can only work if there is sufficient integration in terms of labor, fiscal, financial, and banking policies, price and wage flexibility, and a risk-sharing mechanism (Mundell 1961; Eichengreen 2011:132–3; Lane 2012; Spolaore 2013; Temin and Vines 2013:197–203). This is perhaps why there are so many trade blocs in the world—more than

250—but just a handful of monetary unions, all of them involving very small countries, with the notable exception of the EZ.[1]

The EZ is a tightly-coupled arrangement at the network level due to the very high degree of interconnection among its 19 members, as of 2015, in terms of current account imbalances, trade in intermediates, portfolio investment (especially in government bonds), and cross-border banking. Of the five indicators discussed in chapter 3, the only one that does not contribute to network coupling in the EZ is currency trading, for the obvious reason.

The tight coupling among the current accounts of the various European countries is staggering. EZ members generate at least one-third of their surpluses (or deficits) with other EZ members. Factories across continental Europe feed each other with parts and components, leading to massive cross-border trade in intermediates. As we shall see shortly, foreign banks and households became the largest holders of sovereign debt of other EU states (Blundell-Wignall and Slovik 2010), and the adoption of a common currency led to much cross-border banking activity (see Figure 3.7, upper panel).

In addition to network coupling, the EZ exhibits a high degree of node coupling. More so than the nine EU members who are not part of the EZ, the countries that adopted the euro suffer from a rapid process of population aging, have accumulated enormous amounts of public debt (82% of GDP compared to 69 for the entire high-income OECD), are seeing income and wealth inequality soar (although not as much as in the United Kingdom), and their cities have become more dualistic with the arrival of immigrants and the alarming trend towards urban poverty.

The Premature Launching of the Euro

Given the EU's progressively tighter integration in terms of trade, capital, labor, indirect taxation, regulation, and information, it makes perfect sense to reduce transaction costs and to take another bold step

---

[1] Note that some countries belong to several trade blocs. All bilateral or multilateral trade bloc agreements need to be registered with the World Trade Organization. The complete list can be found at http://rtais.wto.org/UI/PublicAllRTAList.aspx. The only formal monetary unions include: the Euro Zone, Singapore/Brunei, San Marino/Vatican/Euro Zone, the CFA franc, the CFP franc, the East Caribbean dollar, and Lesotho/Swaziland/Namibia/South Africa.

towards a true economic union by agreeing to adopt a common currency. There are two levels to the debate about the euro. The first has to do with whether it was a good idea or not, and the second with whether it was introduced at the best time or not.

There was a considerable debate in the 1990s about the virtues of a common currency, with only a few dissenting voices airing their concern. Prominent among them were two academics, Barry Eichengreen (1997) and Martin Feldstein (2000, 2012). The originator of the idea of optimal currency areas, Robert Mundell, ignored crucial aspects of his own theory (Mundell 1961) when displaying an early enthusiasm for the idea of a European common currency (Mundell 1973a, 1973b). In 1999, the same year the euro became a reality, he was awarded the Prize in Economic Sciences in Honor of Alfred Nobel for his contributions to the study of exchange rates and optimum currency areas. The truth of the matter is that the EZ is far from being an optimal currency area. To illustrate the point, it is useful to compare it with the 50 states of the U.S. in terms of four basic criteria. In terms of trade, inter-state "exports" in the U.S. were equivalent to 66% of U.S. GDP in 2007, just before the crisis started, compared to just 17% for the EZ. In terms of the correlation of local growth between 1997 and 2007, the coefficients were 0.46 and 0.51, respectively. In terms of labor mobility in 2012, 42% of Americans were born outside their state of residence, compared to only 17% in the EZ. Finally, in terms of fiscal matters, 28% of local income in the U.S. could be offset by federal transfers in the event of a macroeconomic shock versus just 0.5% in the case of the EZ (O'Rourke and Taylor 2013:178). Thus, the EZ is far less of an optimal currency area than the U.S. is.

The question of whether the euro was introduced at the best time or, to be more precise, prematurely is the most important one. Integration of capital markets in Europe had long been championed by Germany, Holland, and the UK, but opposed by France. The election of François Mitterrand in 1981 and his failed Keynesian stimulation of the economy created a very different scenario, one in which elite French policymakers saw capital controls as hopelessly ineffective and punitive to the middle class. The *tournant*, or Mitterrand U-turn, paved the way for the unification of European capital markets and provided ammunition for those in support of taking the ultimate step in unification, the introduction of a common currency (Abdelal 2007:56–9). "The euro is fundamentally a political project," argues Barry Eichengreen (2011:70). "This is its weakness, since it explains how it was that the euro was created before all the economic prerequisites needed for its smooth operation were in place." It is, essentially, "a currency without a state. It is the first major currency not backed by a major government" (Eichengreen 2011:130; see also: Ash 2012; Spolaore 2013). But why was the euro created prematurely? The answer lies in the characters involved in the drama.

Prominent among the elite policymakers in favor of more capital integration in Europe was Jacques Delors, Mitterrand's Finance Minister (1981–4), later to become President of the European Commission (1985–94). Delors was a devout Catholic and a staunch technocrat, a rare combination within the Socialist Party elite. Also in the high echelons of government at the time was Michel Camdessus, later to become deputy governor and governor of the Bank of France, and most famously Managing Director of the IMF between 1987 and 2000. He helped spread globally the gospel of the virtues of free cross-border capital flows, and became the target of many criticisms of the IMF's heavy-handed approach to the Latin American and East Asian crises during the 1990s (Abdelal 2007; Guillén 2001:197–8; Bhagwati 1999; Feldstein 1998; Krugman 1998; Sachs 1998; Stiglitz 2002; Wade 1998). Both Delors and Camdessus were the longest-serving officials at the helm of the European Commission and the IMF, respectively, the two supranational institutions that played the most important roles in accelerating the rate of increase in global tight coupling during the 1990s. Both of them were elite French civil servants, educated in Paris, and with experience at the country's central bank. Their belief in the benefits of unfettered capital flows became extremely influential in European policy circles and around the world. Their proposals succeeded when European countries agreed to the formation of a single market for goods, services, labor, and capital, which became a reality at the beginning of 1993 with the coming into effect of the Maastricht Treaty (Abdelal 2007:65–71). They also believed in a long-standing idea among French technocrats that "Europe will be made of money, or it will not be made," as Jacques Rueff, a central banker and advisor to President Charles de Gaulle, once put it (quoted in Eichengreen 2015a:90).

Free capital flows were one side of the issue, with monetary affairs being the other. Back in 1969, the six original European Economic Community (EEC) members had agreed to formulate a plan about monetary union, for which the Werner Report of 1970 created a template (CSEMU 1989). Western European countries had been afflicted by a string of monetary crises since the early 1970s. In August 1971 President Nixon suspended the dollar's convertibility into gold, effectively putting an end to the Bretton Woods system. Also in 1971 the German mark came under speculative attack, and nearly 20 other currencies in Europe were affected as well. When the value of the dollar started to hemorrhage after being floated in 1973, it was Germany which received most of the outflows from the U.S., causing its export competitiveness to decline (Eichengreen 2011:70). Thus, Germany also shared the desire for monetary coordination, although not as urgently as other European countries.

The six members of the EEC agreed in 1972 to maintain somewhat stable exchange rates within a band of 2.25%, a scheme that came to be known as the "European snake." In 1973 they created a European Monetary Cooperation Fund. A second round of monetary instability affecting a similar number of countries took place in 1973. In 1979 the then nine members of the EEC—Denmark, Ireland and the UK joined in 1973—agreed to create a European Monetary System (EMS), including an Exchange Rate Mechanism whereby central banks committed to maintaining the value of their currency within a narrow band of plus or minus 2.25% and a wide band of 6%, depending on the country. The EMS also entailed the creation of the European currency unit (ecu) made of a basket of currencies, an extension of credit facilities, and an enhanced European Monetary Cooperation Fund. Although no currency was designated as the official anchor of the system, the German mark came to effectively play that role. This development generated much anxiety and resentment throughout Europe as governments felt they had lost sovereignty not only to the markets but also to the Deutsche Bundesbank.

Delors saw the creation of a single currency within the scheme of a true Economic and Monetary Union as the solution to these increasing tensions and as a revulsive for the European economy and the entire process of European building. In June 1988 Mitterrand met with

Chancellor Helmut Kohl to discuss the prospects for monetary union. The outcome of that meeting was France's commitment to capital flow liberalization and Germany's acquiescence to form a high-level committee to study a *future* monetary union. Most importantly, however, the Germans did not agree to any specific timetable for currency unification. Still, Mitterrand and Delors pressed on, and the committee—composed of the 12 central bank presidents or governors of the member countries plus three other experts—produced the so-called Delors Report, published in April 1989, establishing a relatively long calendar consisting of the abolition of capital controls by 1990, convergence of macroeconomic policies beginning in 1994, and the definition of the criteria for membership in the eventual monetary union by 1999 (Abdelal 2007:74–7; CSEMU 1989). "Economic and monetary union," the report stated, "would represent the final result of the process of progressive economic integration in Europe" (CSEMU 1989:13). As Abdelal (2007:77) has aptly observed:

> The choice for monetary union appeared to be perfectly logical. Within an asymmetric EMS, France had only limited monetary autonomy. Monetary policy for all of Europe was essentially made by the Bundesbank in Frankfurt. With monetary union, however, a French central banker would at least have a seat at the table with his or her German and other European colleagues to make monetary policy for all of Europe. [...] As [Jacques] de Larosière, then governor of the Banque de France, put in in 1990, "Today I am governor of a central bank who has decided, along with his nation, to follow fully the German monetary policy without voting on it. At least, as part of a European central bank, I'll have a vote."

The Report was a personal triumph for the "animateur, ingénieur, and entrepreneur" that Delors was (Dyson and Featherstone 1999:691–745). However, there would have been no agreement without the support of Karl Otto Pöhl, the powerful President of the Bundesbank, who pressed for budgetary convergence criteria, an independent European Central Bank obligated to maintain price stability, and no transfer of sovereignty at the start. In agreeing to plans for monetary union, Pöhl went against the hardliners within his own central bank (Moravcsik 1998:435).

Then, on November 9, 1989, the Berlin Wall fell. In December Kohl asked Germany's European partners to support his plan for German unification at a meeting in Strasbourg. For his part, Mitterrand asked the German Chancellor to agree to an intergovernmental conference on monetary union to be held the following December, thus accelerating the calendar for the adoption of the common currency by at least two years. French pressure on the Germans resulted in the signing of the Treaty on European Union in December 1991 at Maastricht. Essentially, France wanted a quick transition to monetary union in parallel with German unification while Germany preferred a much longer process prioritizing political union and pursuing monetary union only later (Abdelal 2007:79; Baun 1996; Dyson and Featherstone 1999:195–99, 363–4; Moravcsik 1998:437–40; Temin and Vines 2013:165–9). Mitterrand's goal was to ensure that a united Germany would be "embedded in an integrating Europe" (Katzenstein 1997; see also: Baun 1996; Garrett 2001), a solution that also pleased Margaret Thatcher, George Bush, and Mikhail Gorbachev. As Timothy Garton Ash famously put it, quoting "a wit," the outcome was "the whole of Deutschland for Kohl, half the deutsche Mark for Mitterrand" (Ash 2012). Throughout this process, the key was to reassure the Germans that monetary union would deliver price stability. "Not all Germans believe in God," Delors wryly observed in 1992, "but they all believe in the Bundesbank" (quoted in the *Financial Times* June 8, 2012).

In spite of these efforts at European cooperation and integration, the worst episode of monetary instability occurred in 1992, when the Exchange Rate Mechanism was effectively overrun by market forces, with the British pound and the Italian lira exiting the system (Glick and Rose 1999). Speculators like George Soros had taken positions worth billions of dollars, mostly borrowing the funds. The background context was one of high interest rates in Germany, set by the Bundesbank to prevent inflation in the wake of German unification (Eichengreen 2011:90–3). With pressure on the French franc tightening, governments then agreed to a much wider fluctuation band of 15%. By that time, the number of EU member countries had grown to 12 with the addition of Greece, Portugal, and Spain. By 1995 membership reached 15 after the accession of Austria, Finland, and Sweden.

The impetus for monetary union continued unabated, with 11 of the 15 EU members agreeing to surrender their currencies and to launch the euro on January 1, 1999, namely, France, Germany, Italy, Finland, Austria, Belgium, Holland, Luxembourg, Ireland, Portugal, and Spain, i.e. excluding Greece, Denmark, Sweden, and the UK. Greece joined the EZ in 2001, Slovenia in 2007, Cyprus and Malta in 2008, Slovakia in 2009, Estonia in 2011, Latvia in 2014, and Lithuania in 2015 to complete the list of the present 19 EZ countries (see Figure 6.1). It is important to note that little or no progress was made on the adoption of common policies regarding fiscal affairs or banking supervision, two policy areas discussed in the Delors Report as essential to a successful monetary union (CSEMU 1989). Simply put, there was no time for such niceties. Rushing to monetary union in order to anchor a united Germany came at the cost of not putting in place all of the institutions needed for it to succeed in the long run. More importantly, little was done to effectively create a truly common labor market, as we shall see below. To this day, scholars continue to wonder why Germany was willing to give up some of its power, especially to the smaller EU states (Eichengreen 1996:170–1; Garrett 1994; Katzenstein 1997). Monetary union, from the very moment an agreement was reached in the early 1990s, split the EU into two camps: Germany, the Benelux, and Denmark on one side, and France and the southern periphery on the other, with Britain mostly agreeing with the former (Ash 2012; Lane 2012; Spolaore 2013).

The Mother of all Sovereign Debt Crises

The first nine years of the euro were relatively smooth. Beginning in February 2002, the currency actually appreciated relative to the dollar. At its peak before the sovereign debt crisis, the euro was worth nearly 70% more in dollar terms than when it was introduced in 1999. In further evidence of the euro's gathering strength, the common currency grabbed a larger share of allocated reserves in the world than the currencies it replaced in 1999. At the end of 1998, the German mark, French franc, and Dutch guilder jointly accounted for 17.0% of all allocated reserves in the world, compared to 69.3% for the dollar. The euro's share grew quite rapidly until 2009 to reach 27.7%, while the dollar's share dropped to 62.0%. That was the first year of the sovereign debt crisis. By the end of 2013, the euro's share had slid to 24.4% and the dollar's share to 61.2%, with the Japanese yen, pound sterling, and the Swiss franc edging up.

Convergence in inflation and unemployment rates followed suit after the introduction of the euro, although higher inflation in the European periphery relative to Germany meant that the evolution of the real exchange rate kept on undermining the competitiveness of the EZ's periphery. The Stability and Growth Pact of 1997—which mandated budget deficits of no more than 3% of GDP and a total debt burden not exceeding 60% of GDP—seemed to keep governments in line. Countries continued to formulate their own fiscal and banking policies without much interference from Brussels or Frankfurt as long as they met the criteria (Heipertz and Verdun 2010; Beetsma and Giuliodori 2010; Spolaore 2013), which had to be relaxed after both France and Germany exceeded them in the mid-2000s, the former because of its bad fiscal habits and the latter because of the costs of unification. Economic and Monetary Union, however, ultimately placed the weaker economies between a rock and a hard place, and ended up increasing both network and node coupling.

The sovereign debt crisis of 2009 and the near-demise of the common currency exposed all the good desires and flawed assumptions underpinning the project. The liquidity injections, financial bailouts, and economic stimulus efforts implemented by governments around the world succeeded at containing the crisis. Several economies declared by early 2010 the end of the recession. Brazil, Russia, India, and, especially China, continued to report robust GDP growth figures until 2013, and the United States emerged out of the recession by the second quarter of 2010. Smaller economies like Turkey, Malaysia, South Korea, Taiwan, Thailand, Egypt, and Peru, among others, also grew vigorously since the final months of 2009. The measures adopted to confront the crisis, however, resulted in a rapid deterioration of public finances. By 2010, the sovereign debt burden of the G-7 countries as a percentage of GDP grew to 115%, up from 70% just before the crisis, thus reaching a level not seen since 1950 (IMF 2010b:4).

While unemployment continued to lag, the macroeconomic land-scape had improved considerably by mid-2010 in the world's major economies, with the notable exception of Western Europe in general and the EZ in particular. After 10 years of a seemingly successful implementation of Economic and Monetary Union (EMU), the then 17-country single currency area came under speculative attack begin-ning in December 2009. At the time, the euro was trading slightly above 1.5 U.S. dollars, with the record having been set at nearly 1.6 in July of 2008. By May 2010, the euro plunged to 1.27, though still well above the historical minimum of 0.84 in October 2000. Although the euro had sustained even sharper declines earlier during the crisis, especially in the second half of 2008, the situation in early 2010 was different because speculation was focused on the so-called "peripheral" member countries, also referred to as the PIIGS, namely, Portugal, Ireland, Italy, Greece, and Spain. In fact, the IMF had already called the attention to this group of countries, dryly noting that "financial market participants are increasingly focusing on fiscal stability issues among advanced economies" (IMF 2010a:4; see also Armingeon and Baccaro 2012). Confidence in the euro was undermined by speculation in the markets that these countries would eventually default on their large government debt burden. The recession reduced tax revenue at the same time that it boosted expenditures on unemployment benefits, bringing budget def-icits to levels as high as 12% of GDP. Most importantly, adopting the common currency meant that these countries could no longer resort to two weapons they had used assiduously in the past: printing money to inflate their debt away, and devaluing the currency to restore their export competitiveness.

The risk premiums for sovereign debt skyrocketed along the western and southern periphery. Figure 6.2 shows the effects of monetary union and of the sovereign debt crisis in terms of 10-year government bond spreads over the German Bund. During the early 1990s bond yields within the EZ converged very quickly, giving the impression that lending one euro to the Greek or Spanish governments carried a level of risk largely similar to lending one euro to the German government. Starting in mid-2009, yields for the PIIGS started to rise steeply, first with Greece, which had to request an EU/IMF bailout before the end of the year, and then Ireland, which defaulted in mid-2010, and Portugal,

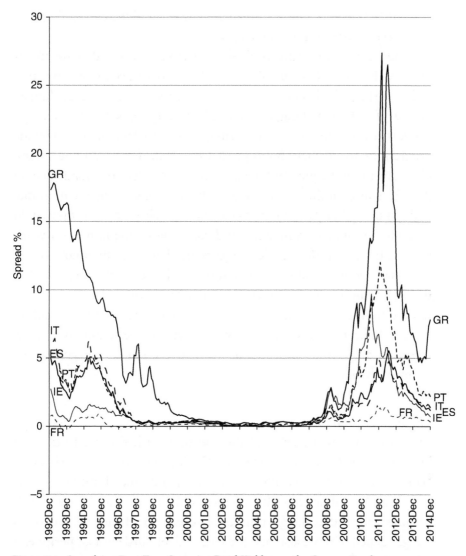

Figure 6.2. Spreads on Euro Zone Sovereign Bond Yields over the German Bund, 1992–2014

Note: 10-year maturity, monthly data.

Key: ES is Spain, FR France, GR Greece, IE Ireland, IT Italy, and PT Portugal.

Source of the data: European Central Bank.

which sought aid a few months later. Yields on Italian and Spanish bonds rose during 2011 to levels that were unsustainable, until European Central Bank (ECB) President Mario Draghi made his famous remarks in the summer of 2012: "Within our mandate, the ECB is ready to do whatever it takes to preserve the euro. And believe me, it will be enough."[2] Tensions almost immediately eased, and the euro was apparently saved from imminent collapse.

Other, more mundane problems, however, persisted. Unemployment remained stubbornly high, and the European economy appeared in late 2014 to be headed towards a third recession and a prolonged period of deflation. Draghi managed in early 2015 to rally enough support within the ECB's governing body to launch a systematic program of government bond purchases worth more than one trillion euros, an amount equivalent to about 10% of outstanding public debt in the EZ. This quantitative easing was aimed at raising the inflation rate and removing bonds from the banks' balance sheets so that they could lend more money to companies and consumers. One important wrinkle was the concession made to Germany that more than 90% of the purchased bonds would stay on national balance sheets as opposed to the ECB's, meaning that no centralized risk pool would be created, thus undermining the credibility of the effort. A few days later, the Coalition of the Radical Left, known as Syriza, won the election in Greece, throwing all Europe into turmoil with its request to renegotiate the terms of the bailout.

The Politics of the Euro Crisis

The euro crisis that started at the end of 2009 had more to do with politics than with economic realities. Greece was certainly in bad shape economically and financially. The markets and other European countries lost all confidence in the country's ability to clean house after it became known that the government had lied about the true size of its budget deficit. Greece also had the largest debt burden of all peripheral EZ countries, at over 120% of GDP, followed by Italy's 110%. The Greek economy had seen its competitiveness eroded due to high taxes, wages, and other types of costs, which had risen well in excess of productivity gains during the subsidy-fueled economic boom of the late 1990s and early 2000s. Greek political institutions—parties, unions, government agencies, and the like—failed miserably to galvanize

---

[2] Speech by Mario Draghi, President of the European Central Bank, at the Global Investment Conference in London, 26 July 2012. http://www.ecb.europa.eu/press/key/date/2012/html/sp120726.en.html, accessed June 21, 2014.

support for a shift in economic policymaking so as to help the country pursue a more sustainable path to economic growth, one not dependent on foreign capital and subsidy inflows, and on the creation of new government jobs.

The major EZ economies—especially Germany and France—and the European Union itself hesitated for weeks as to how to cope with the rapidly unfolding Greek sovereign debt crisis, in part because of domestic political considerations, namely, the reluctance of taxpayers to bail out a country they perceived as a free-rider. This feeling was particularly acute in Germany, where sitting conservative Chancellor Angela Merkel waited until a key regional election in early May 2010 to push hard for the creation of a massive $1 trillion fund to assist EZ countries with sovereign debt problems, of which about 12% to 16% was expected to be allocated to Greece over the following three years. At Germany's insistence, both the EU countries and the IMF contributed to the fund. Markets calmed down in the wake of the more unified and decisive approach to the sovereign debt crisis signaled by the establishment of the fund. In November of 2010 the EU agreed to a €85 billion bailout program for Ireland, and in May of 2011 to a €78 billion rescue package for Portugal. During August 2011, after months of speculative attacks on peripheral European government bonds, the ECB took the unprecedented step of buying Italian and Spanish bonds in order to calm the markets, a measure that the Federal Reserve had adopted earlier during the crisis with respect to U.S. treasuries. There was also a question mark about whether budget imbalances would become a major problem in the other two heavily indebted economies, the United Kingdom and the United States, which were running budget deficits of 13% and 11% of GDP, respectively, had accumulated debts in excess of 60% of GDP, and faced large trade deficits as well (Bergstren 2009).

The European sovereign debt crisis was hard to deal with primarily because European banks own much of the bad debt of peripheral countries, in a clear manifestation of tight coupling. For instance, as of the summer of 2010 German banks carried on their balance sheets €74.3 billion worth of Greek, Spanish, Portuguese, and Irish government bonds, equivalent to 48% of their highest-quality capital, the so-called tier 1. For their part, French banks owned debt worth €25.5 billion or 14% of their tier 1 capital (Blundell-Wignall and Slovik 2010).

This situation essentially presented policymakers and politicians with two options. The first would be to bail out peripheral countries if they became unable to refinance their debts. The second would be to restructure peripheral debt in such a way that bondholders would take a hit, thus making it necessary to bail out some of the banks with the highest exposure, especially the German banks, the Greek banks (whose holdings of Greek debt equaled 226% of their tier 1 capital), and the Portuguese banks (69%). If Spanish government debt were to be restructured, Spanish banks would also be pushed over the precipice because of their huge exposure, equivalent to 113% of their tier 1 capital. In the event that Italian government bonds lost value, the exposure of German banks would double and that of French banks nearly treble, and the capital of Italian banks would be virtually wiped out (Blundell-Wignall and Slovik 2010). Thus, the debate in Europe during the fall of 2011 was about whether to use taxpayer funds to rescue governments or to bail out the banks, i.e. to reduce coupling between the two. One analysis projected that the banks in a most precarious situation were the Royal Bank of Scotland, Deutsche Bank, Société Générale, UniCredit, Groupe BPCE, Commerzbank, and Bankia (*The Economist*, October 15, 2011).

Fiscal Austerity and Economic Growth

Another important aspect of the crisis was the interplay between fiscal austerity and economic reform (Blyth 2013; Gorton 2012). Unfortunately, since the end of 2010 governments in Europe and North America sought to reduce their deficits by cutting spending simultaneously. In a situation in which beggar-thy-neighbor, export-oriented growth was difficult if not impossible and domestic consumer demand remained anemic, government austerity reduced GDP growth in most Western economies (Cameron 2012). The IMF's *Global Financial Stability Report* published in April of 2010 emphasized the need for fiscal adjustment, but in ways that would be politically sustainable:

> To address sovereign risks, credible medium-term fiscal consolidation plans that command public support are needed. This is the most daunting challenge facing governments in the near term. Consolidation plans should be made transparent, and contingency measures

should be in place if the degradation of public finances is greater than expected. Better fiscal frameworks and growth enhancing structural reforms will help ground public confidence that the fiscal consolidation process is consistent with long-term growth. (IMF 2010b:xii)

By October of 2011, many economists predicted that a double-dip recession was in the making and would soon be corroborated by GDP statistics. In August 2011, the newly-installed IMF Managing Director, Christine Lagarde, put it delicately:

Shaping a Goldilocks fiscal consolidation is all about timing. What is needed is a dual focus on medium-term consolidation and short-term support for growth and jobs. That may sound contradictory, but the two are mutually reinforcing. Decisions on future consolidation, tackling the issues that will bring sustained fiscal improvement, create space in the near term for policies that support growth and jobs. (Lagarde 2011)

The IMF correctly diagnosed the problem as one of excessive debt on the balance sheets of households, non-financial corporations, financial institutions, and governments. Until deleveraging took place, it would be hard for banks to resume lending, for investors to feel at ease, for consumers to spend, and for governments not to feel under the gun of the bond vigilantes. Each of these factors contributed to slower growth, persistently high unemployment, and social unrest. At a time of high leverage, however, austerity measures by themselves aggravated the problem, as a growing chorus of economists pointed out (Armingeon and Baccaro 2012; Krugman 2012), especially if all countries in Europe pursued them simultaneously. The IMF has warned about the unwanted effects of one-size-fits-all austerity, although it oftentimes has contradicted itself in actual policy:

This suggests that for many countries, deficit reduction would ideally be deferred to the future, when its output costs would likely be lower. [...] Monetary policy should remain accommodative for the foreseeable future, and structural policies to promote growth should also be pursued. The composition of fiscal adjustment could also be tilted to mitigate its adverse impact on the most vulnerable. (IMF 2013a:37)

In early 2013, the EZ officially went into the feared double-dip recession, from which it only started to emerge later that year. While economic growth in the northern surplus economies was nothing to rave about, unemployment was relatively low. By comparison, the southern economies were deeply into recession and joblessness surpassed 20% in several countries. Austerity measures failed miserably at reining in budget deficits and spurring economic growth.

Spontaneous Protest Movements

In early 2011 the world witnessed the Arab Spring, a series of spontaneous protest movements across the Arab-speaking world that started in Tunisia and Egypt, where long-standing authoritarian regimes were toppled. The Libyan government proved more difficult to dislodge, and fighting between protesters and the security forces continued in Yemen and Syria. Lack of economic opportunity among the young in a part of the world in which over 40% of the population is under the age of 25 was a major background factor. The revolts triumphed when external pressure and the withdrawal of the army's support for the incumbent dictator made regime continuity impossible. It is still unclear, however, whether the Arab Spring will result in a transition to democracy or not.

Spontaneous protests against economic injustice, corporate greed, and runaway financial institutions also took place in developed countries. They started in the United Kingdom in early 2011, and turned violent in August. Peaceful protest movements occurred in Spain starting in May (the so-called "indignados"), Israel in July, and the United States in September ("Occupy Wall Street"). In October a global "Day of Rage" was observed around the world. These protests did not have much impact on policymaking or elections, until Syriza's electoral victory in Greece in January 2015, but they made the problems of unemployment and inequality even more salient and the shortcomings of austerity policies more readily apparent.

Turning Network Coupling into Node Coupling

As mentioned above, one of the initial fears concerning peripheral sovereign risk in Europe had to do with the bond holdings of German and French banks. What happened next was a "nationalization" of the problem, in the sense that domestic banks became even more exposed to their own government's bonds while foreign banks extricated themselves by undoing their positions. This process was primarily driven by the ECB's "free" liquidity window for the banks, which could borrow at often negative interest rates and then buy government bonds with high yields. By the end of 2012, the proportion of government bonds held by domestic banks rose from 10% to 20% in Greece, from 12% to more than 40% in Ireland, from 10% to about 20% in Portugal, from 20% to nearly 40% in Spain, and from 11% to 25% in Italy. Meanwhile, German banks not only unloaded their peripheral bonds but also reduced their share of German public debt from 30% to 23%. The consequence for the peripheral countries was that sovereign risk and bank risk became one and the same (Berges et al. 2014). In other words, tight coupling at the level of the European network was transformed into tight coupling at the node level, i.e. within each country, and with the support of the ECB. Perversely, the banks bought government securities instead of lending to the private sector, thus aggravating the downward spiral in the real economy. This was precisely one of the goals that led ECB President Mario Draghi to announce a massive program to purchase peripheral bonds in January 2015. The other goal was to arrest the dangerous deflationary undercurrents in the European economy. The ECB's decision, however, was not unanimous, further broadening the rift between the surplus and the deficit economies.

Node coupling in Europe has also been characteristic of the labor market. In spite of legal free labor mobility, very few Europeans actually shift their residence or take jobs in other countries. Only 0.2% of the population in the EU-15 changes residence across national borders each year. By contrast, in the United States the proportion is 2.3%, i.e. more than 10 times as high. Labor mobility within individual European countries is also very low, standing at about 1% (EC 2008).

The lack of labor mobility has important implications for the evolution of labor markets. Changes in labor productivity diverged considerably since the introduction of the euro. While in Germany unit labor costs—the labor-related cost of producing one unit of GDP—remained relatively stable between 1995 and 2009, in the peripheral economies and in France they increased by as much as 30% in France, Italy and

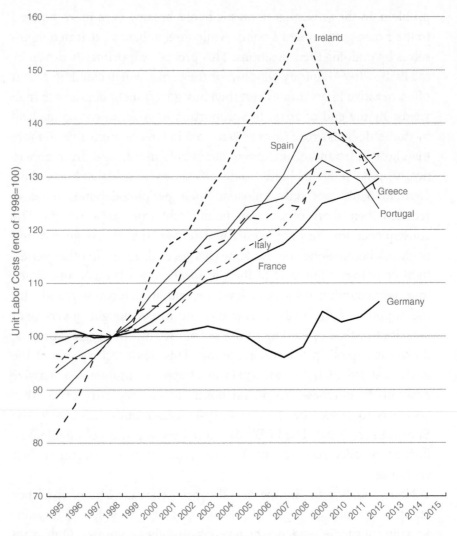

Figure 6.3. Euro Zone Unit Labor Costs, for the Entire Economy, 1995–2012
Source of the data: OECD.

Portugal, 40% in Greece and Spain, and 50% in Ireland (see Figure 6.3; Armingeon and Baccaro 2012; Beetsma and Giuliodori 2010; Dustmann et al. 2014; Wolf 2014:62–4). Before the introduction of the euro, such losses in competitiveness could be easily erased by a devaluation of the national currency. That option, however, was not available after 1999 unless the country decided to leave the EZ altogether. Instead, governments implemented austerity policies in order to appease the bond market and bring about an "internal devaluation" of wages and other prices, which produced a sharp decline in unit labor costs in all countries except for Italy and France (see Figure 6.3). Still, by 2014, no country had closed the gap that had developed with Germany since the adoption of the single currency, although the new German coalition government granted workers wage increases beginning in late 2013.

While unemployment rates throughout the EZ had converged since 1999, the recession, the collapse of domestic demand in the wake of austerity policies (Cameron 2012), and the loss of competitiveness brought about a sharp increase in unemployment rates (Armingeon and Baccaro 2012), especially in Greece and Spain, where it exceeded 25%, while Germany's dropped to about 5% (Figure 6.4). Clearly, at this

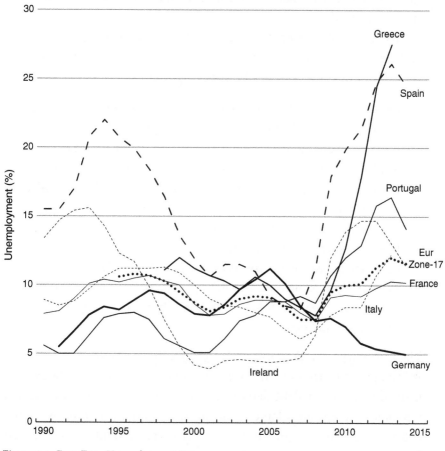

Figure 6.4. Euro Zone Unemployment Rates, 1990–2014

Source: Eurostat.

point a single interest rate set by the ECB for the entire EZ was not optimal. It was too low for the high-unemployment economies, and too high for the low-unemployment economies.

The loss in competitiveness along the European periphery was especially damaging for those economies with a pattern of exports similar to Germany's, that is for countries that are role equivalent with Europe's largest economy. Spain, France, and Italy have an export similarity index in excess of 70% with Germany, meaning that their companies compete head-to-head against German firms for export markets. By contrast, Greece and Ireland have indexes below 45%, and Portugal below 60% (EC 2012). It was this overlap with German exports that was especially worrisome in the cases of Italy and Spain, and not just the fact that they are large economies whose demise could put an end to the euro.

Alison Johnston, Bob Hancké, and Suman Pant (2013:9–10) have captured the essence of how labor market institutions and realities matter to monetary unions when arguing that:

> under a fixed monetary system, where the majority of trade is intra-regional, wage moderation pursued by one group of countries (the North), serves as a "beggar-thy-neighbor" policy vis-à-vis those (the South) that have not pursued such wage moderation. Current account balances, however, are zero-sum games.... [U]nder EMU, savings in the countries with a trade surplus were invested in capital and consumption projects (most notably in real-estate, which further fueled housing bubbles...). The South's failure to adjust its labor costs, and hence is public *and* private borrowing imbalances, vis-à-vis the North preceding the crisis, prompted markets to attach a higher interest rate premium to sovereign bonds in the periphery once the crisis was in full swing.

The Germany/EZ Relationship: A Tightly-Coupled System

Although the German banks were very quick at extricating themselves from the sovereign debt debacle in the periphery of the EZ, the fact remains that Europe's largest and most dynamic economy is tightly coupled with the rest of the EZ, and vice versa. While it is true that Europe has become dependent on Germany for a measure of economic and financial stability, it is no less accurate that Germany has become dependent on Europe for export markets. Generally speaking, the German economy is dependent on exports for growth. In 2013 Germany enjoyed the largest current account surplus in the world, bigger than China's. Most of that surplus, however, was generated with the EZ and the rest of the EU. By contrast, only one-fifth of the trade surplus and one-third of the current account surplus was accounted for by the rest of the world. In fact, Germany runs both a trade and a current account deficit with China (EC 2012; Ash 2012; Spolaore 2013).

It has become commonplace to acknowledge Germany's efforts to help the European periphery. But it is equally important to emphasize that Germany will be a main beneficiary of an eventual economic recovery in Southern Europe. Large German firms and their unionized employees are very dependent on European markets. By contrast, the famous *Mittelstand* of small and medium-sized firms that are major exporters to global markets are less dependent on Europe. German savers are also reluctant to accept the proposition that building a stronger EZ with pooled risks will be to their advantage. In fact, it probably will not. "Germany's reluctance to engage in expansive policies might be informed by a misguided understanding of its own interests...but it is also built on a hard political-economic understanding of monetary policy in Europe that leaves policy-makers and wage setters in the country little choice" (Johnston et al. 2013:40).

In addition to the importance of institutions and institutional prac-tices, I would like to raise an important cultural aspect deeply ingrained in the German psyche that helps explain the divergence in views and perspectives between Europe's largest economy and the Southern Euro-pean countries when it comes to dealing with the crisis. The word in German for debt is *Schuld*, and it just so happens that the same word also means guilt. The linguistic, mental, and cultural association between debt and guilt illustrates the very different values attached to frugality and industriousness in different parts of Europe, thus under-mining the prospects for a truly stable monetary union. When it comes to money, cultural factors matter, as the sociologist Viviana Zelizer

(1994) has demonstrated. From a cultural point of view, it is very hard to see how exactly present-day Europeans can share one single currency. Thus, the core of the European crisis has to do with Germany's insistence on fiscal probity. As Martin Wolf (2014:53–4, 79), the *Financial Times* columnist, has observed,

> inevitably, Germany, like most creditor nations in history, insists that the difficulties of borrowers are entirely their fault. Its own current-account surpluses have nothing to do with the difficulties of deficit countries: the latter are irresponsible, that is all. This is why it has emphasized fiscal deficits as the main problem, not current-account imbalances, and so has also insisted that this is a fiscal crisis rather than a balance-of-payments-cum-financial crisis in which its own financial institutions and regulators were complicit. [...]
>
> Germany's focus on the alleged fiscal crimes of countries now in crisis was an effort at self-exculpation: as the Eurozone's largest supplier of surplus capital, its private sector bore substantial responsibility for the excesses that led to the crisis. As Bagehot indicates, excess borrowing by fools would have been impossible without excess lending by fools: creditors and debtors are joined at the hip.

Barry Eichengreen (2015a:382) throws light into the conundrum facing European countries by putting their almost intractable problems in historical context when arguing that "the single greatest failure to learn appropriate lessons from this earlier history [of the 1920s and the Great Depression] was surely the decision to adopt the euro. The 1920s and 1930s illustrated nothing better than the dangers of tying a diverse set of countries to a single monetary policy." According to him, the core of the problem involves basic economic principles. "Experience under the interwar gold standard highlighted the tendency for large amounts of capital to flow from countries where interest rates were low to where they were high, and the destabilizing consequences that would follow when those flows came to a stop." Most importantly, Eichengreen observes that such a rigid monetary arrangement "highlighted the economic pain and political turmoil that would result when the only available response was austerity. That history should have given European leaders pause before moving ahead with the euro."

How Much Integration is Good for Europe?

Clearly, the EZ was a premature experiment. "From the start, the euro has rested on a gamble," the political scientist Andrew Moravcsik (2012) has argued. "When European leaders opted for monetary union in 1992, they wagered that European economies would converge toward one another: the deficit-prone countries of southern Europe would adopt German economic standards—lower price inflation and wage growth, more saving, and less spending—and Germany would become a little more like them, by accepting more government and private spending and higher wage and price inflation." The arrangement for Economic and Monetary Union created too tightly coupled a system for its own good to begin with. The lack of labor mobility, a fiscal union, and a single banking supervisory and resolution authority further increased tight coupling. In their absence, the system had little margin for deviations, almost no room for error. If the economy slows down in a given country, or if a bubble bursts, there are few, if any, tools available to buffer the effect, to reverse the business cycle, to revive the economy. This is exactly why the EU, however complex, is a much more stable type of system than the EZ. Complexity does not necessarily spell trouble. In fact, it may help nodes and actors within the nodes adjust to unforeseen shocks. Tight coupling, by contrast, can be highly problematic, even fatal.

European integration is a worthy goal to pursue. That part of the world is exceedingly small geographically, though large in terms of population. Each individual country does not have enough scale by itself to be economically efficient on a global scale. The potential benefits to integration are rather obvious. But there are also costs and, most importantly, lost opportunities. The issue is not whether European integration should be pursued, but rather how much of it and involving exactly what aspects.

One of the cornerstones of the post-World War II geopolitical and economic order is that a united Europe is needed to fend off another major conflagration. The horrors visited upon the continent from the 1910s to the 40s are frequently invoked and evoked by political leaders and foreign-policy experts as the main reason for seeking to lock the various European countries—especially France and Germany—into an institutional framework of cooperation and joint decision making. While this integrationist way of thinking about Europe delivered several decades of economic and social progress, it has become someone outdated. The new realities of the twenty-first century require a fundamental reevaluation of the premises underlying the construction of a supranational institutional framework in Europe.

The early architects of European institutions sought to avoid another war, and they saw European integration and unity as the best way to accomplish that goal. In fact, they focused their attention on bringing France and Germany closer together regarding heavy industry, nuclear matters, and trade. Post Bretton Woods European building progressed in the form of a pincer movement, as we analyzed above, simultaneously bringing more countries into the bloc and deepening their commitment across an increasingly ambitious program of integration, including not only trade but also labor and capital markets, government procurement practices, certain aspects of tax policy, product standards, and competition policies, to name but a few areas. The 1990s, as the twentieth century was coming to an end, were the heyday of European integration dreams—and the prelude to the present mayhem.

Central to the debate about the future of Europe is the lack of consensus as to exactly what tighter integration is supposed to accomplish. The original motivations to build a united Europe are no longer as relevant today as they were in the 1950s when Jean Monnet and Robert Schuman were building a united Europe on the ruins of World War II. The Cold War ended more than two decades ago. There is a single German state, one that is resolutely not under Prussia's leadership. Far-right parties have or have had meaningful representation in the national parliaments of Austria, Denmark, France, Holland, Switzerland, and Norway. In the 2014 elections to the European Parliament, far-right and euro-sceptic parties won nearly 21% of the vote and 15% of the seats, a five-fold increase.

No such temptations in Germany, at least thus far. The quality of German democratic life has never been higher. In fact, it is much more vigorous than in France or Spain, let alone Italy. The various German political parties participate in shifting coalitions supporting stable governments focused on social and economic policies with the aim of improving the lot of German citizens as well as helping build a more stable Europe more broadly. Most importantly, the German military is no longer a threat to any other country, whether neighboring or not. In fact, it is fully integrated into NATO, which has now expanded eastwards. Moreover, Germany is not a nuclear power, and it is surrounded by three of them, Russia, France, and Britain, boasting 2,400, 290, and 160 deployed nuclear warheads, respectively. If that were not enough, the U.S. military maintains a strong presence throughout Europe, with some 80,000 deployed troops, 54,000 of them in Germany alone.

When present European leaders mention the avoidance of another European war as a motivation for strengthening European institutions and deepening supranational commitments—especially monetary, financial, and fiscal ones—they are stretching the argument of security based on unity to the point of derision. President Sarkozy certainly did in December 2011 after a meeting with Chancellor Merkel when he referred to the "seventy years of bloody conflict, followed by seventy years of peace," sentencing that Germany and France "had to understand each other." Merkel obliged by adding that "what people should know is that we are working together to find common solutions. . . . We will never confront each other as we did before" (*The Guardian*, December 5, 2011; see also Ash 2012). How exactly these stark statements justify the necessity for Europe to have a common currency is not clear. Beyond the convenience that it offers to businesses, investors, and tourists, the disadvantages and costs of a single currency have become painfully apparent. The response by European leaders has been not to recognize the problems with the concept of the single currency, but rather to deepen the union to include some measure and form of fiscal coordination and co-responsibility—presumably to avoid another war.

European Integration: A Solution Looking for a Problem
Organizations are oftentimes "garbage cans" in which actors, priorities, problems, and solutions interact in unanticipated ways to produce outcomes that do not follow from simple rules of rationality (Cohen, March and Olsen 1973). From this perspective, solutions are looking for problems to address, as opposed to the other way around. States and governments frequently become garbage cans. In particular, state

bureaucrats are trained in certain ways. If homogeneous enough in their training and aspirations, they constitute an "epistemic community, i.e. a network of professionals with recognized expertise and competence in a particular domain and an authoritative claim to policy relevant knowledge within that domain or issue-area" (Haas 1992:3). Epistemic communities prefer certain solutions over others, and they identify, define, and frame problems in ways that make them amenable to the preferred solution.

I argue that the idea of European integration is a solution looking for a problem to solve, crystalized in the standard operating procedures of European institutions such as the Commission and the Council. It comes replete with tools and methodologies for policymaking. It is the kind of philosophy that has become vintage European problem-solving: problems are always constructed as the result of insufficient integration, and therefore solvable with more integration. "La question posée, la solution était indiquée," argued the great French architect Auguste Choisy in the late nineteenth century (Banham 1980:23–4). This classic Cartesian point of view has come to dominate the thinking of policymaking and technocratic elites in Brussels and at the major continental European capitals, especially Paris and Berlin. As I mentioned above, technocrats gained the upper hand during the period Delors headed the European Commission between 1985 and 1994, and the Delors Report was produced by a committee whose members shared a common epistemology. "National governments sought a body of experts who could back up their policy choice, and they could use the experts' collective knowledge and advice to support their decisions. Without the report of the experts, national governments would remain suspicious about the motives and goals of other national governments" (Verdun 1999:323). As Timothy Garton Ash (2012) has noted, "European integration has rightly been described as a project of the elites" (see also Díez Medrano 2003; Fligstein 2001).

The governments of the smaller and poorer member states on Europe's periphery went along with increasing demands for integration, assuming Europe gave them what they really wanted, namely, legitimacy and subsidies. Only London, and to a lesser extent Copenhagen, remained in defiance of the technocratic dogma that any problem can be solved with tighter integration. The dogmatic, almost fanatic, nature of this type of thinking makes it very difficult for European public opinion to even conceive of other types of solutions to the severe economic, financial, and social problems afflicting the continent. The trouble with this "euro-technocratic" view is, of course, that in a bloc of 28 sovereign states, there is a wide spectrum of opinions as to exactly how much integration is necessary for the single market, the continental-wide financial system, and the common currency to work properly.

There is, fortunately, an alternative view to the "fix-it-all-with-integration" approach, one that reduces the degree of tight coupling. It assumes that friendly emulation, competition, and learning among nation-states are inherently good. European countries learned from the United States at the turn of the twentieth century (Guillén 1994). Japan developed by both emulating and learning from other more advanced nations (Westney 1987). Decades later, South Korea followed in its powerful neighbor's steps (Amsden 1989). China is now showing the world that it pays to be open to foreign influences after all—at least as far as the economy and technology are concerned. The three Asian countries, perhaps because of their geopolitical predicament, continue to be fiercely independent in terms of their attitudes towards the rather utopian idea of an East Asian trading bloc.

And Europe? The plan of the elitist euro-technocrats is to intensify and accelerate the process of integration in order to overcome the challenges of the present. They do not seem to grasp that few people in Europe subscribe to a European identity, with national or even subnational identities remaining relevant (Díez Medrano 2003). They have little to say about Europe's relationships with other parts of the world, as if those could interfere with their grand designs. While unity may bring benefits, the way in which the construction of a united Europe is taking place strikes many observers as counterproductive. Sociologist Neil Fligstein (2001) has cogently argued that European governments have sought to create a single market by approving an enormous amount of rules and standards covering every conceivable product, service, market, and government policy. Typically, it has taken European negotiators years to agree on harmonized standards, which are supposed to help create a seamless market. Consider the example of prophylactics. The frequently comical arguments over their optimal length, width, durability, and reliability went on for years before member countries agreed on common standards, which became mandatory in the late 1990s (*The Independent*, February 29, 1996). While harmonization may make sense for certain gadgets, systems or policy arenas—especially technology platforms subject to tipping-point dynamics such as video or telecommunications standards or those at risk of provoking catastrophic failure—it tends to stifle technological innovation, reduce product differentiation, and ultimately hurt the consumer.

Technocracy and Obscurantism
The heart of the problem is that rule-making is what euro-technocrats like to do. It also is what they know how to do, and thereby lies the problem. The European project has long become decoupled from its original motivation of eluding conflict and war, and delivering higher standards of living. European integration has acquired a momentum of its own, driven by the preferences and ways of doing of the bureaucracy. It has effectively become the project of the technocratic elites at both the European and national levels, oftentimes against the desires of the population, and frequently at the expense of the decision-making capacity of member states (Heipertz and Verdun 2010:85–109). As the political scientist and former Labour Member of Parliament David Marquand has accurately observed in his book, *The End of the West: The Once and Future Europe* (2011), back in the 1950s the founding fathers of the European integration did not wish to suppress the sovereignty of the member states. Rather, they wanted to complement it by creating new institutions.

This original idea of a Europe of united nation-states has mutated, especially in the midst of the present debt and monetary crisis, into an all-out attempt to remake Europe as one entity, doing away with whatever little sovereignty and autonomy for policymaking remains at the national and local levels. The euro-technocrats' favorite strategy for having their way is to blame national governments for all present ills because of their fiscal profligacy, and to deprive them of resources by demanding harsh austerity measures. In so doing, they seek to thwart national opposition to their designs and to suppress public debate, effectively rendering any other alternative course of action unviable. They are behaving according to the worst European tradition of obscurantism.

This issue was first pointed out quite a long time ago. In his famous essay, "Obsolete or Obstinate?," political scientist Stanley Hoffman (1966) astutely observed that "the logic of integration deems the uncertainties of the supranational function process creative; the logic of diversity sees them as destructive past a certain threshold." And he continued his brilliant and prescient analysis with a warning against the perils of technocracy:

> As for methods, there was a gamble on the irresistible rise of supranational functionalism. [...] It assumed [...] that the dilemma of governments having to choose between pursuing an integration that ties their hands and stopping a movement that benefits their people could be exploited in favor of integration by men representing the common good, endowed with the advantages of superior expertise, initiating proposals, propped against a set of deadlines, and using for their cause the technique of package deals.

These words are as valid today as they were during the initial stages of European institution-building.

The misguided technocratic attempt to build a united Europe through comprehensive rule-making is suffocating the continent's chances of remaining competitive in the twenty-first century against the backdrop of the rise of the emerging economies as major economic, financial and technological powerhouses. Competition under an increasingly liberalized international trading regime, economists and sociologists remind us, is all about comparative advantage and differentiation, not about harmonization and convergence. After more than half a century of soaring European integration, German firms compete in the global economy in ways that are very different from those that enable French companies to succeed, for instance. Research by Nicholas Ziegler (1995, 1997), Wolfgang Streeck (1991), David Soskice (1999), and Michael Storper and Robert Salais (1997), among others, has documented this important fact (see also Dustman et al. 2014). Even within Germany or France one finds a bewildering array of business models. The tiny exporter of machine tools based in Baden-Württemberg is figuratively worlds away from globe-trotting Daimler, one the of world's largest industrial corporations, which is headquartered in the same German *Land*. And yet, both companies are essential to the roaring performance of the German economy. What's wrong with England being "a nation of shopkeepers," as Adam Smith once put it and Napoleon echoed, while France is driven by Cartesian rationalism? Many aspects of European-level policymaking have the perverse effect of reducing that diversity of approaches to competition. Countries compete successfully when they develop unique institutions that award them some form of societal comparative advantage (Biggart and Orrù 1997; Biggart and Guillén 1999; Guillén 2001).

Consider another example. The infamous Bologna process of standardizing higher education across Europe promises to stymy innovation. According to *Top University Rankings*, a Chinese publication, the EU is home to 29 of the world's top 100 universities, compared to 52 for the United States. Instead of celebrating the diversity of European institutions of higher learning and research, the European Union is intent on standardizing them, as if educational and scholarly excellence could be achieved by decree. Dan Breznitz and Michael Murphree have argued in their recent book, *Run of the Red Queen* (2011) that China has learned the hard way that a national policy of innovation is not the best instrument to promote science and technology. Innovation is increasingly a regional and local phenomenon, as AnnaLee Saxenian (1994) famously demonstrated with her illuminating comparison of Route 128 around Boston and the Silicon Valley. Europe is attempting to foster research and tertiary education at the supranational level, trying to outdo the Chinese—and the Soviets before them—at the game of central planning. European unity understood as harmonization and convergence will most likely undermine Europe's corrosive strength: its resilient diversity. As the sociologist Jack Goldstone argues in his book, *Why Europe?* (2009), European economies rose historically thanks to "close social relations among entrepreneurs, scientists, engineers, and craftspeople," something that occurred at the local not the national, let alone the continental, level.

Perhaps the best illustration of the foolishness of unmitigated European integration has to do with the joint attempt by France and Germany to impose very strict—the more so the better, they argue— fiscal guidelines for countries to follow if they wish to remain part of the single currency, opening themselves to the criticism that they are attempting to create a French–German condominium. Moreover, Berlin and Paris would like technocrats in Brussels to pre-approve and monitor national budgets. Not only is this pretension utterly undemocratic, but it is potentially dangerous. As Paul Krugman (2009, 2012) has repeatedly warned, any rule that deprives governments of the ability to manage the business cycle is a recipe for disaster. Given that European countries mainly trade with each other—both the reason for, and the effect of, the existence of some kind of a European Union—it goes without saying that a coordinated European attempt to bring all national budgets in line simultaneously following a pro-cyclical pattern could seriously backfire by aggravating the recession and raising unemployment across the bloc. The cliffhanger, or "avalanche of thrills," that the struggle to keep the euro alive has become since 2009 is perhaps the best monument one could ever imagine to the failure of the euro-technocrats to deal with the problems generated by their own designs.

Reversing Europe's Tight Coupling and Relative Decline
Contrary to the dogmatic wisdom prevailing in Brussels, historians and social scientists offer evidence that Europe has over the centuries benefited from its political fragmentation, and from the healthy emulation and learning encouraged by it. Jared Diamond argued in his landmark book, *Guns, Germs, and Steel* (1997) that geography and disease, coupled with Europe's fragmentation, led to the "advance of technology, science, and capitalism by fostering competition among states and providing innovators with alternative sources of support and havens from persecution." In *Why the West Rules—For Now*, Stanford University's Ian Morris (2010) pointed out that Europe's rise to global prominence was not accidental, or a historical aberration, because it has lasted for a very long time. It was driven by biology, sociology, and geography, with emulation and competition at all levels playing a pivotal role.

Europe is rapidly becoming irrelevant in global economic, financial, and strategic affairs. While in 1950 Europe, excluding Russia, was home to nearly 18% of the world's population and 30% of global GDP, nowadays the figures are just 9% and 19%, respectively. According to the United Nations Population Division, the medium projection to the year 2100 is for Europe, again without Russia, to hold less than 6% of the world's population. The European economy will be at that time probably less than 10% of the world's total. Europe has the world's most rapidly aging population. In the year 2000 Germany and Italy had, for the first time, more people of age 60 and above than people below age 20. By 2010 Greece, Portugal, Spain, Austria, Bulgaria, Slovenia, Croatia, Finland, Switzerland, Sweden, and Japan had joined the no longer exclusive club of the countries with inverted age pyramids. Projections indicate that France will by 2015 and the UK by 2020. China and Russia are not expected to become members of the graying club until 2030, the United States until 2035, and Brazil until 2040. Unfortunately, the dogmatic emphasis on European unity in the form of tighter integration is accelerating this process of relative demographic and economic decline, not reversing it as the euro-fanatics claim. Europe's global stature continues to dwindle. Both the European network and the country nodes in it are becoming more tightly coupled.

The technocrats' obsession with suppressing diversity and increasing coupling is already having devastating consequences. European institution-building has always been more effective when based on the national interests of the member states, as the political scientist Andrew Moravcsik demonstrated in his landmark book, *The Choice for Europe* (1998). The continent has gone from being an "embattled, mutually antagonistic circle of suspicious and introverted nations," as Tony Judt put it in his controversial 1996 essay, *A Grand Illusion?*, to becoming an uneasy bloc of nations resisting additional transfers of sovereignty to a Brussels-based bureaucracy that has yet to articulate why such a change is necessary. The technocratic dream of a tightly integrated Europe threatens to further diminish its stature in global affairs by reducing the ingenuity and vibrancy of the various European countries to the least common denominator of European-level mediocrity.

The blind push towards more integration also poses a major risk because of its consequences for tight coupling. What Europe desperately needs is economic growth. Whether more integration is the way to achieve growth is unclear, given that innovation and competitiveness tend to stem from other sources, namely, the forces of "creative destruction," as the Austrian economist Joseph Schumpeter famously put it. The technocrats are not interested in debating their ideas, however, only in implementing them. Europe is thus starting to suffer from a yawning democratic deficit which threatens to match its budgetary imbalances. The integration strategy fueled by forced convergence, harmonization, and standardization of everything from markets to elections, and from social policies to monetary affairs, is simply failing to address Europe's short-term unemployment and fiscal imbalances, and at the same time it is weakening its long-term competitiveness. European citizens and the entire world deserve better. Europe has become overregulated and overprotective, and increasingly irrelevant on the global stage (Alesina and Giavazzi 2006).

Much of the European future depends on Germany, which continues to hesitate when it comes to becoming a true leader, and using its economic and financial might to cement a solid relationship with its neighbors, privileging domestic consumption over export growth, and accepting a slightly higher level of inflation. These policies would increase the demand for goods and services produced in the periphery, and help those deeply indebted countries partially inflate their way out of the dire situation in which they find themselves. I personally agree with Tony Judt when he wrote back in 1996:

> I am enthusiastically European; no informed person could seriously wish to return to the embattled, mutually antagonistic circle of suspicious and introverted nations that was the European continent in the quite recent past. But it is one thing to think an outcome desirable, quite another to suppose it is possible. It is my contention that a truly united Europe is sufficiently unlikely for it to be unwise and self-defeating to insist upon it. I am thus, I suppose, a Europessimist.

The blind pursuit of European integration has actually exacerbated the divisions in Europe. The North–South and West–East divides have become wider and deeper over the last few years. It has also increased the degree of tight coupling to dangerous levels, especially within the EZ. There is time to change course, before the far right becomes uncomfortably influential or the global economy makes Europe irrelevant. As Timothy Garton Ash (2012) has put it, without some new driving forces, without a positive mobilization among its elites and peoples, the EU, while probably surviving as an origami palace of treaties and institutions, will gradually decline in efficacy and real significance, like the Holy Roman Empire of yore. Future historians may then identify some time around 2005 as the apogee of the most far-reaching, constructive, and peaceful attempt to unite the continent that history has ever seen.

It is intriguing to note that the sharpest analyses of the long trend of European integration have been made by the likes of Ash and Judt, both British historians. The UK has managed in many ways to take advantage of the benefits of economic and trade liberalization without falling victim to the shortcomings of more ambitious designs like monetary union.

Scholars who are more enthusiastic about the prospects for European integration, like Moravcsik (2012), also sound a cautionary note:

> Whatever the outcome of the crisis, the EU will remain without rival the most ambitious and successful example of voluntary international cooperation in world history. Still, the crisis does signal that the process of European integration is reaching a natural plateau, at least for the foreseeable future, based on a pragmatic division between national policy and supranational policy. The movement toward the "ever-closer union" of which the EU's founding fathers dreamed when they signed the Treaty of Rome in 1957 will have to stop at some point; there will never be an all-encompassing European federal state. But within the increasingly clear mandate of a stable constitutional settlement, Europe will continue to respond to the challenges of an increasingly interdependent world.

His words should be taken literally. The EU will almost certainly survive and play an important role in the world, even if some countries leave the monetary union.

As for the EZ, the future is far less certain. As economists Kevin O'Rourke and Alan Taylor (2013:186–7) have observed, "Europe's current depression drags on. The jury is still out on whether the Eurozone can achieve the minimal collective institutions needed to sustain deep integration and macro-financial stability of the kind that the U.S. economy can take for granted." That institutional deepening requires a banking union, an EZ-wide bond guarantee to decouple sovereign risk from bank risk, and a fiscal union. "But the short-run problems facing countries in the periphery of Europe are now so great that politicians may never get a chance to solve these long-run problems because the eurozone may well have collapsed in the meantime."

The problem is, of course, that a breakup of the EZ would be immensely painful for Europe and for the rest of the world. Trillions of euros of assets and liabilities would need to be redenominated, Argentine-style "corralitos" would be required to avoid a run on the banks, sovereign defaults along the European periphery might be inevitable, and millions of private contracts would require extensive reworking, with the possibility of pervasive and long-lasting litigation and gridlock at the courts. Trade and investment patterns would be hugely affected in the wake of the re-introduction of national currencies. The potential for chaos on a global scale would be enormous.

The exit of a single country would also be painful not just for the affected economy but for the EZ as a whole. The trials and tribulations of the Greek crisis, which seemed to lead to a third rescue package in the summer of 2015, demonstrated the eagerness of many European leaders to keep the EZ intact. This episode makes it readily apparent that the EZ is too tightly coupled to function properly.

7

The Future of the Global System

Economic analysis and advice are not enough. Policies still have to be implemented.

—Barry Eichengreen, *Hall of Mirrors: The Great Depression,*
The Great Recession, and the Uses-and-Misuses of
History by Eichengreen (2015) 13w from pp. 380–81.
By permission of Oxford University Press, USA.

The world as a whole shows increasing structural *similarities of*
form among societies without, however, showing increasing *equal-*
ities of outcomes among societies.

—John W. Meyer and Michael T. Hannan,
National Development and the World System (1979:3)

Is the global system irretrievably unstable and prone to failure? Are certain complex and tightly coupled subsystems like the financial system or the Euro Zone doomed for disaster? In previous chapters I have argued that complexity and tight coupling have created a new situation in which we should expect turbulence, instability, and repeated crises. The best way to reduce risks is to lessen the degree of tight coupling at both the network and node levels so that units within the global system have the opportunity and the time to take corrective action in response to disturbances. Another possibility is to reduce network complexity so that there are fewer moving parts. Finally, one could boost the shock-absorbing properties of node complexity, especially those that have to do with ability of the state to sustain external disturbances. I will analyze these three possibilities in terms of the interplay between isomorphic forces and institutional diversity, documenting the extent to which the global system has evolved towards a structure that hinders the handling of systemic problems.

Tendencies Towards Institutional Isomorphism

The architecture of collapse that characterizes the contemporary global system has not come into being by chance. It has been driven by what sociologists call institutional isomorphism, even in the presence of persistent, and in some cases, increasing inequality (Meyer et al. 1997; Guillén 2001). Isomorphism involves the diffusion of similar structures, practices, and ways of doing around the globe. For example, states have adopted modern economic institutions such as stock markets and central banks (Weber et al. 2009; Polillo and Guillén 2005), certain consumer segments tend to demand similar types of goods and services, and the democratic polity is increasingly seen as the most appropriate form of government (Meyer et al. 1997; Marshall 2013). The trend towards increasing institutional isomorphism is especially acute within subcomponents such as trade blocs (e.g. the European Union), monetary unions (the Euro Zone), dyadic relationships (U.S./China), industries (banking), or organizations (diversified financial institutions), as documented in previous chapters. I will argue that while isomorphism tends to generate structure and order, it can make adaption more difficult and stifle innovative approaches to overcoming episodes of disruption and crisis.

Institutional isomorphism is driven by several forces, including norms, coercion, mimesis, emulation, and competition (DiMaggio and Powell 1983; Westney 1987). Normative isomorphism is fueled by shared ideologies, worldviews, frameworks or templates as to what structures and practices in the economy, the political system, and the society are effective and legitimate. Normative conformity is powered by the world-culture of rationalized modernity, which promotes the formal acceptance of "matters such as citizen and human rights, the natural world and its scientific investigation, socioeconomic development, and education" (Meyer et al. 1997:148). Sociologists have investigated the conformity effects of political, economic, and professional normative frameworks. For instance, Guillén and Suárez (2005) found that democratic freedoms increase the number of Internet users even after controlling for cost and accessibility. Fourcade-Gourinchas and Babb (2002), and Murillo (2002) documented that governments embracing neo-liberal economic ideology engaged in more wide-ranging and deeper liberalization, deregulation, and privatization policies. We saw in chapter 6 another example of normative isomorphism, namely, the process of European institution-building, which was driven by a normative framework based on the technocratic idea that integration was the cure to most if not all problems.

The professions are another key engine of normative isomorphism. Professionals identify, frame, and solve problems in specific ways inspired by their own history, tradition, culture, and technical knowledge (DiMaggio and Powell 1983). Professions are "epistemic communities" that transcend national borders constituting themselves as networks of expertise with a claim to authoritative influence over policy domains (Haas 1992:3). Epistemic communities share a series of beliefs concerning cause–effect relationships, criteria and procedures for validating knowledge, and a toolkit of policies or practices.

The normative effect of the professions when it comes to adopting similar economic policies has been documented in a variety of case studies involving both developing and developed countries (Centeno 1990; Babb 2001; Fourcade-Gourinchas and Babb 2002; Fourcade 2009; Murillo 2002). In the case of economic and financial policymaking, Kogut and Macpherson (2008) found that countries with more economists who are members of the American Economic Association engaged more comprehensively in privatization policies, and Weber et al. (2009) found that countries with a greater number of professional financial associations were more likely to create a stock market. The deregulation of financial markets in Europe and the U.S. during the 1980s and 90s was inspired by ideas drawn from certain economic theories about the efficiency of markets (see chapter 4), and the process of European integration has been driven, to a considerable extent, by logics drawn from economics as well (chapter 6).

Coercive isomorphism is another powerful force in the global system. The underlying causal mechanism involves dependence of the focal actor on another actor that is in a position of power. Dependent countries are more likely to engage in isomorphic change. Thus, Meyer et al. (1997:157) argue that more dependent actors or states in the global system are more inclined to adopt formal structures or practices as they attempt to meet "the expanding externally defined requirements of rational actorhood."

In the cross-national context, sociologists have documented the coercive isomorphic effect of international organizations such as the IMF on the adoption of privatization policies (Henisz et al. 2005), central bank independence (Polillo and Guillén 2005), and stock markets (Weber et al. 2009). Loans from the IMF harbor a potential for coercive isomorphism because they make countries "dependent upon a single (or several similar) sources of support for vital resources" (DiMaggio and Powell 1983:155). In addition, countries dependent on a powerful actor such as the IMF are more likely to adopt formal structures or practices in order to enhance, or at least maintain, their status and legitimacy within the international community of states (Meyer et al. 1997; Rodrik 2006; Gilpin 1987:150–60). In the European Union and in the Euro Zone, smaller states have frequently adopted institutions and practices as a result of pressure from stronger states (see chapter 6). Liberalization of capital flows around the world was also driven by coercive pressure from the IMF and strong states during the 1980s and 90s (chapter 4).

Mimetic isomorphism results from the imitation of the structure or practices deemed to be the most legitimate or effective within a certain field. Fields are spheres of activity within which actors mutually recognize each other's presence and actions (DiMaggio and Powell 1983; Tolbert and Zucker 1983). Organizational theorists have pursued two arguments about mimicry within organizational fields. The first focuses on information under conditions of uncertainty (Lieberman and Asaba, 2006). Field participants are more likely to trust more observable, proximate and direct sources of information when there is ambiguity as to cause–effect relationships and as to the ultimate sources of success (Davis and Greve 1997; Greve 1998).

The second argument stipulates that as the adoption and prevalence of a practice increases, it becomes more "legitimate," that is, it begins to be taken for granted as appropriate or permissible in the eyes of field participants (Abrahamson and Rosenkopf 1993; Scott 2001). Enhanced legitimacy makes it easier for actors in the field to justify the decision to adopt the practice against potential opposition, inertia or plain skepticism. As the legitimacy of the practice increases, actors find it easier to overcome resistance and adopt the practice.

Mimetic policymaking by countries has been documented in case studies involving European and Latin American countries (e.g. Fourcade-Gourinchas and Babb 2002; Murillo 2002). Research based on large samples of countries has found them to engage in policy imitation. For instance, countries with stronger relationships to one another in terms of trade have been found to be more likely to adopt privatization policies (Henisz et al. 2005), and to grant the central bank independent status from the government (Polillo and Guillén 2005). Countries in the same geographical region have been found to be more likely to organize a stock market as the institution becomes more prevalent (Weber et al. 2009). During the 1980s and 90s financial deregulation was in part a process fueled by mimetic behavior (see chapter 4).

While mimetic adoption focuses on peer-to-peer effects, that is, the influence of other actors in the same field of activity, cross-national emulation refers to the imitation of specific actors that are perceived as being leaders, high performers, more prestigious or more legitimate. The difference between adoption through peer imitation and cross-national emulation parallels the classic distinction between "frequency" and "trait" imitation (Haunschild and Miner 1997). Frequency imitation is driven by the legitimacy that the practice acquires as a greater number of actors in a given field adopt it. Trait imitation, by contrast, is driven by the legitimacy of the source of the practice. Past research has established that there are a number of characteristics of an actor that may enhance its legitimacy when it comes to providing a role model for others to imitate, including its performance, size, structural status, and structural centrality (Haveman 1993; Lieberman and Asaba 2006; Strang and Soule 1998; Rogers 1995).

In the context of the cross-national adoption of a policy or practice, research has shown that successful countries provide a role model for others to imitate. In a classic historical study, Westney (1987) documented how the Meiji modernizing elites in Japan draw models and ideas from France for organizing the police and from Britain for setting up the postal system. Similarly, Guillén (1994) showed that elites in various countries sought to emulate American managerial and organizational models such as scientific management and human relations. Another example is the adoption of Japanese quality control and lean production practices by companies around the world (Kenney and Florida 1993; Cole 1985). In each of these instances, the country being emulated was perceived as being at the leading edge of the field. The spread of certain financial innovations and products during the 1990s and early 2000s was driven by emulation of U.S. investment banks by other banks in Europe and elsewhere, a factor that contributed to the financial implosion of 2008 (see chapter 4).

Institutional Isomorphism, Complexity, and Coupling

Institutional isomorphism tends to exacerbate levels of complexity and coupling. The effect of isomorphism on network complexity depends on the nature of the structure, practice, or way of doing being adopted. The worldwide adoption of institutions to facilitate trade, foreign direct investment, tourism, migration, and information flows has greatly enhanced network complexity in the global system (see chapter 2). These institutions include national agencies, regulations, and policies whose purpose is to promote those phenomena. At the international level, the WTO, the World Customs Organization, bilateral investment treaties, the World Tourism Organization, and the International Telecommunication Union have paved the way for increasing network complexity.

Isomorphism has also fostered node complexity through normative, coercive, mimetic, emulative, and competitive pressures. Countries around the world have adopted democracy, added checks and balances, increased the size of their state apparatus, and enhanced state capacity. These processes of adoption have acquired a dynamic of their own driven by institutional forces of isomorphism (Meyer et al. 1997). As documented in previous chapters, node complexity, for the most part, has tended to be shock-absorbing, unlike network complexity, which is largely shock-diffusing, except in the specific cases identified in chapters 1 and 2.

The effect of institutional isomorphism on network coupling is also clear. Trade in intermediates has grown as commercial barriers have vanished, international business transactions have become procedurally easier, and information exchange over large distances has become easier and cheaper. The widespread adoption of policies promoting free capital flows have contributed to the sharp rise in foreign portfolio investment, currency trading, and cross-border banking activity (see chapter 3). It is not as straightforward, however, to trace back the origins of mounting current account imbalances to institutional iso-morphism. On the one hand, institutional convergence around the world has facilitated increasingly unfettered commercial exchange based on the dollar as the world's leading international currency underpinning trade, investment, and the management of reserves. On the other, imbalances have much to do with persistent differences in factor endowments, productivity, societal comparative advantage, and certain policies, especially currency manipulation (see chapter 5).

The effects of isomorphism are even clearer within subcomponents of the global system (Berry et al. 2014). In chapter 6, I examined the isomorphic forces tending towards greater complexity in the European Union, and towards greater coupling with the European Monetary System, certain aspects of the single market, and, especially, the Euro Zone. In particular, I analyzed the effects of common normative frame-works, coercion by the stronger states within the union, and emulation of the most successful countries. In chapter 5, I concluded that the dyadic relationship between the U.S. and China has evolved to become more complex over time, though much less in terms of coupling than the Euro Zone. In this case, isomorphism has not been at work as much, mostly because of the resilience of preexisting Chinese institu-tions in the face of the transition to the market economy and the rise of the middle class, at least for now (Li 2012). In chapter 4 we examined the Great Recession and the role that highly-leveraged and diversified financial institutions played in it. Normative frameworks, coercion, mimicry, emulation, and competition produced a considerable degree of convergence in regulatory, organizational, and managerial structures and practices during the years prior to the crisis, paving the way for the perfect storm of 2008.

Complexity and Coupling over Time

Isomorphic forces operating at different levels of analysis have tended to increase complexity and coupling over the last few decades, although at different rates depending on each case. Figure 7.1 summarizes the case studies analyzed in previous chapters at the different levels of analysis, from the organization to the industry, and from dyadic

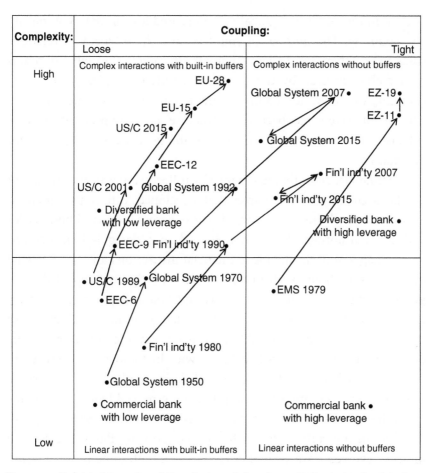

Figure 7.1. Empirical Instances of Complexity and Coupling at Different Levels of Analysis

relationships between pairs of countries to trade blocs, monetary unions, and the global system as a whole.

The 20 indicators I proposed for measuring complexity and coupling at the level of the global system show a clear increase from the 1950s to 2007, with a sharp decrease in some indicators of coupling since the beginning of the crisis, namely, current account imbalances, portfolio investment, and cross-border banking activity (chapter 3). Complexity also fell as a result of the crisis, especially in terms of trade and foreign direct investment, but recovered relatively swiftly (chapter 2). More worrisome is the decline in state capacity, which provides the overall system with a measure of stability.

Back in the 1950s, the global system scored low on both complexity and coupling. The number of countries and the intensity of relationships among them were relatively small. Nowadays, the global system is clearly characterized by the dynamics of high complexity and tight coupling, one in which complex interactions without buffers prevail. The global system has become a structure akin to an architecture of collapse. It is a system prone to instability, disruption, crisis, and breakdown.

The financial crisis that led to the Great Recession was brought about by the architecture of collapse that developed within the financial industry, and whose effects spread swiftly across industrial boundaries and national borders. Between 1980 and 2007 deregulation, mergers, and managerial decisions made financial institutions and the financial industry as a whole much more complex and tightly coupled than in the past (chapter 4). This evolution is captured in Figure 7.1. Commercial banks with low leverage appear to the left of commercial banks with high leverage because they differ from one another in terms of the degree of coupling. Diversified banks with low and high leverage are also different because of the extent of their coupling, but they score much higher in complexity than purely commercial banks. The financial industry as a whole scored relatively low on both complexity and coupling in the early 1980s. After the London Big Bang of 1986, the industry evolved towards higher levels along both dimensions. During the 1990s, the U.S., and other countries like France and Germany, played catch up to the UK. Financial deregulation and cross-border integration was presented as the cure to all ills, present and future (Abadelal 2007; Baghawti 1999). As organizations, banks adapted to the new situation through internal restructurings, mergers, and acquisitions, entering new segments of financial services, and becoming more complex and tightly coupled themselves. The rise of diversified financial institutions with activities in virtually every area of financial services made them more complex. Meanwhile, high degrees of financial leverage during the low-interest-rate era leading up to the crisis made financial institutions and the entire financial system much more tightly coupled. It is noteworthy that banks with more complex operations and with higher leverage ratios were much more likely to go bust or be bailed out when the crisis hit. Meanwhile, banks more focused on commercial banking, and especially better-capitalized banks managed to weather the storm more easily (Berger and Bouwman 2009). As documented in chapter 4, coupling through financial leverage decreased very quickly after the crisis, but complexity came down to a much lesser extent due to the fact that mergers and acquisitions created even larger financial conglomerations than before the crisis.

We analyzed in chapter 5 that the U.S./China relationship is rather intense in terms of trade, primarily in one direction, and portfolio investment, in the opposite direction. By contrast, other indicators of complexity or coupling do not reveal a high degree of interconnection between the two largest economies. In fact, as the world becomes more multipolar, other countries have come into play, putting in perspective the U.S./China relationship, however pivotal at the present time. I argued that this dyadic relationship is more complex than it is coupled, as reflected in Figure 7.1. The growth in complexity, and to a lesser extent in coupling, started after 1989. In the wake of Tiananmen, China relaxed regulations for foreign direct investment, leading to a sharp increase in the presence of U.S. companies, a trend that raised the complexity of the dyadic relationship. It was only after China's entry into the WTO in 2001 that portfolio investment, especially in government bonds, increased in the other direction. Thus, after that point the dyadic relationship grew in terms of coupling (see Figure 7.1). Still, the U.S./China relationship is characterized by relatively loose coupling. As documented in chapter 5, China accounts for less than a quarter of total holdings of U.S. government debt, and investment and banking ties are almost negligible compared to those maintained by either country with other parts of the world.

The example of Europe and its attempt to create a closer union among sovereign nation-states is a clear instance of an architecture of collapse. The initial six members of the European Economic Community (EEC-6) agreed in 1957 to a relatively straightforward, linear, and buffered arrangement focused on merchandise trade. Over the next four decades it became a more complex bloc as it welcomed new members, broadened the scope of areas for collaboration, and deepened certain aspects of the union (EEC-9 and EEC-12 in Figure 7.1). With the coming into effect of the Maastricht Treaty in 1993, the EEC became the European Union in pursuit of an ambitious agenda of economic and political integration that resulted in an increase in the degree of coupling. The Union also became more complex by adding three new members to create the EU-15. Still, that arrangement was not as tightly coupled as the monetary union whose origins date back to the European Monetary System of 1979 (EMS). This path of integration reached its apogee with the premature adoption of the single currency by 11 member states in 1999 (EZ-11). As of early 2015 the Euro Zone included 19 members (EZ-19), after the addition of eight relatively small economies, and was one of the most complex and tightly-coupled systems in the world, as shown in Figure 7.1 and analyzed in chapter 6.

Complexity and coupling can be highly problematic in combination, as illustrated by the global financial crisis of 2008, the Great Recession, and the European sovereign debt crisis. The global system as a whole reached its highest point in terms of node and network complexity and coupling in 2007, with a few indicators dropping as a result of the crisis. At that time, it was a true architecture of collapse. Nowadays the levels may be lower than in 2007, but they are higher than in previous decades, and thus the potential for a disruption, crisis, or systemic breakdown is still there.

The case studies summarized in Figure 7.1 clearly indicate that it is hard to cope with high levels of both complexity and coupling, although human agency, ideologies, and politics were as important if not even more so as triggers (Perrow 2010; Campbell 2010). I documented in chapter 4 that many of the actors involved in the drama leading to the 2008 financial crisis put the system at risk with their greedy behavior while others did not fully understand how reckless their actions were or what the full implications of rising complexity and coupling were. The few regulators and policymakers who identified the issues and fought hard to make the system safer were in the minority. Thus, there is clear evidence of "executive failure" above and beyond the structural characteristics of the system at the time (Perrow 2007; see also Palmer and Maher 2010; Schneiberg and Bartley 2010). Thus, a strict application of Perrow's theory means that the financial implosion was not a "normal accident" because of the role played by human agency in the forms of rampant greed and deception (Perrow 2010). The Euro Zone crisis also took place in the midst of complexity and coupling, but that was the result not of greed and deception but of technocratic hubris and political expediency.

The Future of The Global System

State Capacity as an Antidote to Tight Coupling
While in Perrow's (1994) normal-accident theory high complexity in combination with tight coupling enhances the potential for systemic failure, the analysis proposed in this book deviates from this general principle in one important way. As I argued in chapters 1 and 2, node complexity can be shock-absorbing, thus buffering the system from the ill effects of network complexity and coupling (Allen and Gale 2000; Gai and Kapadia 2010; May et al. 2008; Minoiu and Reyes 2010).

In particular, there is one aspect of node complexity that is associated with more stability and a greater chance of returning to equilibrium in the wake of a systemic disruption. It involves the state as an actor with the ability to intervene during both normal and crisis periods. States are the most important nodes in the global system and the first line of defense, the main buffers, against instability, disruption, crisis, and breakdown, whether the menace has to do with the financial sector, ethnic conflict or a natural disaster. In the case of financial and economic downturns and crises, states can consume or invest in ways that may stabilize the economy and the political system (Katzenstein 1985; Rodrik 1998).

One of the tragedies of the last 30 years is that globalization has undermined the authority and the capacity of the state to take action, especially during times of crisis (see Figure 2.12). The ability of governments to intervene has suffered as a result of the ideological assault on the state by conservative parties and politicians (Evans 1997) as well as a consequence of the liberalization of markets, especially capital markets. Free cross-border capital flows have greatly diminished the ability of policymakers to cope with disruptions and crises, especially in countries with high levels of sovereign debt.

As discussed in chapter 2, states differ from one another in terms of their capacity to formulate and implement policies. Countries characterized by higher levels of state capacity are more likely not only to withstand episodes of distress, disruption, and crisis but also to return to a situation of equilibrium. State capacity helps anticipate problems and propose solutions. States with more capacity have the means to identify and evaluate alternatives proposed or adopted elsewhere in the world, assess their impact, and conduct follow-up studies after implementation takes place (Meyer et al. 1997). A node with sufficient state capacity may become a firewall in the complex global network, providing the overall system with a measure of stability and preventing a shock from spreading further.

One interesting illustration of the role of state capacity during the Great Recession involves independent central banks. The idea that central banks should be independent from political power gained credence during the 1980s and 90s. Dozens of countries shielded their central banks from political influence as a result of normative, coercive, and mimetic pressures. This trend raised the specter of a "democratic deficit" whereby unelected officials wielded much power over the markets and the entire economy with few countervailing forces (Polillo and Guillén 2005; Tognato 2012). It is important to note that central banks continue to be part of the state even after becoming independent from the three branches of government.

During the Great Recession, independent central banks such as the Fed, the Bank of England, and the European Central Bank became key actors when it came to slowing down the spread of the crisis and laying the foundations for a recovery. They were accused by some for not doing enough and by others for doing too much to stimulate growth at the cost of making matters worse. All in all, by deploying trillions of dollars, pounds, and euros, central banks seem to have contributed to averting a more severe crisis (Irwin 2013; Krugman 2012).

The independence and capacity of central banks can be interpreted as an institutional decoupling between the executive branch of government and monetary authority. As we saw in previous chapters, money is a central element of any economy from functional, political, and symbolic points of view. During the Great Recession central banks were in a better position to act than governments, especially those heavily into debt (Europe) or subject to political gridlock (U.S.). Independence made it possible for them to engage in much-needed policymaking aimed at restoring confidence and accelerating growth.

In spite of the buffering effect of a strong, capable state apparatus, it would be a stretch to argue that a tightly-coupled system can be made safe exclusively by putting in place the right kind of node complexity. The evidence presented in previous chapters and summarized in Figure 7.1 suggests that the most intractable and far-reaching crises occurred when both complexity and coupling were high. More research is needed as to exactly what types of complexity tend to absorb shocks rather than diffuse them. The analysis in this book indicates that only node complexity in terms of democracy, checks and balances, and the size of the state apparatus has the potential of turning states into shock-absorbing mechanisms. The evidence regarding network complexity is less supportive of the shock-diffusing argument.

New Geo-Economic Regions

The case studies presented in this book indicate that complexity and coupling concentrated in specific subcomponents of the global system, such as the U.S. financial system (chapter 4) or the Euro Zone (chapter 6), can be particularly troublesome because they are architectures of collapse. It is also clear that isomorphic forces have more of an effect on subcomponents of the global system as opposed to the global system as a whole, as previous research had established (Berry et al. 2014).

One tantalizing question for the future evolution of the global system is whether new geo-economic subcomponents or regions might be emerging. There are two historical patterns of regionalization. One has to do with geographical proximity and adjacency. The land empires of the past, and the European Union or the North American Free Trade Agreement at the present time, are prime examples of this pattern.

The second pattern revolves around the unifying role that bodies of water have often played in global history since antiquity. For instance, Asia-Pacific Economic Cooperation (APEC) is a forum focused on promoting mutual understanding, free trade, and other forms of cooperation among 21 member countries. One tantalizing prospect for the near future is the re-emergence of oceans as catalyzers of economic regions. Figure 7.2 shows the GDP and population sizes of the Pacific, Indian, North Atlantic, South Atlantic, Mediterranean, and Arctic rims. Some countries like Canada, the U.S., Indonesia, or France are part of

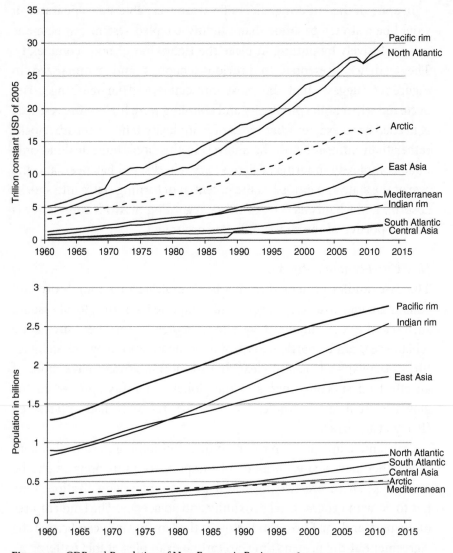

Figure 7.2. GDP and Population of New Economic Regions, 1960–2012
Source of the data: World Development Indicators.

more than one of these regions. In terms of GDP, the Pacific and North Atlantic rims are by far the largest geo-economic regions. In terms of population, however, the North Atlantic falls to fourth place and the Indian rim rises to second place. An interesting case is the Arctic rim, which is the third largest in terms of GDP but one of the smallest in terms of population, barely greater than the Mediterranean. Global warming will turn the Arctic into a navigable ocean during at least part of the year, cutting shipping times from Europe to Asia by more than half and unleashing its great potential in terms of natural resources, with potentially staggering climatic repercussions for the entire world. The South Atlantic rim will also rise in importance, given its natural resources and rapid population growth in West Sub-Saharan Africa. By comparison, the Mediterranean rim will remain relatively small. East Asia will continue to be an important region by itself. One last interesting case is Central Asia, stretching from Turkey to Mongolia, an area that could be more geo-economically relevant if it could articulate a land transportation infrastructure.

The twenty-first century may well be the century of oceans, both from a resource perspective and from the point of view of the organization of economic activity. Such a shift away from land-based regionalization will generate new patterns of complexity and coupling in the global system. It remains to be seen whether they will be less or more severe than those involving land-based regions such as the EU or the Euro Zone, or dyadic relationships such as the one between the U.S. and China.

* * *

The combination of complexity and coupling is generally inimical to the stability of the global system and of the subcomponents within it such as regional blocs, industries, or organizations. Reducing complexity will be hard or counterproductive, for a variety of reasons. At the network level, the number of countries, people movements, and information flows are on the increase, not the decrease. Trade tends to contribute to prosperity over the long run, and one cannot imagine a sharp reduction in foreign direct investment. At the node level, democracy, checks and balances, and the size and capacity of the state apparatus all contribute to turning states into shock-absorbing mechanisms that happen to be essential to preventing crises from spreading, or to coping with them if they do diffuse. Thus, I do not see it as possible or advisable to reduce the degree of complexity in the global system.

The message of this book is that, if we wish to live in a global system less prone to disruption, crisis, and breakdown, we need to either rein in the degree of coupling or enhance the shock-absorbing nature of node complexity, or preferably both. If we truly want to move away from the present architecture of collapse, we must create buffers and make allowances for units in the global system to adjust to disruptions and crises (Schneiberg and Bartley 2010; Bookstaber 2007). Let me offer some examples. There is considerable agreement among experts, policymakers, and politicians that current account imbalances have grown too big (see chapters 3 and 5). They are a source of instability for two reasons, namely, the yawning gap that they create between the surplus and deficit economies, and the pressure they exert on the countries that issue reserve currencies (chapter 5). Most analysts also agree that reducing trade in intermediates is not a solution that comes without costs. There is less agreement concerning foreign portfolio investment, currency trading, and cross-border banking. The debate over unfettered capital flows continues to rage, fuelled by the dozens of (unnecessary) crises they have brought about over the last three decades. I argue that a new institutional framework for international capital mobility is needed. While the IMF and the World Bank must continue to be pivotal agencies in it, the emerging economies must take on larger roles and responsibilities. The global economy has changed massively since 1944, but the institutions underpinning it have not. Some forms of preventive capital controls may also be necessary, even if they come at the cost of inefficient capital allocation across borders. The tradeoff between efficiency and stability cannot be resolved only in favor of the former. This will be, by definition, a political decision that must be carefully examined.

At the node level, there is some agreement as to the negative effects of population aging, rapid urbanization, public debt, income inequality, and wealth inequality, although massive debates as to the policies needed to address the challenges. Population aging in developed countries and emerging economies alike will continue to put pressure on government budgets for decades to come. Urbanization will likely bring food and water systems to the brink of collapse in many emerging economies and developing countries. Income and wealth inequality are already undermining the economy and, even worse, the social and political bases for stability. Discouragingly, there is nothing but disagreement when it comes to policy proposals to address the effects of node coupling, especially regarding proposals seeking to reverse the underlying trends. I suspect that the stability of the global system hinges primarily on how effectively different countries overcome the potentially devastating effects of aging, rapid urbanization, and inequality, subject to the constraint that many states find themselves deeply into debt or otherwise incapacitated to act swiftly in response to these challenges. Network and node coupling must be reduced to make the global system more stable, to escape from the architecture of collapse. If, in addition, we rebuild state capacity to cope with the ever larger problems of global governance, then we will create a much safer global system.

REFERENCES

Abdelal, Rawi. 2007. *Capital Rules: The Construction of Global Finance.* Cambridge: Harvard University Press.

Abrahamson, Eric, and Lori Rosenkopf. 1993. "Institutional and Competitive Bandwagons." *Academy of Management Review* 18:487–517.

Adler, Jerry. 2012. "Raging Bulls: How Wall Street Got Addicted to Light-Speed Trading." *Wired,* http://www.wired.com/2012/08/ff_wallstreet_trading/all/, accessed June 22, 2014.

AFD (African Development Bank). 2011. *The Middle of the Pyramid: Dynamics of the Middle Class in Africa.* Abidjan, Ivory Coast: African Development Bank.

Akerlof, George A., and Robert J. Shiller. 2009. *Animal Spirits: How Human Psychology Drives the Economy, and Why It Matters for Global Capitalism.* Princeton, NJ: Princeton University Press.

Albrow, Martin. 1997. *The Global Age.* Stanford, CA: Stanford University Press.

Alesina, Alberto, and Francesco Giavazzi. 2006. *The Future of Europe: Reform or Decline.* Cambridge, MA: The MIT Press.

Allen, F. and D. Gale. 2000. "Financial Contagion." *Journal of Political Economy* 108(1):1–33.

Alvaredo, Facundo, Anthony B. Atkinson, Thomas Piketty, and Emmanuel Saez. 2014. "The Top 1 Percent in International and Historical Perspective." *Journal of Economic Perspectives* 27(3):3–20.

Amsden, Alice H. 1989. *Asia's Next Giant: South Korea and Late Industrialization.* New York, New York: Oxford University Press.

Andolfatto, David. 2014. "Bitcoin and Beyond: The Possibilities and Pitfalls of Virtual Currencies." Powerpoint presentation. St. Louis, MO: Federal Reserve Bank of St. Louis. March 31. http://www.stlouisfed.org/dialogue-with-the-fed/assets/Bitcoin-3-31-14.pdf, accessed June 22, 2014.

Armingeon, Klaus, and Lucio Baccaro. 2012. "The Sorrows of Young Euro: The Sovereign Debt Crises of Ireland and Southern Europe." In Nancy Bermeo and Jonas Pontusson, eds., *Coping with Crisis: Government Reactions to the Great Recession.* New York: Russell Sage Foundation, pp. 162–97.

Ash, Timothy Garton. 2012. "The Crisis of Europe: How the Union Came Together and Why It's Falling." *Foreign Affairs* 91(5) (September–October):2–15.

Austin, Kenneth. 2014. "Systemic Equilibrium in a Bretton Woods II-Type International Monetary System: The Special Roles of Reserve Issuers and Reserve Accumulators." *Journal of Post Keynesian Economics* 36(4) (Summer):607–33.

Babb, Sarah L. 2001. *Managing Mexico: Economists from Nationalism to Neoliberalism.* Princeton: Princeton University Press.

Banham, Reyner. [1960] 1980. *Theory and Design in the First Machine Age.* Cambridge, MA: The MIT Press.

Baun, Michael. 1996. "The Maastricht Treaty as High Politics." *Political Science Quarterly* 110(4):605–24.

Beckfield, Jason. 2010. "The Social Structure of the World Polity." *American Journal of Sociology* 115(4) (January):1018–68.

Beetsma, Roel, and Massimo Giuliodori. 2010. "The Macroeconomic Costs and Benefits of the EMU and other Monetary Unions: An Overview of Recent Research." *Journal of Economic Literature* 48:603–41.

Berger, Allen N., and Christa H. S. Bouwman. 2009. "Bank Capital, Survival, and Performance around Financial Crises." http://web.mit.edu/cbouwman/www/downloads/BergerBouwmanBankCapPerfFinCrises.pdf, accessed July 23, 2014.

Berges, Angel, Mauro F. Guillén, Juan Pedro Moreno, and Emilio Ontiveros. 2014. *A New Era in Banking: The Landscape after the Battle.* Brookline, MA: Bibliomotion.

Bergsten, Fred C. 2009. "The Dollar and the Deficits: How Washington Can Prevent the Next Crisis." *Foreign Affairs* 88 (6) (November–December 2009):20–38.

Bergsten, Fred C. 2015. "The Truth about Currency Manipulation." *Foreign Affairs* (January 18), digital edition (accessed February 16, 2015).

Berry, Heather, Mauro F. Guillén, and Arun S. Hendi. 2014. "Is there Convergence across Countries? A Spatial Approach." *Journal of International Business Studies* 45:387–404.

Bhagwati, Jagdish. 1998. "The Capital Myth: The Difference between Trade in Widgets and Dollars." *Foreign Affairs* 77(3) (May–June):7–12.

Biggart, Nicole Woolsey and Marco Orrù. 1997. "Societal Strategic Advantage: Institutional Structure and Path Dependence in the Automotive and Electronics Industries of East Asia." Pp. 201–39 in *State, Market and Organizational Form,* edited by Ayse Bugra and Behlul Usdiken. Berlin: Walter de Gruyter.

Biggart, Nicole Woolsey, and Mauro F. Guillén. 1999. "Developing Difference: Social Organization and the Rise of the Auto Industries of South Korea, Taiwan, Spain, and Argentina." *American Sociological Review* 64(5) (October):722–47.

Blanchard, Olivier, and Gian Maria Milesi-Ferretti. 2009. "Global Imbalances: In Midstream?" IMF Staff Position Note SPN/09/29, December 22.

Blau, Peter M., and W. Richard Scott. 1962. *Formal Organizations: A Comparative Approach.* Scranton, Pennsylvania: Chandler Publishing.

Blau, Peter M., and Richard Schoenherr. 1971. *The Structure of Organizations.* New York: Basic.

Blundell-Wignall, Adrian, and Patrick Slovik. 2010. "The EU Stress Test and Sovereign Debt Exposures." Working Paper. Paris: OECD.

Blyth, Mark. 2013. *Austerity: The History of a Dangerous Idea*. Oxford: Oxford University Press.

Boehm, Christoph, Aaron Flaaen, and Nitya Pandalai Nayar. 2015. "Input Linkages and the Transmission of Shocks: Firm-Level Evidence from the 2011 Tohoku Earthquake." Working paper. *http://www.aaronflaaen.com/uploads/3/1/2/4/31243277/flaaen_jobmarketpaper.pdf*, accessed January 30, 2015.

Boix, Carles. 1998. *Political Parties, Growth and Equality: Conservative and Social Democratic Economic Strategies in the World Economy*. New York, New York: Cambridge University Press.

Boix, Carles. 2011. "Democracy, Development, and the International System." *American Political Science Review* 105 (4):809–28.

Bookstaber, Richard. 2007. *A Demon of Our Own Design: Markets, Hedge Funds, and the Perils of Financial Innovation*. New York: Wiley.

Boring, Perianne. 2014. "The U.S. Congress Examines Bitcoin." *Bitcoin Magazine*, April 11. http://bitcoinmagazine.com/12272/congress-divided-bubble-reserve/, accessed June 21, 2014.

Borrelli, Stephen A. 2001. "Finding the Third Way: Bill Clinton, the DLC, and the Democratic Platform of 1992." *The Journal of Policy History*, 13 (4):429–62.

Brandt, Loren, Johannes Van Biesebroeck, and Yifan Zhang. 2012. "Creative Accounting or Creative Destruction: Firm Level Productivity Growth in Chinese Manufacturing," *Journal of Development Economics* 97 (2):339–51.

Bremmer, Ian. 2010. "Democracy in Cyberspace." *Foreign Affairs* (November–December), digital edition, accessed April 28, 2015.

Breznitz, Dan, and Michael Murphree. 2011. *Run of the Red Queen: Government, Innovation, Globalization, and Economic Growth in China*. New Haven, CT: Yale University Press.

Burt, Ronald. 1987. "Social Contagion and Innovation: Cohesion versus Structural Equivalence." *American Journal of Sociology* 92:1287–335.

Burt, Ronald S. 1992. *Structural Holes: The Social Structure of Competition*. Cambridge, MA: Harvard University Press.

Burt, Ronald S. 2005. *Brokerage and Closure: An Introduction to Social Capital*. New York: Oxford University Press.

Cain, J. Salcedo, Rana Hasan, Rhoda Magsombol, and Ajay Tandon. 2008. "Accounting for Inequality in India: Evidence from Household Expenditures." Manila: Asian Development Bank.

Calleo, David. 1978. *The German Problem Reconsidered*. New York: Cambridge University Press.

Cameron, David. 2012. "European Fiscal Responses to the Great Recession." In Nancy Bermeo and Jonas Pontusson, eds., *Coping with Crisis: Government Reactions to the Great Recession*. New York: Russell Sage Foundation, pp. 91–129.

Campbell, John L. 2004. *Institutional Change and Globalization*. Princeton, NJ: Princeton University Press.

Campbell, John L. 2010. "Neoliberalism in Crisis: Regulatory Roots of the U.S. Financial Meltdown." *Research in the Sociology of Organizations* 30B (2010):65–101.

Campbell, John L., and John A. Hall. 2015. *The World of States*. London: Boomsbury.

Capgemini and RBC Wealth Management. 2013. *World Wealth Report 2013*. New York: Capgemini.

Carr, Edward. 2010. "Friend or Foe? A Special Report on China's Place in the World." *The Economist* (December 4), digital edition, accessed April 29, 2015.

Carruthers, Bruce G. 2010. "Knowledge and Liquidity: Institutional and Cognitive Foundations of the Subprime Crisis." *Research in the Sociology of Organizations* 30A (2010):157–82.

Cassidy, John. 2010. "After the Blowup: Laissez-Faire Economists do some Soul-Searching—and Finger-Pointing." *The New Yorker* (January 11):28–33.

Castells, Manuel. 1996. *The Rise of the Network Society*. Cambridge, MA: Blackwell.

Castells, Manuel. 2000. "Toward a Sociology of the Network Society" *Contemporary Sociology* 29(5) (2000):693–9.

Centeno, Miguel Angel. 1990. *The New Científicos: Technocratic Politics in Mexico 1970–1990*. New Haven: Yale University Press.

Centeno, Miguel Angel. 2003. *Blood and Debt: War and the Nation-State in Latin America*. College Park, PA: Penn State University Press.

Chen, Jiandong, Dai Dai, Ming Pu, Wenxuan Hou, and Qiaobin Feng. 2010. "The Trend of the Gini Coefficient of China." Manchester: Brooks World Poverty Industry Working Paper 109.

Cheng, Li. 2011. "Introduction: A Champion for Chinese Optimism and Exceptionalism." In Angang Hu, *China in 2020: A New Type of Superpower*. Washington, DC: Brookings Institution Press, pp. xv–xl.

Cheung, Yin-Wong. 2015. "The Role of Offshore Financial Centers in the Process of Renminbi Internationalization." In Barry Eichengreen and Masahiro Kawai, eds., *Renminbi Internationalization: Achievements, Prospects, and Challenges*. Washington, DC: Brookings Institution Press, chapter 7, Kindle Edition.

Choi, Sang Rim, Daekeun Park and Adrian Tschoegl. 2002. *Banks and the World's Major Banking Centers*. Financial Institutions Center, The Wharton School, Working Paper.

Cohen, Michael D., James G. March, and Johan P. Olsen. 1972. "A Garbage Can Model of Organizational Choice." *Administrative Science Quarterly* 17 (1):1–25.

Cole, Robert E. 1985. "The Macropolitics of Organizational Change: A Comparative Analysis of the Spread of Small-group Activities. *Administrative Science Quarterly* 30(4):560–85.

Credit Suisse. 2014. *Global Wealth Report*. Zurich: Credit Suisse Research Institute.

CSEMU (Committee for the Study of Economic and Monetary Union). 1989. *Report on Economic and Monetary Union in the European Community*. Presented April 17, 1989. Brussels: European Community.

Cusumano, Michael A. 1985. *The Japanese Automobile Industry: Technology and Management at Nissan and Toyota*. Cambridge: The Council on East Asian Studies and Harvard University Press.

Davis, Gerald F. 2009. *Managed by the Markets: How Finance Re-Shaped America.* New York: Oxford University Press.

Davis, Gerald F., and Henrich R. Greve. 1997. "Corporate Elite Networks and Governance Changes in the 1980s." *American Journal of Sociology* 103:1–37.

Dedrick, Jason, Kenneth L. Kraemer, and Greg Linden. 2010. "Who Profits From Innovation in Global Value Chains? A Study of the iPod and Notebook PCs." *Industrial and Corporate Change* 19(1):81–116.

De Jong, Jeroen P. J., and Erik de Bruijn. 2013. "Innovation Lessons from 3D Printing." *Sloan Management Review* (Winter), reprint 54212.

deLisle, Jacques, and Avery Goldstein eds. 2015. *China's Challenges.* Philadelphia, PA: University of Pennsylvania Press.

Diamond, Jared M. [1997] 2005. *Guns, Germs, and Steel: The Fates of Human Societies.* New York: Norton.

Diamond, Jared M. 2005. *Collapse: How Societies Choose to Fail or Succeed.* New York: Viking.

Díez Medrano, Juan. 2003. *Framing Europe: Attitudes to European Integration in Germany, Spain, and the United Kingdom.* Princeton, NJ: Princeton University Press.

DiMaggio, Paul J., and Walter W. Powell. 1983. "The Iron Cage Revisited: Institutional Isomorphism and Collective Rationality in Organizational Fields." *American Sociological Review* 48(2) (April):147–60.

Djelic, Marie-Laure. 1998. *Exporting the American Model.* New York, New York: Oxford University Press.

Dobbin, F., B. Simmons, and G. Garrett. 2007. "The Global Diffusion of Public Policies: Social Construction, Coercion, Competition, or Learning?" *Annual Review of Sociology* 33:449–72.

Dore, Ronald. [1973] 1990. *British Factory, Japanese Factory: The Origins of National Diversity in Industrial Relations.* Berkeley, CA: University of California Press.

Dorius, Shawn F. 2008. "Global Demographic Convergence? A Reconsideration of Changing Intercountry Inequality in Fertility." *Population and Development Review* 34:519–37.

Douglas, Mary. 1986. *How Institutions Think.* Syracuse, New York: Syracuse University Press.

Dustmann, Christian, Bernd Fitzenberger, Uta Schönberg, and Alexandra Spitz-Oener. 2014. "From Sick Man of Europe to Economic Superstar: Germany's Resurgent Economy." *Journal of Economic Perspectives* 28(1):167–88.

Dyson, Kenneth, and Kevin Featherstone. 1999. *The Road to Maastricht: Negotiating Economic and Monetary Union.* New York: Oxford University Press.

Easterly, William. 2007. "Inequality Does Cause Underdevelopment: Insights from a New Instrument." *Journal of Development Economics* 84:755–76.

EC. 2008. *Geographic Mobility in the European Union.* Brussels: European Commission.

EC. 2012. *Current Account Balances in the EU.* Brussels: European Commission.

The Economist. 2009. "High-Frequency Trading: Rise of the Machines." *The Economist,* July 30.

Eichengreen, Barry. 1997. *European Monetary Unification: Theory, Practice, and Analysis.* Cambridge, MA: The MIT Press.

Eichengreen, Barry. 2011. *Exorbitant Privilege.* New York: Oxford University Press.

Eichengreen, Barry. 2013. "Number One Country, Number one Currency?" *World Economy* 36(4):363–74.

Eichengreen, Barry. 2015a. *Hall of Mirrors: The Great Depression, the Great Recession, and the Uses—and Misuses—of History.* New York: Oxford University Press. Kindle Edition.

Eichengreen, Barry, and Masahiro Kawai. 2015. "Introduction and Overview." In Barry Eichengreen and Masahiro Kawai, eds., *Renminbi Internationalization: Achievements, Prospects, and Challenges.* Washington, DC: Brookings Institution Press, chapter 1, Kindle Edition.

Englehart, Ronald, and Christian Welzel. 2005. *Modernization, Cultural Change and Democracy: The Human Development Sequence.* Cambridge, UK: Cambridge University Press.

Esping-Andersen, Gøsta. 1990. *The Three Worlds of Welfare Capitalism.* Cambridge: Polity Press & Princeton: Princeton University Press.

Estevadeordal, Antoni, Kati Suominen and Robert Teh, eds. 2009. *Regional Rules in the Global Trading System.* New York: Cambridge University Press.

Evans, Peter. 1979. *Dependent Development.* Princeton, N J: Princeton University Press.

Evans, Peter. 1997. "The Eclipse of the State? Reflections on Stateness in an Era of Globalization." *World Politics* 50 (October):62–87.

Evans, Peter, and James E. Rauch. 1999. "Bureaucracy and Growth: A Cross-National Analysis of the Effects of 'Weberian' State Structures on Economic Growth." *American Sociological Review* 64(5):748–65.

Feenstra, Robert C., Tzu-Han Yang, and Gary G. Hamilton. 1999. "Business Groups and Product Variety in Trade: Evidence from South Korea, Taiwan, and Japan." *Journal of International Economics* 48:71–100.

Feldstein, Martin. 1998. "Refocusing the IMF." *Foreign Affairs* 77(2) (March–April):20–33.

Feldstein, Martin. 2000. "Europe Can't Handle the Euro." *Wall Street Journal,* February 8, online edition, accessed April 28, 2015.

Feldstein, Martin. 2012. "The Failure of the Euro." *Foreign Affairs* 91 (1) (January–February):105–16.

Fligstein, Neil. 1990. *The Transformation of Corporate Control.* Cambridge, MA: Harvard University Press.

Fligstein, Neil. 2001. *The Architecture of Markets: An Economic Sociology of Twenty-First Century Capitalist Societies.* Princeton, NJ: Princeton University Press.

Fligstein, Neil, and Adam Goldstein. 2010. "The Anatomy of the Mortgage Securitization Crisis." *Research in the Sociology of Organizations* 30A (2010):29–70.

Fligstein, Neil, and Alec Stone Sweet. 2002. "Constructing Markets and Politics: An Institutionalist Account of European Integration." *American Journal of Sociology* 107: 1206–43.

Fourcade, Marion. 2009. *Economists and Societies.* Princeton, NJ: Princeton University Press.

Fourcade-Gourinchas, Marion, and Sarah L. Babb. 2002. "The Rebirth of the Liberal Creed: Paths to Neoliberalism in Four Countries." *American Journal of Sociology* 108:533–79.

Freedman, Charles, et al. 2009. "The Case for a Global Fiscal Stimulus." IMF Staff Position Note 09/03, issued March 6.

Friedman, George. 2009. *The Next 100 Years: A Forecast for the 21st Century.* New York: Anchor Books.

Fukuyama, Francis. 1989. "The End of History?" *The National Interest* (Summer), digital edition, accessed April 28, 2015.

Gai, P. and S. Kapadia. 2010. "Contagion in Financial Networks." *Proceedings of the Royal Society A,* 466(2120):2401–23.

GAO. 2007. *Supervision Can Strengthen Performance Measurement and Collaboration.* Washington, DC: Government Accountability Office, report number GAO-07-154, released March 15.

Garrett, Geoffrey. 1998. *Partisan Politics in the Global Economy.* New York: Cambridge University Press.

Garrett, Geoffrey. 2001. "The Politics of Maastricht." In Barry Eichengreen and Jeffry Frieden, eds., *The Political Economy of European Monetary Unification.* Boulder, CO: Westview, pp. 47–65.

Geertz, Clifford. 1973. *The Interpretation of Cultures: Selected Essays.* New York, New York: Basic Books.

Gereffi, Gary. 2005. "The Global Economy: Organization, Governance, and Development." Pp. 160–82 in Handbook of Economic Sociology, edited by Neil J. Smelser and Richard Swedberg. Princeton, NJ: Princeton University Press.

Gereffi, Gary, J. Humphrey, and T. Sturgeon. 2005. "The Governance of Global Value Chains." *Review of International Political Economy* 12:78–104.

Gerlach, Michael L. 1992. *Alliance Capitalism: The Social Organization of Japanese Business.* Berkeley, CA: University of California Press.

Gerth, Jeff. 2008. "Was AIG Watchdog Not Up To The Job?" November 10. www.propublica.org.

Giddens, Anthony. 1979. *Central Problems in Social Theory: Action, Structure, and Contradiction in Social Analysis.* Berkeley, CA: University of California Press.

Gilpin, Robert. 1987. *The Political Economy of International Relations.* Princeton, NJ: Princeton University Press.

Gilpin, Robert. 2000. *The Challenge of Global Capitalism: The World Economy in the 21st Century.* Princeton, NJ: Princeton University Press.

Gilpin, Robert. 2001. *Global Political Economy: Understanding the International Economic Order.* Princeton, NJ: Princeton University Press.

Girouard N., M. Kennedy, and C. Andre. 2006. "Has The Rise in Debt Made Households More Vulnerable?" OECD Economics Department Working Paper No. 535, OECD.

Glick, Reuven, and Andrew K. Rose. 1999. "Contagion and Trade. Why are Currency Crises Regional?"*Journal of International Money and Finance* 18:603–17.

Goldin, Ian and Mike Mariathasan. 2014. *The Butterfly Defect; How Globalization Creates Systemic Risks, and What to Do about It.* Princeton, NJ: Princeton University Press.

Goldstone, Jack A. 2011. "Understanding the Revolutions of 2011: Weakness and Resilience in Middle Eastern Autocracies." *Foreign Affairs* 90 (3) (May–June):8–16.

Goldstone, Jack A. 2009. *Why Europe? The Rise of the West in World History, 1500–1850.* Boston: McGraw-Hill.

Gorton, Gary B. 2010. *Slapped by the Invisible Hand: The Panic of 2007.* New York: Oxford University Press.

Gorton, Gary. 2012. *Misunderstanding Financial Crises.* Oxford: Oxford University Press.

Granovetter, Mark. 1985. "Economic Action and Social Structure: The Problem of Embeddedness." *American Journal of Sociology* 91(3) (November):481–510.

Greve, Henrich R. 1998. "Managerial Cognition and the Mimetic Adoption of Market Positions: What You See is What You Do." *Strategic Management Journal* 19:967–88.

Grossman, Gene M., and Esteban Rossi-Hansberg. 2006. "Trading Tasks: A Simple Theory of Offshoring." NBER Working Paper No. 12721.

Guillén, Mauro F. 1994. *Models of Management: Work, Authority, and Organization in a Comparative Perspective.* Chicago: University of Chicago Press.

Guillén, Mauro F. 2001. *The Limits of Convergence.* Princeton, NJ: Princeton University Press.

Guillén, Mauro F., and Laurence Capron. 2016. "State Capacity, Minority Shareholder Protections, and Stock Market Development." *Administrative Science Quarterly,* forthcoming.

Guillén, Mauro F., and Emilio Ontiveros. 2012. *Global Turning Points: Understanding the Challenges for Business in the 21st Century.* New York: Cambridge University Press.

Guillén, Mauro F., and Sandra L. Suárez. 2005. "Explaining the Global Digital Divide: Economic, Political and Sociological Drivers of Cross-National Internet Use." *Social Forces* 84(2) (December):681–708.

Guillén, Mauro F., and Sandra L. Suárez. 2010. "The Global Crisis of 2007-2009: Markets, Politics, and Organizations." *Research in the Sociology of Organizations* 30A:257–79.

Guler, Isin, Mauro F. Guillén, and John Muir Macpherson. 2002. "Global Competition, Institutions, and the Diffusion of Organizational Practices: The International Spread of the ISO 9000 Quality Certificates." *Administrative Science Quarterly* 47(June):207–32.

Haas, Peter M. 1992. "Introduction: Epistemic Communities and International Policy Coordination." *International Organization* 46(1):1–35.

Haggard, S. 1990. *Pathways from the Periphery: The Politics of Growth in the Newly Industrializing Countries.* Ithaca, New York: Cornell University Press.

Haggard, Stephan, and Robert R. Kaufman. 1995. *The Political Economy of Democratic Transitions.* Princeton, NJ: Princeton University Press.

Hanson, Jonathan K., and Rachel Sigman. 2013. "Leviathan's Latent Dimensions: Measuring State Capacity for Comparative Political Research." Available at SSRN: http://ssrn.com/abstract=1899933.

Harford, Tim. 2011. "What We Can Learn from a Nuclear Reactor." *Financial Times* (January 14).

Haunschild, Pamela R., and Anne S. Miner. 1997. "Models of Interorganizational Imitation: The Effects of Outcome Salience and Uncertainty." *Administrative Science Quarterly* 42:472–500.

Hausmann, Ricardo, César A. Hidalgo, Sebastián Bustos, Michele Coscia, Alexander Simoes, and Muhammed A. Yildirim. 2014. *The Atlas of Economic Complexity: Mapping Paths to Prosperity.* Cambridge: The MIT Press.

Haveman, H. A. 1993. Follow the Leader: Mimetic Isomorphism and Entry into New Markets. *Administrative Science Quarterly* 38:593–627.

Heipertz, Martin, and Amy Verdun. 2010. *Ruling Europe: The Politics of the Stability and Growth Pact.* New York: Cambridge University Press.

Henisz, Witold J. 2000. "The Institutional Environment for Economic Growth." *Economics & Politics* 12:1–31.

Henisz, Witold J. 2014. POLCON Database. http://www-management.wharton.upenn.edu/henisz/, accessed July 20, 2014.

Henisz, Witold J., Bennet A. Zelner, and Mauro F. Guillén. 2005. "Market-Oriented Infrastructure Reforms, 1977–1999." *American Sociological Review* 70(6) (December):871–97.

Hobsbawm, Eric. 1994. *The Age of Extremes: A History of the World, 1914–1991.* London: Michael Joseph.

Hoffman, Stanley. 1966. "Obstinate or Obsolete? The Fate of the Nation-State and the Case of Western Europe." *Daedalus* 95(3) (Summer):862–915.

Hollingsworth, J. Rogers, Philippe C. Schmitter, and Wolfgang Streeck. 1994. "Capitalism, Sectors, Institutions, and Performance." Pp.3–16 in *Governing Capitalist Economies: Performance and Control of Economic Sectors,* edited by J. Hollingsworth, P. Schmitter, and W. Streeck. New York and Oxford: Oxford University Press.

Howe, Neil, and Richard Jackson. 2012. "Demography and Geopolitics." In Jack A. Goldstone, Eric P. Kaufmann, and Monica Duffy Toft, eds., *Political Demography: How Population Changes are Reshaping International Security and National Politics.* Boulder, Colorado: Paradigm Publishers, pp. 31–48.

Hu, Angang. 2011. *China in 2020: A New Type of Superpower.* Washington, DC: Brookings Institution Press.

Hufbauer, Gary Clyde, and Jared C. Woollacott. 2010. "Trade Disputes Between China and the United States: Growing Pains so Far, Worse Ahead?" Peterson Institute for International Economics Working Paper WP 10–17.

Huntington, Samuel P. 1993. "The Clash of Civilizations?" *Foreign Affairs* 72(3) (Summer):22–49.

Hymer, Stephen. [1960] 1976. *The International Operations of National Firms: A Study of Direct Foreign Investment.* Cambridge, MA: The MIT Press.

Ikenberry, G. John. 2006. *Liberal Order and Imperial Ambition: Essays on American Power and World Politics.* Cambridge, MA: Polity.

IMF. 2007. *Financial Stability Report.* Washington, DC: International Monetary Fund.

IMF. 2009a. *Financial Stability Report.* Washington, DC: International Monetary Fund.

IMF. 2009b. *World Economic Outlook.* Washington, DC: International Monetary Fund.

IMF. 2010a. *Global Financial Stability Report: Market Update* (January). Washington, DC: International Monetary Fund.

IMF. 2010b. *Global Financial Stability Report: Meeting New Challenges to Stability and Building a Safer System* (April). Washington, DC: International Monetary Fund.

IMF. 2010c. "Understanding Financial Interconnectedness." October 4, 2010. Washington, DC: International Monetary Fund.

IMF. 2013. *Fiscal Monitor: Fiscal Adjustment in an Uncertain World* (April). Washington, DC: International Monetary Fund.

IMF. 2014. *Annual Report on Exchange Arrangements and Exchange Restrictions 2014.* Washington, DC: International Monetary Fund.

Irwin, Neil. 2013. *The Alchemists: Three Central Bankers and a World on Fire.* New York: Penguin.

Johnson, Simon, and James Kwak. 2010. *13 Bankers: The Wall Street Takeover and the Next Financial Meltdown.* New York: Random House, Pantheon Books.

Johnston, Alison, Bob Hancké, and Suman Pant. 2013. "Comparative Institutional Advantage in the European Sovereign Debt Crisis." LEQS Paper No. 66/2013, London School of Economics and Political Science. *http://www.lse.ac.uk/eu ropeanInstitute/LEQS/LEQSPaper66.pdf*, accessed January 31, 2015.

Judt, Tony. [1996] 2011. *A Grand Illusion? An Essay on Europe.* New York: New York University Press.

Kapstein, Ethan B., and Nathan Converse. 2008. "Poverty, Inequality, and Democracy." *Journal of Democracy* 19(4) (October):57–68.

Katzenstein, Peter J. 1985. *Small States in World Markets.* Ithaca, NY: Cornell University Press.

Katzenstein, Peter J. 1997. "United Germany in an Integrating Europe." In Peter J. Katzenstein, ed., *Tamed Power: Germany in Europe.* Ithaca, NY: Cornell University Press, pp. 1–48.

Kennedy, Paul. 1987. *The Rise and Fall of the Great Powers.* New York: Random House.

Kenney, Martin, and Richard L. Florida. 1993. *Beyond Mass Production: The Japanese System and its Transfer to the U.S.* Oxford: Oxford University Press.

Kharas, Homis. 2010. *The Emerging Middle Class in Developing Countries*. Paris: OECD.

Kindleberger, Charles P. 1978. *Manias, Panics, and Crashes: A History of Financial Crises*. New York: Macmillan.

Knight, John B. and Sai Ding. 2012. *China's Remarkable Economic Growth* (Oxford: Oxford University Press.

Kliman, Daniel M. 2014. *Fateful Transitions: How Democracies Manage Rising Powers, from the Eve of World War I to China's Ascendance*. Philadelphia, PA: University of Pennsylvania Press.

Kogut, Bruce. 1991. "Country Capabilities and the Permeability of Borders." *Strategic Management Journal* 12:33–47.

Kogut, Bruce and Nalin Kulatilaka. 1993. "Operating Flexibility, Global Manufacturing, and the Option Value of a Multinational Network." *Management Science* 40(1):123–39.

Kogut, Bruce, and J. Muir Macpherson. 2008. "The Decision to Privatize: Economists and the Construction of Ideas and Policies." In Beth A. Simmons, Frank Dobbin, and Geoffrey Garrett, eds., *The Global Diffusion of Markets and Democracy*. New York: Cambridge University Press, pp. 104–40.

Kokubun, Ryosei, and Jisi Wang, eds. 2004. *The Rise of China and a Changing East Asian Order*. Tokyo: Japan Center for International Exchange.

Kozmetsky, George, and Piyu Yue. 2005. *The Economic Transformation of the United States, 1950–2000*. West Lafayette, IN: Purdue University Press.

Krugman, Paul. 1978. "The Theory of Interstellar Trade." Working Paper, Princeton University. http://www.princeton.edu/~pkrugman/interstellar.pdf, accessed June 8, 2014.

Krugman, Paul. 1979. "Increasing Returns, Monopolistic Competition, and International Trade." *Journal of International Economics* 9:469–79.

Krugman, Paul. 1980. "Scale Economies, Product Differentiation, and the Pattern of Trade." *American Economic Review* 70:950–9.

Krugman, Paul. 1994. 1998. "Saving Asia: It's Time to Get Radical." *Fortune* September 7, 75–80.

Krugman, Paul. 2009. *The Return of Depression Economics and the Crisis of 2008*. New York: W. W. Norton.

Krugman, Paul. 2012. *End this Depression Now!* New York: W. W. Norton.

Krugman, Paul. 2013. "How the Case for Austerity has Crumbled." *New York Review of Books* (June 6), online edition, accessed April 28, 2015.

Labaton, Stephen. 1999. "A New Financial Era." *The New York Times* October 23, section A, p. 1.

Laeven, Luc, and Fabian Valencia. 2008. "Systemic Banking Crises: A New Database." IMF Working Paper 08/224. Washington, DC: International Monetary Fund.

Lagarde, Christine. 2011. "Don't Let Fiscal Brakes Stall Global Recovery." *Financial Times* August 15.

Lane, Philip R. 2012. "The European Sovereign Debt Crisis." *Journal of Economic Perspectives* 26(3):49–68.

Lauder Global TrendLab. 2011. *Global Risk: New Perspectives and Opportunities.* Philadelphia, PA: The Lauder Institute. http://lauder.wharton.upenn.edu/pages/pdf/other/Global%20TrendLab%202011%20Global%20Risk.pdf, accessed June 25, 2014.

Lauder Global TrendLab. 2012. *Sustainability: New Perspectives and Opportunities.* Philadelphia, PA: The Lauder Institute. http://lauder.wharton.upenn.edu/pages/pdf/other/Global_TrendLab_2012_Sustainability.pdf, accessed June 25, 2014.

Lauder Global TrendLab. 2013. *Poverty and Inequality: Persistent Challenges and New Solutions.* Philadelphia, PA: The Lauder Institute. http://lauder.wharton.upenn.edu/pages/pdf/other/Global_TrendLab_2013_Poverty.pdf, accessed June 25, 2014.

Lauder Global TrendLab. 2014. *The Future of the State.* Philadelphia, PA: The Lauder Institute. http://lauder.wharton.upenn.edu/pages/pdf/other/Global_TrendLab_2014_State.pdf, accessed June 25, 2014.

Lazonick, William, and Mary O'Sullivan. 1996. "Organization, Finance, and International Competition." *Industrial and Corporate Change* 5(1):1–49.

Lee, Il Houng, Murtaza Syed, and Liu Xueyan. 2012. "Is China Over-Investing and Does It Matter?" IMF Working Paper 12/277. Washington, DC: International Monetary Fund.

Lee, Timothy B. 2013. "Here's How Bitcoin Charmed Washington." *The Washington Post* November 21.

Leiner, Barry M., Vinton G. Cerf, David D. Clark, Robert E. Kahn, Leonard Kleinrock, Daniel C. Lynch, Jon Postel, Larry G. Roberts, and Stephen Wolff. n.d. *A Brief History of the Internet.* Downloadable from the Internet Society http://www.internetsociety.org/internet/what-internet/history-internet/brief-history-internet, accessed June 20, 2014.

Lerner, Josh, and Peter Tufano. 2011. "The Consequences of Financial Innovation: A Counterfactual Research Agenda." Working Paper 16780. Cambridge, MA: NBER.

Levi, Margaret. 1988. *Of Rule and Revenue.* Berkeley: University of California Press.

Lewis, Michael. 2014. *Flash Boys: A Wall Street Revolt.* New York: W. W. Norton.

Li, Cheng. 2012. "The End of the CCP's Resilient Authoritarianism? A Tripartite Assessment of Shifting Power in China." *The China Quarterly* 211 (September):595–623.

Lin, Justin Yifu. 2012. *Demystifying the Chinese Economy.* Cambridge: Cambridge University Press.

Lieberman, Marvin B., and Shigeru Asaba. 2006. "Why Do Firms Imitate Each Other?" *Academy of Management Review* 31:366–85.

Lipset, Martin Seymour. 1959. "Some Social Requisites of Democracy: Economic Development and Political Legitimacy." *American Political Science Review* 53(1) (March):69–105.

Lo, Andrew W. 2012. "Reading about the Financial Crisis: A Twenty-One-Book Review." *Journal of Economic Literature* 50(1):151–78.

McKinnon, Ronald I. 2013. *The Unloved Dollar Standard: From Bretton Woods to the Rise of China*. New York: Oxford University Press.

McKinsey Global Institute. 2014. *Global Flows in a Digital Age: How Trade, Finance, People and Data Connect the World Economy*. McKinsey & Co. http://www.mckinsey.com/insights/globalization/global_flows_in_a_digital_age?utm_content=buffer2abc6&utm_medium=social&utm_source=twitter.com&utm_campaign=buffer, accessed June 22, 2014.

McNeill, William H. 1978. "Human Migration: A Historical Overview." In W. H. McNeill and R. S. Adams, eds., *Human Migrations: Patterns and Policies*, Bloomington, IN: Indiana University Press, pp. 3–19.

Maddison, Angus. 2012. *Historical Statistics of the World Economy: 1–2008 AD*. http://www.ggdc.net/maddison/maddison-project/home.htm, accessed June 20, 2014.

Mann, Michael. 1984. "The Autonomous Power of the State: Its Origins, Mechanisms and Results." *European Journal of Sociology* 25(02):185–213.

Mann, Michael. 1992. *States, War and Capitalism*. Cambridge, MA: Blackwell.

Mann, Michael. 1993. *The Sources of Social Power*. Cambridge: Cambridge University Press.

Mansfield, Edward D., and Helen V. Milner. 1999. "The New Wave of Regionalism." *International Organization* 53(3) (Summer):589–627.

Marquand, David. 2011. *The End of the West: The Once and Future Europe*. Princeton, NJ: Princeton University Press.

Marshall, Monty G. 2013. "Polity IV Project: Political Regime Characteristics and Transitions, 1800–2013." http://www.systemicpeace.org/polity/polity4.htm, accessed July 20, 2014.

Matsuo, Hirofumi. 2014. "Implications of the Tohoku Earthquake for Toyota's Coordination Mechanism: Supply Chain Disruption of Automotive Semiconductors." Mimeo, Graduate School of Business Administration, Kobe University.

Maurer, Andreas. n.d. "Trade in Value Added: What is the Country of Origin in an Interconnected World" Geneva: World Trade Organization. http://www.wto.org/english/res_e/statis_e/miwi_e/background_paper_e.htm, accessed June 8, 2014.

May, Robert M., Simon A. Levin, and George Sugihara. 2008. "Complex Systems: Ecology for Bankers." *Nature* 451 (February 21):893–5.

Meyer, John W., and Michael T. Hannan. 1979. "National Development in a Changing World System: An Overview." In *National Development and the World System: Educational, Economic, and Political Change, 1950–1970*, edited by John W. Meyer and Michael T. Hannan. Chicago, IL: The University of Chicago Press, pp. 3–16.

Meyer, John W., John Boli, George M. Thomas and Francisco O. Ramirez. 1997. "World Society and the Nation-State." *American Journal of Sociology* 103(1) (July):144–81.

Milanovic, Branko. 2009. "Global Inequality Recalculated: The Effect of New 2005 PPP Estimates on Global Inequality." Policy Research Working Paper 5061. Washington, DC: The World Bank.

Minoiu, Camelia, Chanhyun Kang, V. S. Subrahmanian, and Anamaria Berea. 2015. "Does Financial Connectedness Predict Crises?" *Quantitative Finance* 15(4):607–24.

Minoiu, Camelia, and Javier A. Reyes. 2011. "A Network Analysis of Global Banking: 1978-2009." IMF Working Paper WP/11/74. Washington, DC: International Monetary Fund.

Mishkin, Frederic S. 2011. "Over the Cliff: From the Subprime to the Global Financial Crisis." *Journal of Economic Perspectives* 25(1):49–70.

Mizruchi, Mark S. 1993. "Cohesion, Equivalence, and Similarity of Behavior: A Theoretical and Empirical Assessment." *Social Networks* 15:275–307.

Mizruchi, Mark S. 2010. "The American Corporate Elite and the Historical Roots of the Financial Crisis of 2008." *Research in the Sociology of Organizations* 30B (2010):103–39.

Moore, Barrington. 1966. *Social Origins of Dictatorship and Democracy: Lord and Peasant in the Making of the Modern World.* Boston: Beacon.

Moravcsik, Andrew. 1998. *The Choice for Europe: Social Purpose and State Power from Messina to Maastricht.* Ithaca, NY: Cornell University Press.

Moravcsik, Andrew. 2012. "Europe after the Crisis: How to Sustain a Common Currency." *Foreign Affairs* 91(3)(May–June):54–68.

Morris, Ian. 2010. *Why the West Rules—For Now: The Patterns of History, and What They Reveal about the Future.* New York: Straus and Giroux.

Mundell, Robert A. 1961. *"A Theory of Optimum Currency Areas." American Economic Review* 51 (4): 657–65.

Mundell, Robert A. 1973a. "Uncommon Arguments for Common Currencies." In H. G. Johnson and A.K. Swoboda, eds., *The Economics of Common Currencies.* London: Allen and Unwin, pp. 114–32.

Mundell, Robert A. 1973b. "A Plan for a European Currency." In H. G. Johnson and A. K. Swoboda, eds., *The Economics of Common Currencies.* London: Allen and Unwin, pp. 143–72.

Murillo, Maria Victoria. 2002. "Political Bias in Policy Convergence: Privatization Choices in Latin America." *World Politics* 54:462–943.

Murmann, Johann Peter. 2006. *Knowledge and Competitive Advantage: The Coevolution of Firms, Technology, and National Institutions.* New York: Cambridge University Press.

Nash, Nathaniel. 1987. "Treasury Now Favors the Creation of Huge Banks." *The New York Times* June 7.

North, Douglass. 1981. *Structure and Change in Economic History.* New York: Norton.

Nye, Joseph S., Jr. 2004. *Soft Power: The Means to Success in World Politics.* New York: Public Affairs.

Nye, Joseph S., Jr. 2011. *The Future of Power.* New York: Public Affairs.

O'Rourke, Kevin H. and Alan M. Taylor. 2013. "Cross of Euros." *Journal of Economic Perspectives* 27(3) (Summer):167–92.

O'Sullivan, Mary. 2000. *Contests for Corporate Control: Corporate Governance and Economic Performance in the United States and Germany,* Oxford: Oxford University Press.

OECD-WTO. 2013. "Trade in Value-Added: Concepts, Methodologies, and Challenges." Joint note. http://www.oecd.org/sti/ind/49894138.pdf, accessed February 16, 2015.

Olson, Mancur. 1965. *The Logic of Collective Action: Public Goods and the Theory of Groups.* Cambridge, MA: Harvard University Press.

Olson, Mancur. 1982. *The Rise and Decline of Nations: Economic Growth, Stagflation, and Social Rigidities.* New Haven, CT: Yale University Press.

Orrù, M., N. W. Biggart, and G. G. Hamilton. 1997. *The Economic Organization of East Asian Capitalism.* Thousand Oaks, CA: Sage.

Osterhammel, Jürgen. 2014. *The Transformation of the World: A Global History of the Nineteenth Century.* Princeton, NJ: Princeton University Press.

Palmer, Donald, and Michael Maher. 2010. "A Normal Accident Analysis of the Mortgage Meltdown." *Research in the Sociology of Organizations* 30A (2010):219–56.

Panagariya, Arvind. 2008. *India: The Emerging Giant.* New York: Oxford University Press.

Patrick, Stewart. 2014. "The Unruled World: The Case for Good Enough Global Governance." *Foreign Affairs* 93(1) (January–Februrary):58–73.

Perrow, Charles. 1986. *Complex Organizations.* New York: Random House.

Perrow, Charles. 1984. *Normal Accidents: Living with High-Risk Technologies.* New York: Basic Books.

Perrow, Charles. 2007. *The Next Catastrophe: Reducing our Vulnerabilities to Natural, Industrial, and Terrorist Disasters.* Princeton, NJ: Princeton University Press.

Perrow, Charles. 2010. "The Meltdown Was not an Accident." *Research in the Sociology of Organizations* 30A (2010):309–30.

Pettis, Michael. 2013. *The Great Rebalancing: Trade, Conflict, and the Perilous Road Ahead for the World Economy.* Princeton, NJ: Princeton University Press.

Pettis, Michael. 2013. *Restructuring the Chinese Economy: Economic Distortions and the Next Decade of Chinese Growth.* Washington, DC: Carnegie Endowment.

Philippon, Thomas, and Ariell Reshef. 2013. "An International Look at the Growth of Modern Finance." *Journal of Economic Perspectives* 27(2) (Spring):73–96.

Piketty, Thomas. 2014. *Capital in the 21st Century.* Cambridge, MA: The Belknap Press of Harvard University Press.

Piketty, Thomas, and Emmanuel Saez. 2014. "Inequality in the Long Run." *Science* 344(6186):838–43.

Polanyi, Karl. [1944] 1957. *The Great Transformation.* Boston: Beacon Press.

Polidano, Charles. 2000. "Measuring Public Sector Capacity." *World Development* 28 (5):805–22.

Polillo, Simone and Mauro F. Guillén. 2005. "Globalization Pressures and the State: The Global Spread of Central Bank Independence." *American Journal of Sociology* 110(6) (May):1764–802.

Porter, Michael E. 1990. *The Competitive Advantage of Nations.* New York: Free Press.

Portes, Alejandro. 1997. "Neoliberalism and the Sociology of Development: Emerging Trends and Unanticipated Facts." *Population and Development Review* 23(2) (June):229–59.

Prasad, Eswar S. 2014. *The Dollar Trap: How the U.S. Dollar Tightened its Grip on Global Finance*. Princeton, NJ: Princeton University Press.

Przeworski, Adam, and Fernando Limongi. 1993. "Political Regimes and Economic Growth." *Journal of Economic Perspectives* 7(3) (Summer):51–69.

Rajan, Raghuram. 2005. "Has Financial Development Made the World Riskier?" Cambridge, MA: NBER Working Paper 11728.

Rajan, Raghuram G. 2010. *Fault Lines: How Hidden Fractures Still Threaten the World Economy*. Princeton, NJ: Princeton University Press.

Reinhardt, Carmen M., and Kenneth S. Rogoff. 2009. *This Time is Different: Eight Centuries of Financial Folly*. Princeton, NJ: Princeton University Press.

Roach, Stephen. 2014. *Unbalanced: The Codependency of America and China*. New Haven, CT: Yale University Press.

Roach, Stephen. 2014. *Unbalanced: The Codependency of America and China*. New Haven: Yale University Press. Kindle Edition.

Robertson, Roland. 1992. *Globalization: Social Theory and Global Culture*. London: Sage Publications.

Rodrik, Dani. 1998. "Why Do More Open Economies Have Bigger Governments?" *Journal of Political Economy* 106(5):997–1032.

Rodrik, Dani. 2006. "Goodbye Washington Consensus, Hello Washington Confusion?" *Journal of Economic Literature* 44 (December):973–87.

Rogers, Everett. 2003. *The Diffusion of Innovations*. New York: Free Press.

Rona-Tas, Akos, and Stefanie Hiss. 2010. "The Role of Ratings in the Subprime Mortgage Crisis: The Art of Corporate and the Science of Consumer Credit Rating." *Research in the Sociology of Organizations* 30A (2010):115–55.

Rose, Andrew K. 2011. "Exchange Rate Regimes in the Modern Era: Fixed, Floating, and Flaky." *Journal of Economic Literature* 49(3):652–72.

Roubini, Nouriel, and Stephen Mihm. 2010. *Crisis Economics: A Crash Course in the Future of Finance*. New York: Penguin Press.

Rueschemeyer, Dietrich, Evelyn Huber Stephens, and John D. Stephens.1992. *Capitalist Development and Democracy*. Chicago: University of Chicago Press.

Sachs, Jeffrey. 1998. "The IMF and the Asian Flu." *The American Prospect* (March–April):16–21.

Salmon, Felix. 2009. "Recipe for Disaster: The Formula that Killed Wall Street." *Magazine* February 23, 2009.

Saxenian, AnnaLee. 1994. *Regional Advantage: Culture and Competitionin Silicon Valley and Route 128*. Cambridge, MA: Harvard University Press.

Schneiberg, Marc, and Tim Bartley. 2010. "Regulating or Redesigning Finance? Market Architectures, Normal Accidents, and Dilemmas of Regulatory Reform." *Research in the Sociology of Organizations* 30A (2010):281–307.

Scott, W. R. 2001. *Institutions and Organizations*. Thousand Oaks, CA: Sage.

Shambaugh, David. 2013. *China Goes Global: The Partial Power*. New York: Oxford University Press.

Shiller, Robert J. 2008. *The Subprime Solution: How Today's Global Financial Crisis Happened, and What to Do about It*. Princeton, NJ: Princeton University Press.

Shinn, David H., and Joshua Eisenman. 2012. *China and Africa: A Century of Engagement*. Philadelphia, PA: University of Pennsylvania Press.

Simchi-Levi, David, William Schmidt, and Yehua Wei. 2014. "From Superstorms to Factory Fires: Managing Unpredictable Supply Chain Disruptions." *Harvard Business Review* Jan–Feb.

Skocpol, Theda. 1979. *States and Social Revolutions*. Cambridge: Cambridge University Press.

Skocpol, Theda. 1985. "Bringing the State Back In: Strategies of Analysis in Current Research." In Peter B. Evans, Dietrich Rueschemeyer, and Theda Skocpol, eds., *Bringing the State Back In*. Cambridge: Cambridge University Press, pp. 3–37.

Smith, Dave A. and Douglas R. White. 1992. "Structure and Dynamics of the Global Economy: Network Analysis of International Trade, 1965–1980." *Social Forces* 70:857–93.

Soros, George. 2002. *George Soros on Globalization*. New York: Public Affairs.

Soskice, David. 1999. "Divergent Production Regimes: Coordinated and Uncoordinated Market Economies in the 1980s and 1990s." In *Continuity and Change in Contemporary Capitalism*, edited by Herbert Kitschett et al. New York: Cambridge University Press, pp. 101–34.

Spolaore, Enrico. 2013. "What is European Integration Really about? A Political Guide for Economists." *Journal of Economic Perspectives* 27(3):125–44.

Sposi, Michael, and Janet Koech. 2013. "Value-Added Data Recast U.S.-China Trade Deficit." *Economic Letter, Federal Reserve Bank of Dallas*, 8(5) (July). http://www.dallasfed.org/assets/documents/research/eclett/2013/el1305.pdf, accessed February 17, 2015.

Stepan, Alfred, Juan J. Linz, and Yogendra Yadav. 2011. *Crafting State-Nations: India and other Multinational Democracies*. Baltimore, MD: Johns Hopkins University Press.

Stewart, James B. 2009. "Eight Days: The Battle to Save the American Financial System." *The New Yorker* (September 21):58–81.

Stiglitz, Joseph E. 2002. *Globalization and Its Discontents*. New York: W. W. Norton.

Stiglitz, Joseph E. 2010. *Freefall: America, Free Markets, and the Sinking of the World Economy*. New York: W. W. Norton.

Stinchcombe, Arthur L. 1983. *Economic Sociology*. New York, New York: Academic Press.

Storper, Michael and Robert Salais. 1997. *Worlds of Production: The Action Frameworks of the Economy*. Cambridge, MA: Harvard University Press.

Strang, David, and Sarah A. Soule. 1998. "Diffusion in Organizations and Social Movements." *Annual Review of Sociology* 24:265–90.

Streeck, Wofgang. 1991. "On the Institutional Conditions of Diversified Quality Production." In *Beyond Keynesianism: The Socio-Economics of Production and Full Employment*, edited by E. Matzner and W. Streeck. Hants, England: Edward Elgar Publishing, pp. 21–61.

Streeck, Wolfgang. 1995. "German Capitalism: Does it Exist? Can it Survive?" Discussion Paper 95/5. Cologne: Max-Planck Institut für Gesellschaftsforschung.

Sturgeon, Timothy J., and Olga Memedovic. 2011. "Mapping Global Value Chains: Intermediate Goods Trade and Structural Change in the World Economy." Working paper Development Policy and Strategic Research Branch Working Paper 05/2010. Vienna: United Nations Industrial Development Organization.

Suárez, Sandra L. 2000. *Does Business Learn? Taxes, Uncertainty and Political Strategies*. Ann Arbor: The University of Michigan Press.

Suárez, Sandra L. 2006. "Mobile Democracy: Text Messages, Voter Turnout and the 2004 Spanish Elections." *Representation* 42(2) (July):117–28.

Suárez, Sandra L. 2011. "Social media and regime change in Egypt." *Campaigns & Elections* 32 (3):30.

Suárez, Sandra L. 2012. "Reciprocal Policy Diffusion: The Regulation of Executive Compensation in the UK and US." *Journal of Public Affairs* 12(4) (November):303–14.

Suárez, Sandra L. 2014. "Symbolic Politics and the Regulation of Executive Compensation: A Comparison of the Great Depression and Great Recession." *Politics & Society* 42 (March): 73–105.

Suarez, Sandra L., and Robin Kolodny. 2011. "Paving the Road to 'Too Big to Fail': Business Interests and the Politics of Financial Deregulation in the U.S." *Politics & Society* 39:74–102.

Subramanian, Arvind. 2011. *Eclipse: Living in the Shadow of China's Economic Dominance*. Washington, DC: Petersen Institute for International Economics.

Subramanian, Arvind, and Martin Kessler. 2013. "The Renminbi Bloc is Here." Working Paper 12–19. Washington, DC: Peterson Institute.

Swidler, Ann. 1986. "Culture in Action." *American Sociological Review* 51(2) (April):273–86.

Temin, Peter, and David Vines. 2013. *The Leaderless Economy: Why the World Economic System Fell Apart and how to Fix It*. Princeton, NJ: Princeton University Press.

Tett, Gillian. 2009. *Fool's Gold: How the Bold Dream of a Small Tribe at J.P. Morgan Was Corrupted by Wall Street Greed and Unleashed a Catastrophe*. New York: Free Press.

The New York Times. 1997. "State Farm Plans Banking Subsidiary" *The New York Times* July 1.

Thomson Reuters. 2013. *Building BRICS: Exploring the Global Research and Innovation Impact of Brazil, Russia, India, China, and South Korea*. New York: Thomson Reuters.

Tilly, Charles. 1992. *Coercion, Capital and European States, AD 990–1992*. Cambridge, MA: Blackwell.

Tilly, Charles. 1997. *Roads from Past to Present*. Lanham, MD: Rowman and Littlefield.

Timmer, Marcel P., Abdul Azeez Erumban, Bart Los, Robert Stehrer, and Gaaitzen J. de Vries. 2014. "Slicing Up Global Value Chains." *Journal of Economic Perspectives* 28(2):99–118.

Tognato, Carlo. 2012. *Central Bank Independence: Cultural Codes and Symbolic Performance*. New York: Palgrave Macmillan.

Tolbert, Pamela S. and Lynne G. Zucker. 1983. "Institutional Sources of Change in the Formal Structure of Organizations." *Administrative Science Quarterly* 28:22–39.

Truell, Peter. 1997. "A Wall Street Behemoth." *The New York Times* September 25.

U.S. House of Representatives. 2014. "Hearing: 4-2-2014 Bitcoin: Examining the Benefits and Risks for Small Business." Washington, DC: U.S. House of Representatives, Committee on Small Business. http://docs.house.gov/Committee/Calendar/ByEvent.aspx?EventID=101978, accessed June 21, 2014.

U.S. Senate. 2013. "Beyond Silk Road: Potential Risks, Threats, and Promises of Virtual Currencies." November 18. Washington, DC: U.S. Senate Committee on Homeland Security & Governmental Affairs. http://www.hsgac.senate.gov/hearings/beyond-silk-road-potential-risks-threats-and-promises-of-virtual-currencies, accessed June 21, 2014.

UNCTAD. 2009. *World Investment Report 2009: Transnational Corporations, Agricultural Production, and Development*. New York: United Nations Conference on Trade and Development.

UNCTAD. 2012. *World Investment Report 2012: Towards a New Generation of Investment Policies*. New York: United Nations Conference on Trade and Development.

UNCTAD. 2013. *World Investment Report 2013: Global Value Chains*. New York: United Nations Conference on Trade and Development.

UNCTAD. 2014. *World Investment Report 2014: Investing in the SDGs*. New York: United Nations Conference on Trade and Development.

Van Rossem, Ronald. 1996. "The World-System Paradigm as General Theory of Development: A Cross-National Test." *American Sociological Review* 61:508–27.

Velde, François R. 2013. "Bitcoin: A Primer." Essays on Issues, Federal Reserve Bank of Chicago, No. 317.

Verdun, Amy. 1999. "The Role of the Delors Committee in Creating EMU: An Epistemic Community?" *Journal of European Public Policy* 6(2):308–28.

Verdun, Amy. 2000. *European Responses to Globalization and Financial Market Integration: Perceptions of Economic and Monetary Union in Britain, France, and Germany*. New York: Palgrave.

Wade, Robert. 1998. "The Asian Debt-and-Development Crisis of 1997-?: Causes and Consequences." *World Development* 26(8):1535–53.

Wallerstein, Immanuel. 1974. *The Modern World-System*. New York: Academic Press.

Waters, Malcolm. 1995. *Globalization*. New York: Routledge.

Weaver, R. K. and Bert A. Rockman. 1993. *Do Institutions Matter? Government capabilities in the United States and Abroad*. Washington, DC: Brookings Institution Press.

Weber, Klaus, Gerald F. Davis, and Michael Lounsbury. 2009. "Policy as Myth and Ceremony: The Global Spread of Stock Exchanges, 1980–2005." *Academy of Management Journal* 52(6):1319–47.

Wei, Shang-Jin, and Xiaobo Zhang. 2011. "The Competitive Saving Motive: Evidence from Rising Sex Ratios and Savings Rates in China." *Journal of Political Economy* 119(3):511–64.

Westney, D. Eleanor. 1987. *Imitation and Innovation: The Transfer of Western Organizational Patterns to Meiji Japan.* Cambridge, MA: Harvard University Press.

Whitley, Richard. 1992. *Business Systems in East Asia: Firms, Markets, and Societies.* London: Sage Publications.

Wilmarth, Arthur E. 2002. "The Transformation of the U.S. Financial Services Industry, 1975-2000." *University of Illinois Law Review* 215, online edition, accessed April 28, 2015.

Wilmarth, Arthur E. 2009. "The Dark Side of Universal Banking: Financial Conglomerates and the Origins of the Subprime Financial Crisis." *University of Illinois Law Review* 41(4):963–1050.

Wilson, Chris. 2011. "Understanding Global Demographic Convergence since 1950." *Population and Development Review* 37:375–88.

Wolf, Martin. 2014. *The Shifts and the Shocks: What We've Learned—and Have Still to Learn from the Financial Crisis.* New York: Penguin. Kindle Edition.

Woodruff, W. 1966. *Impact of Western Man: A Study of Europe's Role in the World Economy, 1750-1960.* New York: MacMillan.

World Bank. 2011. *Multipolarity: The New Global Economy.* Washington, DC: The World Bank.

Yang, Dennis Tao. 2012. "Aggregate Savings and External Imbalances in China." *Journal of Economic Perspectives* 26(4):125–46.

Yu, Yongding. 2012. "Rebalancing the Chinese Economy." *Oxford Review of Economic Policy* 28(3):551–68.

Yu, Yongding. 2015. "How Far Can Renminbi Internationalization Go?" In Barry Eichengreen and Masahiro Kawai, eds., *Renminbi Internationalization: Achievements, Prospects, and Challenges.* Washington DC: Brookings Institution Press, chapter 3, Kindle Edition.

Z/Yen Group. 2014. *The Global Financial Centres Index 15* (March). http://www.longfinance.net/images/GFCI15_15March2014.pdf, accessed June 21, 2014.

Zelizer, Viviana. 1994. *The Social Meaning of Money.* Princeton, NJ: Princeton University Press.

Ziegler, J. Nicholas. 1995. "Institutions, Elites, and Technological Change in France and Germany." *World Politics* 47(3) (April):341–72.

Ziegler, J. Nicholas. 1997. *Governing Ideas: Strategies for Innovation in France and Germany.* Ithaca, New York: Cornell University Press.

INDEX